Duquesne Studies

Philosophical Series — Volume Twenty-Four

Totality and Infinity

Philosophical Series
Volume Twenty-Four

Totality and Infinity

An Essay on Exteriority

by
EMMANUEL LEVINAS

Translated by Alphonso Lingis

Duquesne University Press, Pittsburgh

To Marcelle *and* Jean Wahl

TABLE OF CONTENTS

SECTION III. Exteriority and the Face

SECTION IV. Beyond the Face

INTRODUCTION

Ever since the beginning of the modern phenomenological movement disciplined attention has been paid to various patterns of human experience as they are actually lived through in the concrete. This has brought forth many attempts to find a general philosophical position which can do justice to these experiences without reduction or distortion. In France, the best known of these recent attempts have been made by Sartre in his *Being and Nothingness* and by Merleau-Ponty in his *Phenomenology of Perception* and certain later fragments. Sartre has a keen sense for life as it is lived, and his work is marked by many penetrating descriptions. But his dualistic ontology of the en-soi versus the pour-soi has seemed over-simple and inadequate to many critics, and has been seriously qualified by the author himself in his latest Marxist work, *The Critique of Dialetical Reason*. Merleau-Ponty's major work is a lasting contribution to the phenomenology of the pre-objective world of perception. But aside from a few brief hints and sketches, he was unable, before his unfortunate death in 1961, to work out carefully his ultimate philosophical point of view.

This leaves us then with the German philosopher, Heidegger, as the only contemporary thinker who has formulated a total ontology which claims to do justice to the stable results of phenomenology and to the living existential thought of our time. There is no doubt that Heidegger's early work, *Sein und Zeit,* is a highly original contribution to philosophy. But as critics have pointed out, it is marked by certain special features and one-sided emphases which are open to serious question. The author himself has apparently recognized the exaggerated anthropocentrism or subjectivism of its point of view which he has tried to correct by an opposite emphasis on a quasi-independent Being in his later and more obscure writings. Another fact needs to be noted. Since the publication of *Sein und Zeit* in 1927 there has been a great outpouring of German works attacking or defending certain special theses of Heidegger in different fields. But he does not seem to have stirred up original thinking along new lines in his native country.

The present book *Totality and Infinity,* of Emmanuel Levinas, shows,

11

however, that this is definitely not true in France. The author is thoroughly familiar with recent phenomenology and existential philosophy, and has an exhaustive knowledge of Husserl, Heidegger, Sartre, and Merleau-Ponty. Without these new developments, his work would have been impossible. It contains many penetrating descriptions of patterns of experience as we live them through, and many far-ranging reflections on these. It is basically phenomenological in character. But it is far more than a mere elaboration or correction of past insights. It is not often that one finds a philosophical work that is both radically original and carefully thought through. This book is both. It is striking out along new lines to formulate a general position which is opposed to Husserl's transcendental idealism as well as to Heidegger's hermeneutic philosophy of Being. In this way it shows the inexhaustible richness of our lived experience and the fruitfulness of reflecting on its forms and patterns. The radical empiricists who, since the time of William James, have doubted that the methods of transcendental idealism fit the patterns of experience, will find much supporting evidence in this work, which is full of novel insights and argument.

According to Levinas, I find myself existing in a world of alien things and elements which are other than, but not negations of myself. The latter is a logical relation which brings its terms together into a neutral system in the light of which each can be understood impartially, as we say. But the world as I originally experience it is not a logical system of this kind, in which no term takes precedence over the rest. My primary experience is definitely biased and egocentric. I take precedence over the various objects I find around me, and in so far as my experience is normal, I learn to manipulate and control them to my advantage, either as the member of a group which I identify with myself or simply as myself alone. In general, these objects are at my disposal, and I am free to play with them, live on them, and to enjoy them at my pleasure.

Levinas finds that this primordial experience of enjoyment (*jouissance*) has been neglected by Heidegger and other phenomenologists, and he devotes many pages to describing it in its major manifestations. There is a strong tendency in all human individuals and groups to maintain this egocentric attitude and to think of other individuals either as extensions of the self, or as alien objects to be manipulated for the advantage of the individual or social self. According to Levinas, neither of these egocentric views does justice to our original experience of the other person, and the most fundamental part of the book is devoted to the description and analysis of this experience—*the phenomenology of the other,* as we may call it.

The other person as he comes before me in a face to face encounter is not an *alter ego,* another self with different properties and accidents but in all essential respects like me. This may be the expression of an optimistic hope from a self-centered point of view which is often verified. The other may, indeed, turn out to be, on the surface at least, merely an analogue of myself. But not necessarily! I may find him to be inhabiting a world that is basically other than mine and to be essentially different from me. He is not a mere object to be subsumed under one of my categories and given a place in my world. Most of us are now familiar with this other-reducing theory which Sartre propounds in his *Being and Nothingness.* It may describe a widespread manner of dealing with the other person but it fails to do justice to his own existence, as is clearly indicated by the slavery and rebellion to which it leads. Nor finally do we take account of these inner depths of alien existence by regarding the other along Hegelian lines as a mere negation of the self. This only encompasses him in a supposedly neutral system that is readily identified with the rational self. Can it be that the underlying, unifying *one* of our monistic systems has been the avaricious, power-seeking, organizing, self-same self?

In any case, whether or not they are truly rational, these traditional theories are one-sidedly egocentric and reductive. None of them does justice to the other as I meet him for the first time in his strangeness face to face. I see this countenance before me nude and bare. He is present in the flesh. But as Levinas points out in his revealing descriptions, there is also a sense of distance and even of absence in his questioning glance. He is far from me and other than myself, a stranger, and I cannot be sure of what this strangeness may conceal. Hence the need to show friendly intent which brought forth the earliest forms of introduction and greeting. For example, the closed fist might conceal a knife, and coming "open handed" means no enmity, as Ortega y Gasset has shown in his reflections on the handshake in his *Man and People.* But this is only a bare beginning. Even if he comes with no ill will, he remains a stranger inhabiting an alien world of his own. Of course, I may simply treat him as a different version of myself, or, if I have the power, place him under my categories and use him for my purposes. But this means reducing him to what he is not. How can I coexist with him and still leave his otherness intact?

According to Levinas, there is only one way, by language, and some of the more provocative sections of the book are devoted to this topic. The questioning glance of the other is seeking for a meaningful response. Of course, I may give only a casual word, and go on my own way with indifference, passing the other by. But if communication and community is to be achieved, a real response, a responsible answer must be given. This means that I must be ready to put my world into words, and to offer it to the other. There can be no free interchange without something to give. Responsible communication depends on an initial act of generosity, a giving of my world to him with all its dubious assumptions and arbitrary features. They are then exposed to the questions of the other, and an escape from egotism becomes possible.

It has been and is still widely held that this can be achieved only by a joint sacrifice of self to a neutral, englobing system. But Levinas brings forth very strong evidence to show that this is not the case. By speaking to the other I enter into a relation with him. But this speaking does not bind me down or limit me, because I remain at a distance from what is said. Hence real conversation with an other cannot be exhaustively planned. I am never sure just what he will say, and there is always room for reinterpretation and spontaneity on both sides. My autonomy remains intact. In fact, in so far as I have any, it is stimulated to further intensity by searching questions from a point of view that is not merely opposite and therefore correlative to mine, but genuinely other. I can always say what I wish, and even begin once again *de novo*. The same is true of the other. He does not merely present me with lifeless signs into which I am free to read meanings of my own. His expressions bear *his* meanings, and he is himself present to bring them out and defend them. There is no difference between the active expression and what is expressed. The two coincide. The other is not an object that must be interpreted and illumined by my alien light. He shines forth with his own light, and speaks for himself.

Levinas, of course, is not denying that a great part of our speaking and thinking is systematic and bound by logic of some kind. What he is interested in showing is that prior to these systems, which are required to meet many needs, and presupposed by them is the existing individual and his ethical choice to welcome the stranger and to share his world by speaking to him. In other words, we do not become social by first being systematic. We become systematic and orderly in our thinking by first freely making a choice for generosity and communication, i.e., for the social. What we call thinking and speaking is very often only a playing with our own words and concepts or a succession of egocentric monologues. But according to Levinas, speaking becomes serious only when we pay attention to the other and take account of him and the strange world he inhabits. It is only by responding to him that I become aware of the arbitrary views and attitudes into which my uncriticized freedom always leads me, and become responsible, that is, able to respond. It is only then that I see the need of justifying my egocentric attitudes, and of doing justice to the other in my thought and in my action.

Hegel and his followers have also seen the accidental biases and eccentricities that make the personal freedom of the individual unreliable and open to criticism. They have therefore attacked the personal existence, which Levinas calls "the inner life," as capricious and subjective, and have defended those objective rational systems and social organizations which subordinate, or even repress, the individual. Levinas grants that they have dominated the course of human history. He points out, however, that while this view may have weakened the influence of individual fantasies and delusions, it has led to forms of social suppression and tyranny which are even worse. Must we always choose one or the other of these evils? Anarchy on the one hand and tyranny on the other?

In politics, in education, in every phase of our cultural life, are we not constantly presented with alternatives of this kind? One may say that a main argument of this book is the working out of a third way between the horns of this recurrent dilemma. Totalitarian thinking accepts vision rather than language as its model. It aims to gain an all-inclusive, panoramic view of all things, including the other, in a neutral, impersonal light like the Hegelian *Geist* (Spirit), or the Heideggerian Being. It sees the dangers of an uncontrolled, individual freedom, and puts itself forth as the only rational answer to anarchy. To be free is the same as to be rational, and to be rational is to give oneself over to the total system that is developing in world history. Since the essential self is also rational, the development of this system will coincide with the interests of the self. All otherness will be absorbed in this total system of harmony and order.

According to Levinas, however, there is another way, not yet fully explored, which he is suggesting in this book. It cannot be identified with subjective anarchism since it takes account of the other and his criticism. But it also differs from the holistic thinking of traditional philosophy in the following ways. Instead of referring to the panoramic sense of vision as its model for understanding, it refers to language where there is always room for the diversity of dialogue, and for further growth through the dynamics of question and answer. This other-regarding way of thought rejects the traditional assumption that reason has no plural, and asks why we should not recognize what our lived experience shows us, that reason has many centers, and approaches the truth in many different ways. Instead of building great systems in which the singular diversities of things and persons are passed over and diluted, this way of thinking prefers to start with the careful analysis of the peculiar features of each being in its otherness, and only then to clarify its relations with other things in the light of its peculiar and distinctive features.

This other-oriented mode of speaking and thinking will pay less attention to things as they appear to the separated self, and more attention to the search for what they are in themselves, in their radical otherness, even though this is less certain and always more difficult to find. This will mean less interest in conceptual constructions and a greater readiness to listen and learn from experience. It will not think of knowing, in the sense of gathering, as the primary aim of man from which action will follow as a matter of course, but rather of action and of the achievement of justice and peace as prior to speaking and thinking.

The basic difference is between a mode of thought which tries to gather all things around the mind, or self, of the thinker, and an externally oriented mode which attempts to pentrate into what is radically other than the mind that is thinking it. This difference emerges with peculiar clarity in the case of my meeting with the other person. I may either decide to remain within myself, assimilating the other and trying to make use of him, or I may take the risk of going out of my way and trying to speak and to give to him. This does not fulfill a *need*. I can satisfy my needs more adequately by keeping to myself and the members of the in-group with which I am identified. And yet it is the expression of a *desire,* as Levinas calls it, for that which transcends me and my self-centered categories. This desire is never satisfied, but it seems insatiable, and feeds on itself.

By communicating with the other, I enter into a relation with him which does not necessarily lead to my dependence on him. Nor does he become dependent on me. He can *absolve* himself from this relation with his integrity intact. Hence Levinas calls it absolving, or absolute.

And he finds many other relations of this kind, for example, that of truth. In so far as I am related to another entity and share in its being, it must be really changed. But as classical metaphysics pointed out, in so far as I discover the truth about something, it is absolved from this relation and remains unchanged. The same is true of the idea of absolute perfection which is clearly radically other than what I am. But I can strive for such an other without changing it, or losing my own integrity, just as I can respond to another person and engage in dialogue without jeopardizing his or my own being. Levinas suggests that this may be the reason for Plato's well-known statement at *Republic* 509 that the good lies beyond being, and relates it to his own view that the conclusions of our basic philosophical questions are to be found beyond metaphysics in ethics. My way of existing conveys my final answer.

As Levinas points out, one answer is given by the totalizers who are satisfied with themselves and with the systems they can organize around themselves as they already are. A very different answer is given by those who are dissatisfied, and who strive for what is other than themselves, the infinitizers, as we may call them. The former seek for power and control; the latter for a higher quality of life. The former strive for order and system; the latter for freedom and creative advance. This leads to the basic contrast which is expressed in the title of the book, between totality on the one hand and infinity on the other. Many examples of the former can be found in the history of our Western thought. The latter is largely unknown and untried.

It is this outwardly directed but self-centered totalistic thinking that organizes men and things into power systems, and gives us control over nature and other people. Hence it has dominated the course of human history. From this point of view, only the neutral and impersonal, Being, for example, is important. "What is it?" is the most basic question that requires an answer in terms of a context, a system. The real is something that can be brought before the senses and the mind as an object. The acts of sensing, thinking, existing, as they are lived through, are discounted as subjective. A priority is, therefore, placed on objective thinking, and the objective. The group is more powerful, more inclusive, and, therefore, more important than the individual. To be free is to sacrifice the arbitrary inner self and to fit into a rationally grounded system. Inner feelings and thoughts cannot be observed. They are private and unstable. So men are judged by what they do,

their works that are visible and remain. Since they endure, they can be
judged by the group which also remains. They are what they are judged
to be by the ongoing course of history. Since this is the inclusive system,
with nothing beyond, there is no appeal from this judgment. It is final.
As Hegel said, *Die Weltgeschichte ist die Weltgericht*. History itself
is the final judge of history.

To the infinitizers on the other hand, this seems like a partial and
biased doctrine. Systematic thinking, no doubt, has its place. It is
required for the establishment of those power structures which satisfy
necessary needs. But when absolutized in this way and applied to free
men, it constitutes violence, which is not merely found in temporary
and accidental displays of armed force, but in the permanent tyranny of
power systems which free men should resist. Slavery is the dominance
of the neutral and impersonal over the active and personal. In a living
dialogue and even in a written monologue of many volumes it is more
important to find out who is speaking and why, than merely to know
what is said. We do not *need* to know the other person (or thing) as
he is in himself, and we shall never know him apart from acting with
him. But unless we *desire* this, and go on trying, we shall never escape
from the subjectivism of our systems and the objects that they bring
before us to categorize and manipulate. We do not get rid of our
thoughts and feelings by ignoring them or by any other means. But we
may seek to transcend them, first as individuals and only later, perhaps,
as a group. The individual person becomes free and responsible not by
fitting into a system but rather by fighting against it and by acting on
his own.

Those who are not limited to visible objects and who have some sense
of the inner life that is revealed in dialogue will not judge a man ex-
clusively by his works. They will recognize the alien factors that always
intervene between the man himself and the objects he produces. They
will also be aware of the difference between those who judge and the
other whom they are judging. They will understand that the judgment of history is made by survivors on the works of the dead who are
no longer present to explain and defend them. They will see that this
judgment is crude and subjective, varying with the otherness of those
who judge differently from place to place and from time to time. So
they will never accept it as final. They will seek rather to separate
themselves from this course of history to make judgments of their own
with reference to a standard of perfection that is radically other and

transcendent. To this "idea of the infinite," as Levinas calls it, an appeal can be made. We are not bound to accept the *status quo* as right, and history itself is not the final judge of history.

This is only the bare suggestion of a few major points in the careful exposition of a pluralistic point of view which is supported by a wealth of concrete illustration and phenomenological description. This is particularly true of the author's studies of our human meeting and communication with the other, which underlies the whole work. But it is also true of his studies of suffering and patience, of the lived human body which is neither a thing nor a purely subjective principle as Merleau-Ponty sometimes seems to think, and of the condition of violence as a systemic condition to which man is always subject, and which should be of special interest to the contemporary reader. Levinas' description between *need* which seeks to fill a negation or lack in the subject, and *desire* which is positively attracted by something other not yet possessed or needed, is worked out in very original ways and grounded on a rich array of phenomenological evidence. The same is true of his suggestive interpretations of time, the parental relation, and the family which is not a mere step on the way to the state, as Hegel supposed.

The careful reader may find certain deficiencies in the argument. He may wonder why the original state of enjoyment is called purely subjective and even solipsistic when this separated self is clearly encompassed by the elements, and existing, in some sense not fully clear, with others in the world. He may seek for more light on what the author calls the "inner life" and on its specific differences from the preceding subjective condition. He may find himself doubting whether his experience of the other person is a sufficient ground for "the idea of the infinite" as the author seems to suppose. Furthermore, he may wonder about the strange asymmetry, the complete supremacy of the other, that the author finds in the self-other relation. He may be finally puzzled about some of the things Levinas seems to read into the parent-child relation. Other difficulties may arise for the critical reader.

But whatever his point of view may be, he will not be the same after reading this work with any care. It is the disciplined development of a pluralistic point of view that has not been thought through before. It takes account of a wide array of empirical patterns that are carefully and accurately described and analyzed. The book shows the lasting fertility of the phenomenological movement in the broad sense of this phrase with which we are now becoming familiar. But it is not merely a reinterpretation of what has been said before. It is something highly original and, to use its own language, radically other. For example, though it comes, as we have indicated, from a phenomenological background, and without Husserl and Heidegger could not have been written, it is highly critical of Husserl and constitutes one of the most basic attacks on the thought of Heidegger that has yet been formulated. Alphonso Lingis is thoroughly familiar with recent French philosophy and with the background of this work. The original French of the author is not written in a popular style. But Lingis has given us a translation which is accurate and discerning. The work deserves to be widely read not only by professional philosophers, for it is carefully thought out by an original mind, but by intelligent laymen as well, for it is close to life.

John Wild
Yale University

PREFACE

Everyone will readily agree that it is of the highest importance to know whether we are not duped by morality.

Does not lucidity, the mind's openness upon the true, consist in catching sight of the permanent possibility of war? The state of war suspends morality; it divests the eternal institutions and obligations of their eternity and rescinds ad interim the unconditional imperatives. In advance its shadow falls over the actions of men. War is not only one of the ordeals—the greatest—of which morality lives; it renders morality derisory. The art of foreseeing war and of winning it by every means— politics—is henceforth enjoined as the very exercise of reason. Politics is opposed to morality, as philosophy to naïveté.

We do not need obscure fragments of Heraclitus to prove that being reveals itself as war to philosophical thought, that war does not only affect it as the most patent fact, but as the very patency, or the truth, of the real. In war reality rends the words and images that dissimulate it, to obtrude in its nudity and in its harshness. Harsh reality (this sounds like a pleonasm!), harsh object-lesson, at the very moment of its fulguration when the drapings of illusion burn war is produced as the pure experience of pure being. The ontological event that takes form in this black light is a casting into movement of beings hitherto anchored in their identity, a mobilization of absolutes, by an objective order from which there is no escape. The trial by force is the test of the real. But violence does not consist so much in injuring and annihilating persons as in interrupting their continuity, making them play roles in which they no longer recognize themselves, making them betray not only commitments but their own substance, making them carry out actions that will destroy every possibility for action. Not only modern war but every war employs arms that turn against those who wield them. It establishes an order from which no one can keep his distance; nothing henceforth is exterior. War does not manifest exteriority and the other as other; it destroys the identity of the same.

The visage of being that shows itself in war is fixed in the concept of totality, which dominates Western philosophy. Individuals are reduced to being bearers of forces that command them unbeknown to themselves.

The meaning of individuals (invisible outside of this totality) is derived from the totality. The unicity of each present is incessantly sacrificed to a future appealed to to bring forth its objective meaning. For the ultimate meaning alone counts; the last act alone changes beings into themselves. They are what they will appear to be in the already plastic forms of the epic.

The moral consciousness can sustain the mocking gaze of the political man only if the certitude of peace dominates the evidence of war. Such a certitude is not obtained by a simple play of antitheses. The peace of empires issued from war rests on war. It does not restore to the alienated beings their lost identity. For that a primordial and original relation with being is needed.

Morality will oppose politics in history and will have gone beyond the functions of prudence or the canons of the beautiful to proclaim itself unconditional and universal when the eschatology of messianic peace will have come to superpose itself upon the ontology of war. Philosophers distrust it. To be sure they profit from it to announce peace also; they deduce a final peace from the reason that plays out its stakes in ancient and present-day wars: they found morality on politics. But for them eschatology—a subjective and arbitrary divination of the future, the result of a revelation without evidences, tributary of faith—belongs naturally to Opinion.

However, the extraordinary phenomenon of prophetic eschatology certainly does not intend to win its civic rights within the domain of thought by being assimilated to a philosophical evidence. In religions and even in theologies eschatology, like an oracle, does indeed seem to "complete" philosophical evidences; its beliefs-conjectures mean to be more certain than the evidences—as though eschatology added information about the future by revealing the finality of being. But, when reduced to the evidences, eschatology would then already accept the ontology of totality issued from war. Its real import lies elsewhere. It does not introduce a teleological system into the totality; it does not consist in teaching the orientation of history. Eschatology institutes a relation with being *beyond the totality* or beyond history, and not with being beyond the past and the present. Not with the void that would surround the totality and where one could, arbitrarily, think what one likes, and thus promote the claims of a subjectivity free as the wind. It is a relationship with *a surplus always exterior to the totality,* as though the objective totality did not fill out the true measure of being, as though another concept, the concept of *infinity,* were needed to express this transcendence with regard to totality, non-encompassable within a totality and as primordial as totality.

This "beyond" the totality and objective experience is, however, not to be described in a purely negative fashion. It is reflected *within* the totality and history, *within* experience. The eschatological, as the "beyond" of history, draws beings out of the jurisdiction of history and the future; it arouses them in and calls them forth to their full responsibility. Submitting history as a whole to judgment, exterior to the very wars that mark its end, it restores to each instant its full signification in that very instant: all the causes are ready to be heard. It is not the last judgment that is decisive, but the judgment of all the instants in time, when the living are judged. The eschatological notion of judgment (contrary to the judgment of history in which Hegel wrongly saw its rationalization) implies that beings have an identity "before" eternity, before the accomplishment of history, before the fullness of time, while there is still time; implies that beings exist in relationship, to be sure, but on the basis of themselves and not on the basis of the totality. The idea of being overflowing history makes possible *existents* [*étants*] both involved in being and personal, called upon to answer at their trial and consequently already adult—but, for that very reason, *existents* that can speak rather than lending their lips to an anonymous utterance of history. Peace is produced as this aptitude for speech. The eschatological vision breaks with the totality of wars and empires in which one does not speak. It does not envisage the end of history within being understood as a totality, but institutes a relation with the infinity of being which exceeds the totality. The first "vision" of eschatology (hereby distinguished from the revealed opinions of positive religions) reveals the very possibility of eschatology, that is, the breach of the totality, the possibility of a *signification without a context.* The experience of morality does not proceed from this vision—it *consummates* this vision; ethics is an optics. But it is a "vision" without image, bereft of the synoptic and totalizing objectifying virtues of vision, a relation or an intentionality of a wholly different type—which this work seeks to describe.

---

* We are translating *"étant"* throughout by "existent," reserving "being" to translate *"être."* It will become clear that the distinction between *"être"* and *"étant"* in this work alludes to but does not reproduce the Heideggerian distinction between *"Sein"* and *"Seiendes."*
We shall distinguish between *"étant"* and the less employed term *"existant"* by using the form "existant" to translate the latter term.—Trans.

Is relationship with Being produced only in representation, the natural locus of evidence? Does objectivity, whose harshness and universal power is revealed in war, provide the unique and primordial form in which Being, when it is distinguished from image, dream, and subjective abstraction, *imposes itself* on consciousness? Is the apprehension of an object equivalent to the very movement in which the bonds with truth are woven? These questions the present work answers in the negative. Of peace there can be only an eschatology. But this does not mean that when affirmed objectively it is believed by faith instead of being known by knowledge. It means, first of all, that peace does not take place in the objective history disclosed by war, as the end of that war or as the end of history.

But does not the experience of war refute eschatology, as it refutes morality? Have we not begun by acknowledging the irrefutable evidence of totality?

To tell the truth, ever since eschatology has opposed peace to war the evidence of war has been maintained in an essentially hypocritical civilization, that is, attached both to the True and to the Good, henceforth antagonistic. It is perhaps time to see in hypocrisy not only a base contingent defect of man, but the underlying rending of a world attached to both the philosophers and the prophets.

But does not the experience of war and totality coincide, for the philosopher, with experience and evidence as such? And is not philosophy itself after all defined as an endeavor to live a life beginning in evidence, opposing the opinion of one's fellow-men, the illusions and caprice of one's own subjectivity? Does not the eschatology of peace, outside of this evidence, live on subjective opinions and illusions? Unless philosophical evidence refers from itself to a situation that can no longer be stated in terms of "totality" . . . Unless the non-knowing with which the philosophical knowing begins coincides not with pure nothingness but only with a nothingness of objects. . . . Without substituting eschatology for philosophy, without philosophically "demonstrating" eschatological "truths," we can proceed from the experience of totality back to a situation where totality breaks up, a situation that conditions the totality itself. Such a situation is the gleam of exteriority or of transcendence in the face of the Other.* The rigorously developed con-

---

* *Le visage d'autrui.* With the author's permission, we are translating *"autrui"* (the personal Other, the you) by "Other," and *"autre"* by "other." In

cept of this transcendence is expressed by the term infinity. This revelation of infinity does not lead to the acceptance of any dogmatic content, whose philosophical rationality cannot be argued for in the name of the transcendental truth of the idea of infinity. For the way we are describing to work back and remain this side of objective certitude resembles what has come to be called the transcendental method (in which the technical procedures of transcendental idealism need not necessarily be comprised).

Would the violence which, for a mind, consists in welcoming a being to which it is inadequate contradict the ideal of autonomy that guides philosophy—which in evidence is mistress of her own truth? But the relation with infinity—the idea of the Infinite, as Descartes calls it— overflows thought in a wholly different sense than does opinion. Opinion vanishes like the wind when thought touches it—or is revealed to be already within that thought. What remains ever exterior to thought is thought in the idea of infinity. It is the condition for every opinion as also for every objective truth. The idea of infinity is the mind before it lends itself to the distinction between what it discovers by itself and what it receives from opinion.

The relation with infinity cannot, to be sure, be stated in terms of experience, for infinity overflows the thought that thinks it. Its very *infinition* is produced precisely in this overflowing. The relation with infinity will have to be stated in terms other than those of objective experience; but if experience precisely means a relation with the absolutely other, that is, with what always overflows thought, the relation with infinity accomplishes experience in the fullest sense of the word.

Finally, the eschatological vision does not oppose to the experience of totality the protestation of a person in the name of his personal egoism or even of his salvation. Such a proclamation of morality based on the pure subjectivism of the I is refuted by war, the totality it reveals, and the objective necessities. We oppose to the objectivism of war a subjectivity born from the eschatological vision. The idea of infinity delivers the subjectivity from the judgment of history to declare it ready for judgment at every moment and, we shall show,[1] called to participate in this judgment, impossible without it. The harsh law of war breaks up not

---

doing so, we regrettably sacrifice the possibility of reproducing the author's use of capital or small letters with both these terms in the French text.

The very important term *"visage"* shall always be translated "face."—Trans.

[1] Cf. pp. 240 ff.

against an impotent subjectivism cut off from being, but against the infinite, more objective than objectivity.

Do the particular beings yield their truth in a Whole in which their exteriority vanishes? Or, on the contrary, is the ultimate event of being enacted in the outburst of this exteriority? Our initial question now assumes this form.

This book then does present itself as a defense of subjectivity, but it will apprehend the subjectivity not at the level of its purely egoist protestation against totality, nor in its anguish before death, but as founded in the idea of infinity.

It will proceed to distinguish between the idea of totality and the idea of infinity, and affirm the philosophical primacy of the idea of infinity. It will recount how infinity is produced in the relationship of the same with the other,* and how the particular and the personal, which are unsurpassable, as it were magnetize the very field in which the production of infinity is enacted. The term "production" designates both the effectuation of being (the event "is produced," an automobile "is produced") and its being brought to light or its exposition (an argument "is produced," an actor "is produced").** The ambiguity of this verb conveys the essential ambiguity of the operation by which the being of an entity simultaneously is brought about [*s'évertue*] and is revealed.

The idea of infinity is not an incidental notion forged by a subjectivity to reflect the case of an entity encountering on the outside nothing that limits it, overflowing every limit, and thereby infinite. The production of the infinite entity is inseparable from the idea of infinity, for it is precisely in the disproportion between the idea of infinity and the infinity of which it is the idea that this exceeding of limits is produced. The idea of infinity is the mode of being, the *infinition,* of infinity. Infinity does not first exist, and *then* reveal itself. Its infinition is produced as revelation, as a positing of its idea in *me.* It is produced in the im-

---

* The same and the other: these categories are frequently capitalized in the French text. Since we are in every case rendering *"l'autre"* by "the other," we are forced to drop the capital from the corresponding term *"le même"* ("the same").—Trans.

** *The Shorter Oxford Dictionary* (Oxford, 1955, p. 1592) illustrates the two meanings of the term thus:

1. Art may make a Suit of Clothes, But Nature must produce a Man. Hume.
2. Produce your cause, saith the Lord, bring forth your strong reasons. *Isa.* xli, 21. The books must be produced, as we cannot receive parole evidence on their contents 1776.—Trans.

probable feat whereby a separated being fixed in its identity, the same, the I, nonetheless contains in itself what it can neither contain nor receive solely by virtue of its own identity. Subjectivity realizes these impossible exigencies—the astonishing feat of containing more than it is possible to contain. This book will present subjectivity as welcoming the Other, as hospitality; in it the idea of infinity is consummated. Hence intentionality, where thought remains an *adequation* with the object, does not define consciousness at its fundamental level. All knowing qua intentionality already presupposes the idea of infinity, which is preeminently *non-adequation.*

To contain more than one's capacity does not mean to embrace or to encompass the totality of being in thought or, at least, to be able to account for it after the fact by the inward play of constitutive thought. To contain more than one's capacity is to shatter at every moment the framework of a content that is thought, to cross the barriers of immanence—but without this descent into being reducing itself anew to a concept of descent. Philosophers have sought to express with the concept of act (or of the incarnation that makes it possible) this descent into the real, which the concept of thought interpreted as a pure knowing would maintain only as a play of lights. The act of thought—thought as an act —would precede the thought thinking or becoming conscious of an act. The notion of act involves a violence essentially: the violence of transitivity, lacking in the transcendence of thought. For the transcendence of thought remains closed in itself despite all its adventures—which in the last analysis are purely imaginary, or are adventures traversed as by Ulysses: on the way home. What, in action, breaks forth as essential violence is the surplus of being over the thought that claims to contain it, the marvel of the idea of infinity. The incarnation of consciousness is therefore comprehensible only if, over and beyond adequation, the overflowing of the idea by its ideatum, that is, the idea of infinity, moves consciousness. The idea of infinity (which is not a representation of infinity) sustains activity itself. Theoretical thought, knowledge, and critique, to which activity has been opposed, have the same foundation. The idea of infinity, which is not in its turn a representation of infinity, is the common source of activity and theory.

Consciousness then does not consist in equaling being with representation, in tending to the full light in which this adequation is to be sought, but rather in overflowing this play of lights—this phenomenology —and in accomplishing *events* whose ultimate signification (contrary to the Heideggerian conception) does not lie in *disclosing*. Philosophy does indeed dis-cover the signification of these events, but they are produced without discovery (or truth) being their destiny. No prior disclosure illuminates the production of these essentially noctural events. The welcoming of the face and the work of justice—which condition the birth of truth itself—are not interpretable in terms of disclosure. Phenomenology is a method for philosophy, but phenomenology—the comprehension effected through a bringing to light—does not constitute the ultimate event of being itself. The relation between the same and the other is not always reducible to knowledge of the other by the same, nor even to the *revelation* of the other to the same, which is already fundamentally different from disclosure.[2]

We were impressed by the opposition to the idea of totality in Franz Rosenzweig's *Stern der Erlösung,* a work too often present in this book to be cited. But the presentation and the development of the notions employed owe everything to the phenomenological method. Intentional analysis is the search for the concrete. Notions held under the direct gaze of the thought that defines them are nevertheless, unbeknown to this naïve thought, revealed to be implanted in horizons unsuspected by this thought; these horizons endow them with a meaning—such is the essential teaching of Husserl.[3] What does it matter if in the Husserlian phenomenology taken literally these unsuspected horizons are in their turn interpreted as thoughts aiming at objects! What counts is the idea of the overflowing of objectifying thought by a forgotten experience from which it lives. The break-up of the formal structure of thought (the noema of a noesis) into events which this structure dissimulates, but which sustain it and restore its concrete significance, constitutes a *deduction*—necessary and yet non-analytical. In our exposition it is indicated by expressions such as "that is," or "precisely," or "this accomplishes that," or "this is produced as that."

The signification that, in the present work, phenomenological deduc-

---

[2] In broaching, at the end of this work, the study of relations which we situate beyond the face, we come upon events that cannot be described as noeses aiming at noemata, nor as active interventions realizing projects, nor, of course, as physical forces being discharged into masses. They are conjunctures in being for which perhaps the term "drama" would be most suitable, in the sense that Nietzsche would have liked to use it when, at the end of *The Case of Wagner,* he regrets that it has always been wrongly translated by action. But it is because of the resulting equivocation that we forego this term.

[3] Cf. our article "La Ruine de la Représentation," in *Edmund Husserl 1859-1959* (The Hague, 1959), pp. 73-85.

tion shows to underlie the theoretical thought concerning being and the panoramic exposition of being itself is not irrational. The aspiration to radical exteriority, thus called metaphysical, the respect for this metaphysical exteriority which, above all, we must "let be," constitutes truth. It animates this work and evinces its allegiance to the intellectualism of reason. But theoretical thought, guided by the ideal of objectivity, does not exhaust this aspiration; it remains this side of its ambitions. If, as this book will show, ethical relations are to lead transcendence to its term, this is because the essential of ethics is in its *transcendent intention*, and because not every transcendent intention has the noesis-noema structure. Already *of itself* ethics is an "optics." It is not limited to preparing for the theoretical exercise of thought, which would monopolize transcendence. The traditional opposition between theory and practice will disappear before the metaphysical transcendence by which a relation with the absolutely other, or truth, is established, and of which ethics is the royal road. Hitherto the relation between theory and practice was not conceivable other than as a solidarity or a hierarchy: activity rests on cognitions that illuminate it; knowledge requires from acts the mastery of matter, minds, and societies—a technique, a morality, a politics—that procures the peace necessary for its pure exercise. We shall go further, and, at the risk of appearing to confuse theory and practice, deal with both as modes of metaphysical transcendence. The apparent confusion is deliberate and constitutes one of the theses of this book. Husserlian phenomenology has made possible this passage from ethics to metaphysical exteriority.

How far we are in this preface from the theme of the work announced by its first sentence! Already there is question of so many other things, even in these preliminary lines, which ought to state without detours the intent of the work undertaken. Philosophical research in any case does not answer questions like an interview, an oracle, or wisdom. And can one speak of a book as though one had not written it, as though one were its first critic? Can one thus undo the inevitable dogmatism that gathers up and gauges an exposition in pursuit of its theme? It will appear in the eyes of the reader, so naturally indifferent to the vicissitudes of this chase, as a thicket of difficulties where nothing guarantees the presence of game. We should like at least to invite him not to be rebuffed by the aridity of certain pathways, by the labor of the first section, whose preparatory character is to be emphasized, but in which the horizon of this whole research takes form.

The word by way of preface which seeks to break through the screen stretched between the author and the reader by the book itself does not give itself out as a word of honor. But it belongs to the very essence of language, which consists in continually undoing its phrase by the fore-word or the exegesis, in unsaying the said, in attempting to restate without ceremonies what has already been ill understood in the inevitable ceremonial in which the said delights.

SECTION I

THE SAME AND THE OTHER

A. METAPHYSICS AND TRANSCENDENCE

1. Desire for the Invisible

"The true life is absent." But we are in the world. Metaphysics arises and is maintained in this alibi. It is turned toward the "elsewhere" and the "otherwise" and the "other." For in the most general form it has assumed in the history of thought it appears as a movement going forth from a world that is familiar to us, whatever be the yet unknown lands that bound it or that it hides from view, from an "at home" ["chez soi"]* which we inhabit, toward an alien outside-of-oneself [hors-de-soi], toward a yonder.

The term of this movement, the elsewhere or the other, is called *other* in an eminent sense. No journey, no change of climate or of scenery could satisfy the desire bent toward it. The other metaphysically desired is not "other" like the bread I eat, the land in which I dwell, the landscape I contemplate, like, sometimes, myself for myself, this "I," that "other." I can "feed" on these realities and to a very great extent satisfy myself, as though I had simply been lacking them. Their *alterity* is thereby reabsorbed into my own identity as a thinker or a possessor. The metaphysical desire tends toward *something else entirely,* toward the *absolutely other*. The customary analysis of desire can not explain away its singular pretension. As commonly interpreted need would be at the basis of desire; desire would characterize a being indigent and incomplete or fallen from its past grandeur. It would coincide with the consciousness of what has been lost; it would be essentially a nostalgia, a longing for return. But thus it would not even suspect what the veritably other is.

The metaphysical desire does not long to return, for it is desire for a

---

* "*Chez soi*"—translating the Hegelian *bei sich*—will for Levinas express the original and concrete form in which an existent comes to exist "for itself." We shall (rather clumsily!) translate "*chez soi*" by "at home with oneself." But it should be remembered that it is in the being "at home," i.e. in the act of inhabiting, that the circuit of the self arises.—Trans.

land not of our birth, for a land foreign to every nature, which has not been our fatherland and to which we shall never betake ourselves. The metaphysical desire does not rest upon any prior kinship. It is a desire that can not be satisfied. For we speak lightly of desires satisfied, or of sexual needs, or even of moral and religious needs. Love itself is thus taken to be the satisfaction of a sublime hunger. If this language is possible it is because most of our desires and love too are not pure. The desires one can satisfy resemble metaphysical desire only in the deceptions of satisfaction or in the exasperation of non-satisfaction and desire which constitutes voluptuosity itself. The metaphysical desire has another intention; it desires beyond everything that can simply complete it. It is like goodness—the Desired does not fulfill it, but deepens it.

It is a generosity nourished by the Desired, and thus a relationship that is not the disappearance of distance, not a bringing together, or—to circumscribe more closely the essence of generosity and of goodness—a relationship whose positivity comes from remoteness, from separation, for it nourishes itself, one might say, with its hunger. This remoteness is radical only if desire is not the possibility of anticipating the desirable, if it does not think it beforehand, if it goes toward it aimlessly, that is, as toward an absolute, unanticipatable alterity, as one goes forth unto death. Desire is absolute if the desiring being is mortal and the Desired invisible. Invisibility does not denote an absence of relation; it implies relations with what is not given, of which there is no idea. Vision is an adequation of the idea with the thing, a comprehension that encompasses. Non-adequation does not denote a simple negation or an obscurity of the idea, but—beyond the light and the night, beyond the knowledge measuring beings—the inordinateness of Desire. Desire is desire for the absolutely other. Besides the hunger one satisfies, the thirst one quenches, and the senses one allays, metaphysics desires the other beyond satisfactions, where no gesture by the body to diminish the aspiration is possible, where it is not possible to sketch out any known caress nor invent any new caress. A desire without satisfaction which, precisely, *understands* [*entend*] the remoteness, the alterity, and the exteriority of the other. For Desire this alterity, non-adequate to the idea, has a meaning. It is understood as the alterity of the Other and of the Most-High. The very dimension of height[1] is opened up by meta-

---

[1] " . . . in my opinion, that knowledge only which is of being and of the unseen can make the soul look upwards . . ." Plato, *Republic*, 529b. (Trans. B. Jowett, *The Dialogues of Plato*, New York, 1937.)

physical Desire. That this height is no longer the heavens but the Invisible is the very elevation of height and its nobility. To die for the invisible—this is metaphysics. This does not mean that desire can dispense with acts. But these acts are neither consumption, nor caress, nor liturgy.

Demented pretension to the invisible, when the acute experience of the human in the twentieth century teaches that the thoughts of men are borne by needs which explain society and history, that hunger and fear can prevail over every human resistance and every freedom! There is no question of doubting this human misery, this dominion the things and the wicked exercise over man, this animality. But to be a man is to know that this is so. Freedom consists in knowing that freedom is in peril. But to know or to be conscious is to have time to avoid and forestall the instant of inhumanity. It is this perpetual postponing of the hour of treason—infinitesimal difference between man and non-man—that implies the disinterestedness of goodness, the desire of the absolutely other or nobility, the dimension of metaphysics.

2. The Breach of Totality

This absolute exteriority of the metaphysical term, the irreducibility of movement to an inward play, to a simple presence of self to self, is, if not demonstrated, claimed by the word transcendent. The metaphysical movement is transcendent, and transcendence, like desire and inadequation, is necessarily a transascendence.[2] The transcendence with which the metaphysician designates it is distinctive in that the distance it expresses, unlike all distances, enters into the *way of existing* of the exterior being. Its formal characteristic, to be other, makes up its content. Thus the metaphysician and the other can not be *totalized*. The metaphysician is absolutely separated.

The metaphysician and the other do not constitute a simple correlation, which would be reversible. The reversibility of a relation where the terms are indifferently read from left to right and from right to left would couple them the *one* to the *other;* they would complete one another in a system visible from the outside. The intended transcendence would be thus reabsorbed into the unity of the system, destroying the radical

---

[2] We borrow this term from Jean Wahl. Cf. "Sur l'idée de la transcendance" in *Existence humaine et transcendance* (Neuchâtel, 1944). We have drawn much inspiration from the themes evoked in that study.

alterity of the other. Irreversibility does not only mean that the same goes unto the other differently than the other unto the same. That eventuality does not enter into account: the radical separation between the same and the other means precisely that it is impossible to place oneself outside of the correlation between the same and the other so as to record the correspondence or the non-correspondence of this going with this return. Otherwise the same and the other would be reunited under one gaze, and the absolute distance that separates them filled in.

The alterity, the radical heterogeneity of the other, is possible only if the other is other with respect to a term whose essence is to remain at the point of departure, to serve as *entry* into the relation, to be the same not relatively but absolutely. *A term can remain absolutely at the point of departure of relationship only as I.*

To be I is, over and beyond any individuation that can be derived from a system of references, to have identity as one's content. The I is not a being that always remains the same, but is the being whose existing consists in identifying itself, in recovering its identity throughout all that happens to it. It is the primal identity, the primordial work of identification.

The I is identical in its very alterations. It represents them to itself and thinks them. The universal identity in which the heterogenous can be embraced has the ossature of a subject, of the first person. Universal thought is an "I think."

The I is identical in its very alterations in yet another sense. The I that thinks hearkens to itself thinking or takes fright before its depths and is to itself an other. It thus discovers the famous naïveté of its thought, which thinks "straight on" as one "follows one's nose."* It hearkens to itself thinking and surprises itself being dogmatic, foreign to itself. But faced with this alterity the I is the same, merges with itself, is incapable of apostasy with regard to this surprising "self." Hegelian phenomenology, where self-consciousness is the distinguishing of what is not distinct, expresses the universality of the same identifying itself in the alterity of objects thought and despite the opposition of self to self. "I distinguish myself from myself; and therein I am immediately aware that this factor distinguished from me is not distinguished. I, the selfsame being, thrust myself away from myself; but this which is distinguished, which is set up as unlike me, is immediately on its being distinguished no

---

* ". . . qui pense 'devant elle', comme and marche 'devant soi'."

distinction for me."[3] The difference is not a difference; the I, as other, is not an "other." We will not retain from this citation Hegel's affirmation of the provisional character of immediate evidence. The I that repels the self, lived as repugnance, the I riveted to itself, lived as ennui, are modes of self-consciousness and rest on the unrendable identity of the I and the self. The alterity of the I that takes itself for another may strike the imagination of the poet precisely because it is but the play of the same: the negation of the I by the self is precisely one of the modes of identification of the I.

The identification of the same in the I is not produced as a monotonous tautology: "I am I." The originality of identification, irreducible to the A is A formalism, would thus escape attention. It is not to be fixed by reflecting on the abstract representation of self by self; it is necessary to begin with the concrete relationship between an I and a world. The world, foreign and hostile, should, in good logic, alter the I. But the true and primordial relation between them, and that in which the I is revealed precisely as preeminently the same, is produced as a *sojourn* [*séjour*] in the world. The *way* of the I against the "other" of the world consists in *sojourning*, in *identifying oneself* by existing here *at home with onself* [*chez soi*]. In a world which is from the first other the I is nonetheless autochthonous. It is the very reversion of this alteration. It finds in the world a site [lieu] and a home [maison]. Dwelling is the very mode of *maintaining oneself* [*se tenir*],* not as the famous serpent grasping itself by biting onto its tail, but as the body that, on the earth exterior to it, holds *itself* up [*se* tient] and *can*. The "at home" [Le "chez soi"] is not a container but a site where *I can,* where, dependent on a reality that is other, I am, despite this dependence or thanks to it, free. It is enough to walk, to *do* [*faire*], in order to grasp anything, to take. In a sense everything is in the site, in the last analysis everything is at my disposal, even the stars, if I but reckon them, calculate the intermediaries or the means. The site, a medium [Le lieu, milieu], affords means. Everything is here, everything belongs to me; everything is caught up in advance with the primordial occupying of a site, everything

---

[3] G. W. F. Hegel, *The Phenomenology of Mind,* Eng. trans. J. B. Baillie, 2nd ed. (London & New York, 1955), p. 211.

* "Se tenir" involves the notion of containing oneself; it is the idea of an active identity with oneself. It also involves the notion of holding oneself up, of standing, of having a stance—which is at the same time a position and an attitude, a posture and an intention. Hence Levinas immediately passes to the idea of the "I can" it implicates.—Trans.

is com-prehended.* The possibility of possessing, that is, of suspending the very alterity of what is only at first other, and other relative to me, is the *way* of the same. I am at home with myself in the world because it offers itself to or resists possession. (What is absolutely other does not only resist possession, but contests it, and accordingly can consecrate it.) This reversion of the alterity of the world to self-identification must be taken seriously; the "moments" of this identification—the body, the home, labor, possession, economy—are not to figure as empirical and contingent data, laid over the formal skeleton of the same; they are the articulations of this structure. The identification of the same is not the void of a tautology nor a dialectical opposition to the other, but the concreteness of egoism. This is important for the possibility of metaphysics. If the same would establish its identity by simple *opposition to the other,* it would already be a part of a totality encompassing the same and the other. The pretension of metaphysical desire, with which we began, the relationship with the absolutely other, would be belied. But the metaphysician's separation from the metaphysical, which is maintained within the relationship by being produced as an egoism, is not the simple obverse of that relationship.

But how can the same, produced as egoism, enter into relationship with an other without immediately divesting it of its alterity? What is the nature of this relationship?

The metaphysical relation can not be properly speaking a representation, for the other would therein dissolve into the same: every representation is essentially interpretable as a transcendental constitution. The other with which the metaphysician is in relationship and *which he recognizes as other* is not simply in another locality; this other recalls Plato's Ideas which, according to Aristotle's formula, are not in a site. The *sway* [*pouvoir*] of the I will not cross the distance marked by the alterity of the other. To be sure my own most inward sphere of intimacy appears to me as foreign or hostile; usage-objects, foods, the very world we inhabit are other in relation to us. But the alterity of the I and the world inhabited is only formal; as we have indicated, in a world in which I sojourn this alterity falls under my powers. The metaphysical other is other with an alterity that is not formal, is not the simple reverse of identity, and is not formed out of resistance to the same, but is prior to every

---

* ". . . tout à l'avance est pris avec la prise originelle du lieu, tout est compris."

initiative, to all imperialism of the same. It is other with an alterity constitutive of the very content of the other. Other with an alterity that does not limit the same, for in limiting the same the other would not be rigorously other: by virtue of the common frontier the other, within the system, would yet be the same.

The absolutely other is the Other.* He and I do not form a number. The collectivity in which I say "you" or "we" is not a plural of the "I." I, you—these are not individuals of a common concept. Neither possession nor the unity of number nor the unity of concepts link me to the Stranger [l'Etranger], the Stranger who disturbs the being at home with oneself [le chez soi]. But Stranger also means the free one. Over him I have no *power*.** He escapes my grasp by an essential dimension, even if I have him at my disposal. He is not wholly in my site. But I, who have no concept in common with the Stranger, am, like him, without genus. We are the same and the other. The conjunction *and* here designates neither addition nor power of one term over the other. We shall try to show that the *relation* between the same and the other—upon which we seem to impose such extraordinary conditions—is language. For language accomplishes a relation such that the terms are not limitrophe within this relation, such that the other, despite the relationship with the same, remains transcendent to the same. The relation between the same and the other, metaphysics, is primordially enacted as conversation,† where the same, gathered up in its ipseity as an "I," as a particular existent unique and autochthonous, leaves itself.

A relation whose terms do not form a totality can hence be produced within the general economy of being only as proceeding from the I to the other, as a *face to face,* as delineating a distance in depth—that of conversation, of goodness, of Desire—irreducible to the distance the synthetic activity of the understanding establishes between the diverse terms, other with respect to one another, that lend themselves to its synoptic operation. The I is not a contingent formation by which the same and the other, as logical determinations of being, can in addition be reflected *within a thought*. It is in order that alterity be produced *in being* that a "thought" is needed and that an I is needed. The irreversibility of the relation can be produced only if the relation is effected by one of the terms as the very movement of transcendence, as the *traversing* of this

---

* "L'absolument Autre, c'est Autrui."
** ". . . je ne peux *pouvoir*."
† *discours*—this term shall often be rendered by "discourse."

distance, and not as a recording of, or the psychological invention of this movement. "Thought" and "interiority" are the very break-up of being and the production (not the reflection) of transcendence. We know this relation only in the measure that we effect it; this is what is distinctive about it. Alterity is possible only starting from *me*.

Conversation, from the very fact that it maintains the distance between me and the Other, the radical separation asserted in transcendence which prevents the reconstitution of totality, cannot renounce the egoism of its existence; but the very fact of being in a conversation consists in recognizing in the Other a *right* over this egoism, and hence in justifying oneself. Apology, in which the I at the same time asserts itself and inclines before the transcendent, belongs to the essence of conversation. The goodness in which (as we will see further) conversation issues and from which it draws signification will not undo this apologetic moment.

The breach of totality is not an operation of thought, obtained by a simple distinguishing of terms that evoke one another or at least line up opposite one another. The void that breaks the totality can be maintained against an inevitably totalizing and synoptic thought only if thought finds itself *faced* with an other refractory to categories. Rather than constituting a total with this other as with an object, *thought consists in speaking*. We propose to call "religion" the bond that is established between the same and the other without constituting a totality.

But to say that the other can remain absolutely other, that he enters only into the relationship of conversation, is to say that history itself, an identification of the same, cannot claim to totalize the same and the other. The absolutely other, whose alterity is overcome in the philosophy of immanence on the allegedly common plane of history, maintains his transcendence in the midst of history. The same is essentially identification within the diverse, or history, or system. It is not I who resist the system, as Kierkegaard thought; it is the other.

3. Transcendence Is Not Negativity

The movement of transcendence is to be distinguished from the negativity by which discontent man refuses the condition in which he is established. Negativity presupposes a being established, placed in a site where he is at home [chez soi]; it is an economic fact, in the etymological sense of this adjective. Labor transforms the world, but is sustained by the world it transforms. The labor that matter resists puts to profit the resistance of materials; the resistance is still within the same. The negator and the negated are posited together, form a system, that is, a totality. The doctor who missed an engineering career, the poor man who longs for wealth, the patient who suffers, the melancholic who is bored for nothing oppose their condition while remaining attached to its horizons. The "otherwise" and the "elsewhere" they wish still belong to the here below they refuse. The desperate person who wills nothingness or eternal life pronounces a total refusal of the here below; but death, for the one bent on suicide and for the believer, remains catastrophic. God always calls us to Himself too soon; we want the here below. In the horror of the radical unknown to which death leads is evinced the limit of negativity.[4] This mode of negating while taking refuge in what one negates delineates the same or the I. The alterity of a world refused is not the alterity of the Stranger but that of the fatherland which welcomes and protects. Metaphysics does not coincide with negativity.

One may indeed endeavor to deduce the metaphysical alterity from beings that are familiar to us, and thus contest its radical character. Is not metaphysical alterity obtained by the superlative expression of perfections whose pale image fills the here below? But the negation of imperfections does not suffice for the conception of this alterity. Precisely perfection exceeds conception, overflows the concept; it designates distance: the idealization that makes it possible is a passage to the limit, that is, a transcendence, a passage to the other absolutely other. The idea of the perfect is an idea of infinity. The perfection designated by this passage to the limit does not remain on the common plane of the *yes* and the *no* at which negativity operates; on the contrary, the idea of infinity designates a height and a nobility, a transascendence. The Cartesian primacy of the idea of the perfect over the idea of the imperfect thus remains entirely valid. The idea of the perfect and of infinity is not reducible to the negation of the imperfect; negativity is incapable of transcendence. Transcendence designates a relation with a reality infinitely distant from my own reality, yet without this distance destroying this relation and without this relation destroying this distance, as would happen with relations within the same; this relation does not be-

---

[4] Cf. our remarks on death and the future in "Le Temps et l'Autre" (*La Choix, le monde, l'existence* [Grenoble, 1947], p. 166), which agree on so many points with Blanchot's admirable analyses in *Critique*, t. VIII, n. 66 (Nov., 1952), pp. 915 ff.

come an implantation in the other and a confusion with him, does not affect the very identity of the same, its ipseity, does not silence the *apology,* does not become apostasy and ecstasy.

We have called this relation metaphysical. It is premature and in any case insufficient to qualify it, by opposition to negativity, as positive. It would be false to qualify it as theological. It is prior to the negative or affirmative proposition; it first institutes language, where neither the no nor the yes is the first word. The description of this relation is the central issue of the present research.

4. Metaphysics Precedes Ontology

It is not by chance that the theoretical relation has been the preferred schema of the metaphysical relation. Knowledge or theory designates first a relation with being such that the knowing being lets the known being manifest itself while respecting its alterity and without marking it in any way whatever by this cognitive relation. In this sense metaphysical desire would be the essence of theory. But theory also designates comprehension [intelligence]—the logos of being—that is, a way of approaching the known being such that its alterity with regard to the knowing being vanishes. The process of cognition is at this stage identified with the freedom of the knowing being encountering nothing which, other with respect to it, could limit it. This mode of depriving the known being of its alterity can be accomplished only if it is aimed at through a third term, a neutral term, which itself is not a being; in it the shock of the encounter of the same with the other is deadened. This third term may appear as a concept thought. Then the individual that exists abdicates into the general that is thought. The third term may be called sensation, in which objective quality and subjective affection are merged. It may appear as *Being* distinguished from the *existent:* Being, which at the same time is not (that is, is not posited as an existent) and yet corresponds to the work plied by the existent, which is not a nothing. Being, which is without the density of existents, is the light in which existents become intelligible. To theory as comprehension of beings the general title ontology is appropriate. Ontology, which reduces the other to the same, promotes freedom—the freedom that is the identification of the same, not allowing itself to be alienated by the other. Here theory enters upon a course that renounces metaphysical Desire, renounces the marvel of exteriority from which that Desire lives.

But theory understood as a respect for exteriority delineates another structure essential for metaphysics. In its comprehension of being (or ontology) it is concerned with critique. It discovers the dogmatism and naïve arbitrariness of its spontaneity, and calls into question the freedom of the exercise of ontology; it then seeks to exercise this freedom in such a way as to turn back at every moment to the origin of the arbitrary dogmatism of this free exercise. This would lead to an infinite regression if this return itself remained an ontological movement, an exercise of freedom, a theory. Its critical intention then leads it beyond theory and ontology: critique does not reduce the other to the same as does ontology, but calls into question the exercise of the same. A calling into question of the same—which cannot occur within the egoist spontaneity of the same—is brought about by the other. We name this calling into question of my spontaneity by the presence of the Other ethics. The strangeness of the Other, his irreducibility to the I, to my thoughts and my possessions, is precisely accomplished as a calling into question of my spontaneity, as ethics. Metaphysics, transcendence, the welcoming of the other by the same, of the Other by me, is concretely produced as the calling into question of the same by the other, that is, as the ethics that accomplishes the critical essence of knowledge. And as critique precedes dogmatism, metaphysics precedes ontology.

Western philosophy has most often been an ontology: a reduction of the other to the same by interposition of a middle and neutral term that ensures the comprehension of being.

This primacy of the same was Socrates's teaching: to receive nothing of the Other but what is in me, as though from all eternity I was in possession of what comes to me from the outside—to receive nothing, or to be free. Freedom does not resemble the capricious spontaneity of free will; its ultimate meaning lies in this permanence in the same, which is reason. Cognition is the deployment of this identity; it is freedom. That reason in the last analysis would be the manifestation of a freedom, neutralizing the other and encompassing him, can come as no surprise once it was laid down that sovereign reason knows only itself, that nothing other limits it. The neutralization of the other who becomes a theme or an object—appearing, that is, taking its place in the light—is precisely his reduction to the same. To know ontologically is to surprise in an existent confronted that by which it is not this existent, this stranger, that by which it is somehow betrayed, surrenders, is given in the horizon in which it loses itself and appears, lays itself open to grasp, ɔmes a concept. To know amounts to grasping being out of nothing or reducing it to nothing, removing from it its alterity. This result is obtained from the moment of the first ray of light. To illuminate is to remove from being its resistance, because light opens a horizon and empties space—delivers being out of nothingness. Mediation (characteristic of Western philosophy) is meaningful only if it is not limited to reducing distances. For how could intermediaries reduce the intervals between terms infinitely distant? Will not the intervals between the mid-points progressively staked out ad infinitum appear always equally untraversable? If an exterior and foreign being is to surrender itself to intermediaries there must be produced somewhere a great "betrayal." As far as the things are concerned, a surrender is carried out in their conceptualization. As for man, it can be obtained by the terror that brings a free man under the domination of another. For the things the work of ontology consists in apprehending the individual (which alone exists) not in its individuality but in its generality (of which alone there is science). The relation with the other is here accomplished only through a third term which I find in myself. The ideal of Socratic truth thus rests on the essential self-sufficiency of the same, its identification in ipseity, its egoism. Philosophy is an egology.

Berkeley's idealism, which passes for a philosophy of the immediate, also answers to the ontological problem. Berkeley found in the very qualities of objects the hold they offered to the I; in recognizing in qualities, which remove the things from us most, their lived essence he spanned the distance separating the subject from the object. The coinciding of lived experience with itself was revealed to be a coinciding of thought with an existent. The work of comprehension lay in this coincidence. Thus Berkeley immerses all sensible qualities in the lived experience of affection.

Phenomenological mediation follows another route, where the "ontological imperialism" is yet more visible. It is the Being of existents that is the *medium* of truth; truth regarding an existent presupposes the prior openness of Being. To say that the truth of an existent proceeds from the openness of Being is in any event to say that its intelligibility is due not to our coinciding, but to our non-coinciding with it. An existent is comprehended in the measure that thought transcends it, measuring it against the horizon whereupon it is profiled. Since Husserl the whole of phenomenology is the promotion of the idea of *horizon,* which for it plays a role equivalent to that of the *concept* in classical idealism; an existent arises upon a ground that extends beyond it, as an individual arises from a concept. But what commands the non-coinciding of thought with the existent—the Being of the existent, which guarantees the independence and the extraneity of the existent—is a phosphorescence, a luminosity, a generous effulgence. The existing of an existant is converted into intelligibility; its independence is a surrender in radiation. To broach an existent from Being is simultaneously to let it be and to comprehend it. Reason seizes upon an existent through the void and nothingness of existing—wholly light and phosphorescence. Approached from Being, from the luminous horizon where it has a silhouette, but has lost its face, an existent is the very appeal that is addressed to comprehension. *Being and Time* has argued perhaps but one sole thesis: Being is inseparable from the comprehension of Being (which unfolds as time) ; Being is already an appeal to subjectivity.

The primacy of ontology for Heidegger[5] does not rest on the truism: "to know an *existent* it is necessary to have comprehended the Being of existents." To affirm the priority of *Being* over *existents* is to already decide the essence of philosophy; it is to subordinate the relation with *someone,* who is an existent, (the ethical relation) to a relation with the *Being of existents,* which, impersonal, permits the apprehension, the domination of existents (a relationship of knowing), subordinates justice to freedom. If freedom denotes the mode of remaining the same in the midst of the other, knowledge, where an existent is given by interposition of impersonal Being, contains the ultimate sense of freedom. It would be opposed to justice, which involves obligations with regard to an existent that refuses to give itself, the Other, who in this sense would be an existent par excellence. In subordinating every relation with existents to the relation with Being the Heideggerian ontology affirms the primacy of freedom over ethics. To be sure, the freedom involved in the essence of truth is not for Heidegger a principle of free will. Freedom comes from an obedience to Being: it is not man who possesses freedom; it is freedom that possesses man. But the dialectic which thus reconciles freedom and obedience in the concept of truth presupposes the primacy of the same, which marks the direction of and defines the whole of Western philosophy.

The relation with Being that is enacted as ontology consists in neutral-

---

[5] Cf. our article "L'ontologie est-elle fondamentale?" in the *Revue de Métaphysique et de Morale* (janvier, 1951).

izing the existent in order to comprehend or grasp it. It is hence not a relation with the other as such but the reduction of the other to the same. Such is the definition of freedom: to maintain oneself against the other, despite every relation with the other to ensure the autarchy of an I. Thematization and conceptualization, which moreover are inseparable, are not peace with the other but suppression or possession of the other. For possession affirms the other, but within a negation of its independence. "I think" comes down to "I can"—to an appropriation of what is, to an exploitation of reality. Ontology as first philosophy is a philosophy of power. It issues in the State and in the non-violence of the totality, without securing itself against the violence from which this non-violence lives, and which appears in the tyranny of the State. Truth, which should reconcile persons, here exists anonymously. Universality presents itself as impersonal; and this is another inhumanity.

The "egoism" of ontology is maintained even when, denouncing Socratic philosophy as already forgetful of Being and already on the way to the notion of the "subject" and technological power, Heidegger finds in Presocratism thought as obedience to the truth of Being. This obedience would be accomplished in existing as builder and cultivator, effecting the unity of the site which sustains space. In bringing together presence on the earth and under the firmament of the heavens, the waiting for the gods and the company of mortals in the presence to the things —which is to build and to cultivate—Heidegger, with the whole of Western history, takes the relation with the Other as enacted in the destiny of sedentary peoples, the possessors and builders of the earth. Possession is preeminently the form in which the other becomes the same, by becoming mine. In denouncing the sovereignty of the technological powers of man Heidegger exalts the pre-technological powers of possession. His analyses do not start with the thing-object, to be sure, but they bear the mark of the great landscapes to which the things refer. Ontology becomes ontology of nature, impersonal fecundity, faceless generous mother, matrix of particular beings, inexhaustible matter for things.

A philosophy of power, ontology is, as first philosophy which does not call into question the same, a philosophy of injustice. Even though it opposes the technological passion issued forth from the forgetting of Being hidden by existents, Heideggerian ontology, which subordinates the relationship with the Other to the relation with Being in general, remains under obedience to the anonymous, and leads inevitably to another power, to imperialist domination, to tyranny. Tyranny is not the pure and simple extension of technology to reified men. Its origin lies back in the pagan "moods," in the enrootedness in the earth, in the adoration that enslaved men can devote to their masters. *Being* before the *existent,* ontology before metaphysics, is freedom (be it the freedom of theory) before justice. It is a movement within the same before obligation to the other.

The terms must be reversed. For the philosophical tradition the *conflicts* between the same and the other are resolved by theory whereby the other is reduced to the same—or, concretely, by the community of the State, where beneath anonymous power, though it be intelligible, the I rediscovers war in the tyrannic oppression it undergoes from the totality. Ethics, where the same takes the irreducible Other into account, would belong to opinion. The effort of this book is directed toward apperceiving in discourse a non-allergic relation with alterity, toward apperceiving Desire—where power, by essence murderous of the other, becomes, faced with the other and "against all good sense," the impossibility of murder, the consideration of the other, or justice. Concretely our effort consists in maintaining, within anonymous community, the society of the I with the Other—language and goodness. This relation is not prephilosophical, for it does not do violence to the I, is not imposed upon it brutally from the outside, despite itself, or unbeknown to it, as an opinion; more exactly, it is imposed upon the I beyond all violence by a violence that calls it entirely into question. The ethical relation, opposed to first philosophy which identifies freedom and power, is not contrary to truth; it goes unto being in its absolute exteriority, and accomplishes the very intention that animates the movement unto truth.

The relationship with a being infinitely distant, that is, overflowing its idea, is such that its authority as an existent is already *invoked* in every question we could raise concerning the meaning of its Being. One does not question oneself concerning him; one questions him. Always he faces. If ontology—the comprehension, the embracing of Being—is impossible, it is not because every definition of Being already presupposes the knowledge of Being, as Pascal had said and Heidegger refutes in the first pages of *Being and Time;* it is because the comprehension of Being in general cannot *dominate* the relationship with the Other. The latter relationship commands the first. I cannot disentangle myself from society with the Other, even when I consider the Being of the existent he is. Already the comprehension of Being is said to the existent, who again arises behind the theme in which he is presented. This "saying to the Other"—this relationship with the Other as interlocutor, this relation with an *existent*—precedes all ontology; it is the ultimate relation in Being. Ontology presupposes metaphysics.

5. *Transcendence as the Idea of Infinity*

The schema of theory in which metaphysics was found distinguished theory from all ecstatic behavior. Theory excludes the implantation of the knowing being in the known being, the entering into the Beyond by ecstasy. It remains knowledge, relationship. To be sure, representation does not constitute the primordial relation with being. It is nonetheless privileged, precisely as the possibility of recalling the separation of the I. And to have substituted for the magical communion of species and the confusion of distinct orders a spiritual relation in which beings remain at their post but communicate among themselves will have been the imperishable merit of the "admirable Greek people," and the very institution of philosophy. In condemning suicide, at the beginning of the *Phaedo,* Socrates refuses the false spiritualism of the pure and simple and immediate union with the Divine, characterized as desertion; he proclaims ineluctable the difficult itinerary of knowledge starting from the here below. The knowing being remains separated from the known being. The ambiguity of Descartes's first evidence, revealing the I and God in turn without merging them, revealing them as two distinct moments of evidence mutually founding one another, characterizes the very meaning of separation. The separation of the I is thus affirmed to be non-contingent, non-provisional. The distance between me and God, radical and necessary, is produced in being itself. Philosophical transcendence thereby differs from the transcendence of religions (in the current thaumaturgic and generally lived sense of this term), from the transcendence that is already (or still) participation, submergence in the being toward which it goes, which holds the transcending being in its invisible meshes, as to do it violence.

This relation of the same with the other, where the transcendence of the relation does not cut the bonds a relation implies, yet where these bonds do not unite the same and the other into a Whole, is in fact fixed in the situation described by Descartes in which the "I think" maintains with the Infinite it can nowise contain and from which it is separated a relation called "idea of infinity." To be sure, things, mathematical and moral notions are also, according to Descartes, presented to us through their ideas, and are distinct from them. But the idea of infinity is exceptional in that its *ideatum* surpasses its idea, whereas for the things the total coincidence of their "objective" and "formal" realities is not precluded; we could conceivably have accounted for all the ideas, other than that of Infinity, by ourselves. Without deciding anything for the moment as to the veritable significance of the presence of the ideas of things in us, without holding to the Cartesian argumentation that *proves* the separated existence of the Infinite by the finitude of the being having an idea of infinity (for there perhaps is not much sense to proving an existence by describing a situation prior to proof and to the problems of existence), it is of importance to emphasize that the transcendence of the Infinite with respect to the I which is separated from it and which thinks it measures (so to speak) its very infinitude. The distance that separates *ideatum* and idea here constitutes the content of the *ideatum* itself. Infinity is characteristic of a transcendent being as transcendent; the infinite is the absolutely other. The transcendent is the sole *ideatum* of which there can be only an idea in us; it is infinitely removed from its idea, that is, exterior, because it is infinite.

To think the infinite, the transcendent, the Stranger, is hence not to think an object. But to think what does not have the lineaments of an object is in reality to do more or better than think. The distance of transcendence is not equivalent to that which separates the mental act from its object in all our representations, since the distance at which the object stands does not exclude, and in reality implies, the *possession* of the object, that is, the suspension of its being. The "intentionality" of transcendence is unique in its kind; *the difference between objectivity and transcendence will serve as a general guideline for all the analyses of this work.* We find that this presence in thought of an idea whose *ideatum* overflows the capacity of thought is given expression not only in Aristotle's theory of the agent intellect, but also, very often, in Plato. Against a thought that proceeds from him who "has his own head to himself,"[6] he affirms the value of the delirium that comes from God, "winged thought."[7] Delirium here does not have an irrationalist significance; it is only a "divine release of the soul from the yoke of custom and convention."[8] The fourth type of delirium is reason itself, rising to the

---

[6] *Phaedrus*, 244a.

[7] *Phaedrus*, 249a.

[8] *Phaedrus*, 265a.

ideas, thought in the highest sense. Possession by a god, enthusiasm, is not the irrational, but the end of the solitary (and which we will later call "economic") or inward thought, the beginning of a true experience of the *new* and of the noumenon—already Desire.

The Cartesian notion of the idea of the Infinite designates a relation with a being that maintains its total exteriority with respect to him who thinks it. It designates the contact with the intangible, a contact that does not compromise the integrity of what is touched. To affirm the presence in us of the idea of infinity is to deem purely abstract and formal the contradiction the idea of metaphysics is said to harbor, which Plato brings up in the *Parmenides*[9]—that the relation with the Absolute would render the Absolute relative. The absolute exteriority of the exterior being is not purely and simply lost as a result of its manifestation; it "absolves" itself from the relation in which it presents itself. But the infinite distance of the Stranger despite the proximity achieved by the idea of infinity, the complex structure of the unparalleled relation designated by this idea, has to be described; it is not enough to distinguish it formally from objectification.

We must now indicate the terms which will state the deformalization or the concretization of the idea of infinity, this apparently wholly empty notion. The infinite in the finite, the more in the less, which is accomplished by the idea of Infinity, is produced as Desire—not a Desire that the possession of the Desirable slakes, but the Desire for the Infinite which the desirable arouses rather than satisfies. A Desire perfectly disinterested—goodness. But Desire and goodness concretely presuppose a relationship in which the Desirable arrests the "negativity" of the I that holds sway in the Same—puts an end to power and emprise. This is positively produced as the possession of a world I can bestow as a gift on the Other—that is, as a presence before a face. For the presence before a face, my orientation toward the Other, can lose the avidity proper to the gaze only by turning into generosity, incapable of approaching the other with empty hands. This relationship established over the things henceforth possibly common, that is, susceptible of being said, is the relationship of conversation. The way in which the other presents himself, exceeding *the idea of the other in me,* we here name face. This *mode* does not consist in figuring as a theme under my gaze, in spreading itself forth as a set of qualities forming an image. The face of the

---

[9] *Parmenides,* 133b-135c, 141e-142b.

Other at each moment destroys and overflows the plastic image it leaves me, the idea existing to my own measure and to the measure of its *ideatum*—the adequate idea. It does not manifest itself by these qualities, but καθ'αὐτό. It *expresses itself*. The face brings a notion of truth which, in contradistinction to contemporary ontology, is not the disclosure of an impersonal Neuter, but *expression*: the existent breaks through all the envelopings and generalities of Being to spread out in its "form" the totality of its "content," finally abolishing the distinction between form and content. This is not achieved by some sort of modification of the knowledge that thematizes, but precisely by "thematization" turning into conversation. The condition for theoretical truth and error is the word of the other, his expression, which every lie already presupposes. But the first content of expression is the expression itself. To approach the Other in conversation is to welcome his expression, in which at each instant he overflows the idea a thought would carry away from it. It is therefore to *receive* from the Other beyond the capacity of the I, which means exactly: to have the idea of infinity. But this also means: to be taught. The relation with the Other, or Conversation, is a non-allergic relation, an ethical relation; but inasmuch as it is welcomed this conversation is a teaching [enseignement]. Teaching is not reducible to maieutics; it comes from the exterior and brings me more than I contain. In its non-violent transitivity the very epiphany of the face is produced. The Aristotelian analysis of the intellect, which discovers the agent intellect coming in by the gates, absolutely exterior, and yet constituting, nowise compromising, the sovereign activity of reason, already substitutes for maieutics a transitive action of the master, since reason, without abdicating, is found to be in a position to *receive*.

Finally, infinity, overflowing the idea of infinity, puts the spontaneous freedom within us into question. It commands and judges it and brings it to its truth. The analysis of the idea of Infinity, to which we gain access only starting from an I, will be terminated with the surpassing of the subjective.

The notion of the face, to which we will refer throughout this work, opens other perspectives: it brings us to a notion of meaning prior to my *Sinngebung* and thus independent of my initiative and my power. It signifies the philosophical priority of the existent over Being, an exteriority that does not call for power or possession, an exteriority that is not reducible, as with Plato, to the interiority of memory, and yet maintains the I who welcomes it. It finally makes possible the description of the notion of the immediate. The philosophy of the immediate is realized neither in Berkeley's idealism nor in modern ontology. To say that the *existent* is disclosed only in the openness of Being is to say that we are never directly with the existent as such. The immediate is the interpellation and, if we may speak thus, the imperative of language. The idea of contact does not represent the primordial mode of the immediate. Contact is already a thematization and a reference to a horizon. The immediate is the face to face.

Between a philosophy of transcendence that situates elsewhere the true life to which man, escaping from here, would gain access in the privileged moments of liturgical, mystical elevation, or in dying—and a philosophy of immanence in which we would truly come into possession of being when every "other" (cause for war), encompassed by the same, would vanish at the end of history—we propose to describe, within the unfolding of terrestrial existence, of economic existence (as we shall call it), a relationship with the other that does not result in a divine or human totality, that is not a totalization of history but the idea of infinity. Such a relationship is metaphysics itself. History would not be the privileged plane where Being disengaged from the particularism of points of view (with which reflection would still be affected) is manifested. If it claims to integrate myself and the other within an impersonal spirit this alleged integration is cruelty and injustice, that is, ignores the Other. History as a relationship between men ignores a position of the I before the other in which the other remains transcendent with respect to me. Though of myself I am not exterior to history, I do find in the Other a point that is absolute with regard to history—not by amalgamating with the Other, but in speaking with him. History is worked over by the ruptures of history, in which a judgment is borne upon it. When man truly approaches the Other he is uprooted from history.

B. SEPARATION AND DISCOURSE

1. Atheism or the Will

The idea of Infinity implies the separation of the same with regard to the other, but this separation cannot rest on an opposition to the other which would be purely anti-thetical. Thesis and antithesis, in repelling one another, call for one another. They appear in opposition to a synoptic gaze that encompasses them; they already form a totality which, by integrating the metaphysical transcendence expressed by the idea of infinity, relativizes it. An absolute transcendence has to be produced as non-integrateable. If separation then is necessitated by the production of Infinity overflowing its idea and therefore separated from the I inhabited by this idea (the preeminently inadequate idea), this separation must be accomplished in the I in a way that would not only be correlative and reciprocal to the transcendence in which the infinite maintains itself with respect to its idea in me, it must not only be the logical rejoinder of that transcendence; the separation of the I with regard to the other must result from a positive movement. *Correlation does not suffice as a category for transcendence.*

A separation of the I that is not the reciprocal of the transcendence of the other with regard to me is not an eventuality thought of only by quintessential abstractors. It imposes itself upon meditation in the name of a concrete moral experience: what I permit myself to demand of myself is not comparable with what I have the right to demand of the Other. This moral experience, so commonplace, indicates a metaphysical asymmetry: the radical impossibility of seeing oneself from the outside and of speaking in the same sense of oneself and of the others, and consequently the impossibility of totalization—and, on the plane of social experience, the impossibility of *forgetting* the intersubjective experience that leads to that social experience and endows it with meaning (as, to believe the phenomenologists, perception, impossible to conjure away, endows scientific experience with meaning).

53

The separation of the Same is produced in the form of an inner life, a psychism. The psychism constitutes an *event* in being; it concretizes a conjuncture of terms which were not first defined by the psychism and whose abstract formulation harbors a paradox. The original role of the psychism does not, in fact, consist in only *reflecting* being; it is already *a way of being [une manière d'être]*, resistance to the totality. Thought or the psychism opens the dimension this *way* requires. The dimension of the psychism opens under the force of the resistance a being opposes to its totalization; it is the feat of radical separation. The *cogito*, we said, evinces separation. The being infinitely surpassing its own idea in us— God in the Cartesian terminology—subtends the evidence of the *cogito*, according to the third *Meditation*. But the discovery of this metaphysical relation in the *cogito* constitutes chronologically only the second move of the philosopher. That there could be a chronological order distinct from the "logical" order, that there could be several moments in the progression, that there is a progression—here is separation. For by virtue of time this being is not *yet*—which does not make it the same as nothingness, but maintains it at a distance from itself. It is not all at once. Even its cause, older than itself, is still to come. The cause of being is thought or known by its effect *as though* it were posterior to its effect. We speak lightly of the possibility of this "as though," which is taken to indicate an illusion. But this illusion is not unfounded; it constitutes a positive event. The posteriority of the anterior—an inversion logically absurd—is produced, one would say, only by memory or by thought. But the "improbable" phenomenon of memory or of thought must precisely be interpreted as a revolution in being. Thus already theoretical thought—but in virtue of a still more profound structure that sustains it, the psychism—articulates separation. Separation is not reflected in thought, but produced by it. For in it the *After* or the *Effect* conditions the *Before* or the *Cause:* the Before *appears* and is only welcomed. Likewise, by virtue of the psychism the being that is in a *site* remains free with regard to that site; posited in a site in which it maintains itself, it is that which comes thereto from elsewhere. The present of the *cogito,* despite the support it discovers for itself *after the fact* in the absolute that transcends it, maintains itself all by itself— be it only for an instant, the space of a *cogito.* That there could be this instant of sheer youth, heedless of its slipping into the past and of its recovered self-possession in the future (and that this uprooting be necessary if the I of the *cogito* is to cling to the absolute), in short, that there be the very order or distance of time—all this articulates the ontological separation between the metaphysician and the metaphysical. The conscious being may very well involve something unconscious and implicit, and one may denounce as much as one likes its freedom as already enchained to an ignored determinism; ignorance here is a detachment, incomparable to the self-ignorance in which things lie. It is founded in the interiority of a psychism; it is positive in the enjoyment of itself. The imprisoned being, ignorant of its prison, is at home with itself. Its power for illusion—if illusion there was—constitutes its separation.

The being that thinks at first seems to present itself, to a gaze that conceives it, as integrated into a whole. In reality it is so integrated only once it is dead. Life permits it an as-for-me, a leave of absence, a postponement, which precisely is interiority. Totalization is accomplished only in history—in the history of the historiographers, that is, among the survivors. It rests on the affirmation and the conviction that the chronological order of the history of the historians outlines the plot of being in itself, analogous to nature. The time of universal history remains as the ontological ground in which particular existences are lost, are computed, and in which at least their essences are recapitulated. Birth and death as punctual moments, and the interval that separates them, are lodged in this universal time of the historian, who is a survivor. Interiority as such is a "nothing," "pure thought," nothing but thought. In the time of the historiographer interiority is the non-being in which everything is possible, for in it nothing is impossible—the "everything is possible" of madness. This possibility is not an essence, that is, is not the possibility of a being. But for there to be a separated being, for the totalization of history to not be the ultimate schema of being, it is necessary that death which for the survivor is an end be not only this end; it is necessary that there be in dying another direction than that which leads to the end as to a point of impact in the duration of survivors. Separation designates the possibility of an *existent* being set up and having its own destiny to itself, that is, being born and dying without the place of this birth and this death in the time of universal history being the measure of its reality. Interiority is the very possibility of a birth and a death that do not derive their meaning from history. Interiority institutes an order different from historical time in which totality is constituted, an order where everything is *pending*, where what is no longer possible historically remains always possible. The birth of a separated being that must proceed from nothingness, absolute beginning, is an event historically absurd. So also is the activity issuing from a will which, within historical continuity, at each instant marks the point of a new origin. These paradoxes are overcome by the psychism.

Memory recaptures and reverses and suspends what is already accomplished in birth—in nature. Fecundity escapes the punctual instant of death. By memory I ground myself after the event, retroactively: I assume today what in the absolute past of the origin had no subject to receive it and had therefore the weight of a fatality. By memory I assume and put back in question. Memory realizes impossibility: memory, after the event, assumes the passivity of the past and masters it. Memory as an inversion of historical time is the essence of interiority.

In the totality of the historiographer the death of the other is an *end,* the point at which the separated being is cast into the totality, and at which, consequently, *dying* can be passed through and past, the point from which the separated being will continue by virtue of the heritage his existence had amassed. But the psychism extracts an existence resistant to a fate that would consist in becoming "nothing but past"; interiority is the refusal to be transformed into a pure loss figuring in an alien accounting system. The death agony is precisely in this impossibility of ceasing, in the ambiguity of a time that has run out and of a mysterious time that yet remains; death is consequently not reducible to the end of a being. What "still remains" is totally different from the future that one welcomes, that one projects forth and in a certain measure draws from oneself. For a being to whom everything happens in conformity with projects, death is an absolute event, absolutely a posteriori, open to no power, not even to negation. Dying is agony because in dying a being does not come to an end while coming to an end; he has no more time, that is, can no longer wend his way anywhere, but thus he goes where one cannot go, suffocates—how much longer. . . . The non-reference to the common time of history means that mortal existence unfolds in a dimension that does not run parallel to the time of history and is not situated with respect to this time as to an absolute. This is why the life between birth and death is neither folly nor absurdity nor flight nor cowardice. It flows on in a dimension of its own where it has meaning, and where a triumph over death can have meaning. This triumph is not a new *possibility* offered after the end of every possibility—but a resurrection in the son in whom the rupture of death is embodied. Death—suffocation in the impossibility of the possible—opens a passage toward descent. Fecundity is yet a personal relation, though it be not given to the "I"* as a possibility.[1]

There would be no separated being if the time of the One could fall into the time of the other. This is what was expressed, always negatively, by the idea of the eternity of the soul: the dead one's refusal to fall into the time of the other, the personal time free from common time. If the common time were to absorb the time of the "I"** death would be the end. But if refusal to be purely and simply integrated into history would indicate the continuation of life after death or its preexistence prior to its beginning in terms of the time of the survivor, then commencement and end would in no wise have marked a separation that could be characterized as radical and a dimension that would be interiority. For this would still be to insert the interiority into the time of history, as though perenniality throughout a time common to the plurality—the totality—dominated the fact of separation.

The non-correspondance of death to an end a survivor observes hence does not mean that the existence that is mortal but incapable of passing away would still be present after its death, that the mortal being would survive the death that strikes at the hour common to men. And one would be wrong to situate the interior time within objective time, as Husserl does, and so to prove the eternity of the soul.

Commencement and end taken as points of universal time reduce the I to the third person, such as it is spoken of by the survivor. Interiority is essentially bound to the first person of the I. The separation is radical only if each being has its own time, that is, its *interiority,* if each time is not absorbed into the universal time. By virtue of the dimension of interiority each being declines the concept and withstands totalization—a refusal necessary for the idea of Infinity, which does not produce this separation by its own force. The psychic life, which makes birth and death possible, is a dimension in being, a dimension of non-essence, beyond the possible and the impossible. It does not exhibit itself in history; the discontinuity of the inner life interrupts historical time. The thesis of the primacy of history constitutes an option for the comprehension of being in which interiority is sacrificed. The present work proposes another option. The real must not only be determined

---

* "Je."
[1] Cf. p. 267 ff.
** "Je."

in its historical objectivity, but also from interior intentions, from the *secrecy* that interrupts the continuity of historical time. Only on the basis of this secrecy is the pluralism of society possible. It attests this secrecy. We have always known that it is impossible to form an idea of the human totality, for men have an inner life closed to him who does, however, grasp the comprehensive movements of human groups. The way of access to social reality starting with the separation of the I is not engulfed in "universal history," in which only totalities appear. The experience of the other starting from a separated I remains a source of meaning for the comprehension of totalities, just as concrete perception remains determinative for the signification of scientific universes. Cronos, thinking he swallows a god, swallows but a stone.

The interval of discretion or of death is a third notion between being and nothingness.

The interval is not to life what potency is to act. Its originality consists in being between two times. We propose to call this dimension dead time. The rupture of historical and totalized duration, which dead time marks, is the very rupture that creation operates in being. The discontinuity of Cartesian time, which requires a continuous creation, indicates the very dispersion and plurality of created being. Each instant of historical time in which action commences is, in the last analysis, a birth, and hence breaks the continuous time of history, a time of works and not of wills. The inner life is the unique *way* for the real to exist as a plurality. We shall later study closely this separation that is an ipseity, in the fundamental phenomenon of enjoyment.[2]

One can call atheism this separation so complete that the separated being maintains itself in existence all by itself, without participating in the Being from which it is separated—eventually capable of adhering to it by belief. The break with participation is implied in this capability. One lives outside of God, at home with oneself; one is an I, an egoism. The soul, the dimension of the psychic, being an accomplishment of separation, is naturally atheist. By atheism we thus understand a position prior to both the negation and the affirmation of the divine, the breaking with participation by which the I posits itself as the same and as I.

It is certainly a great glory for the creator to have set up a being capable of atheism, a being which, without having been *causa sui,* has an

---

[2] Cf. Section II.

independent view and word and is at home with itself. We name "will" a being conditioned in such a way that without being *causa sui* it is first with respect to its cause. The psychism is the possibility for such a being.

The psychism will be specified as sensibility, the element of enjoyment, as egoism. In the egoism of enjoyment dawns the *ego,* source of the will. It is the psychism and not matter that provides a principle of individuation. The particularity of the τόδε τι does not prevent the singular beings from being integrated into a whole, from existing in function of the totality, in which this singularity vanishes. Individuals belonging to the extension of a concept are *one* through this concept; concepts, in their turn, are *one* in their hierarchy; their multiplicity forms a whole. If the individuals of the extension of the concept owe their individuality to an accidental or an essential attribute, this attribute nowise opposes the unity latent in their multiplicity. This unity will be actualized in the knowing of an impersonal reason, which integrates the particularities of the individuals in becoming their idea or in totalizing them by history. The absolute interval of separation cannot be obtained by distinguishing the terms of the multiplicity by some qualitative specification that would be ultimate, as in Leibniz's *Monadology,* where a *difference,* without which one monad would remain indistinguishable from an "other," is inherent in the terms.[3] As qualities the differences still refer to the community of a genus. The monads, echos of the divine substance, form a totality within its thought. The plurality required for conversation results from the interiority with which each term is "endowed," the psychism, its egoist and sensible self-reference. Sensibility constitutes the very egoism of the I, *which is sentient and not something sensed.* Man as measure of all things, that is, measured by nothing, comparing all things but incomparable, is affirmed in the sensing of sensation. Sensation breaks up every system; Hegel places at the origin of his dialectic the sensed, and not the unity of sensing and sensed in sensation. It is not by chance that in the *Theaetetus*[4] Protagoras's and Heraclitus's theses are brought together, as though the singularity of the sentient would be required for Parmedidean being to be able to be pulverized into becoming and to unfold otherwise than as an objective flux of things. A multiplicity of sentients would be the

---

[3] *Monadology,* art. 8.
[4] 152 a-e.

very *mode* in which a becoming is possible—a becoming in which thought would not simply find again, now in movement, a being subject to a universal law, producing unity. Only in this way does becoming acquire the value of an idea radically opposed to the idea of being, does it designate the resistance to every integration expressed by the image of the river, in which, according to Heraclitus, one does not bathe twice, and according to Cratylus, not even once. A notion of becoming destructive of Parmenidean monism is acquired only through the singularity of sensation.

2. Truth

We shall show further how separation or ipseity is produced primordially in the enjoyment of happiness, how in this enjoyment the separated being affirms an independence that owes nothing, neither dialectically nor logically, to the other which remains transcendent to it. This absolute independence, which does not posit itself by opposing, and which we have called atheism, does not exhaust its essence in the formalism of abstract thought. It is accomplished in all the plenitude of economic existence.[5]

While the atheist independence of the separated being does not posit itself by opposition to the idea of infinity, it alone makes possible the relation denoted by this idea. The atheist separation is *required* by the idea of Infinity, but is not dialectically brought about by it. The idea of Infinity, the relation between the same and the other, does not undo the separation attested in transcendence. Indeed the same can rejoin the other only in the hazards and risks of the quest for truth; it does not rest on the other in complete security. Without separation there would not have been truth; there would have been only being. Truth, a lesser contact than tangency, in the risk of ignorance, illusion, and error, does not undo "distance," does not result in the union of the knower and the known, does not issue in totality. Despite the theses of the philosophy of existence, this contact is not nourished from a prior enrootedness in being. The quest for truth unfolds in the apparition of forms. The distinctive characteristic of forms is precisely their epiphany at a distance. Enrootedness, a primordial preconnection, would maintain participation as one of the sovereign categories of being, whereas the

---

[5] Cf. Section II.

notion of truth marks the end of this reign. Participation is a way of referring to the other: it is to have and unfold one's own being without at any point losing contact with the other. To break with participation is, to be sure, to maintain contact, but no longer derive one's being from this contact: it is to see without being seen, like Gyges.[6] For this it is necessary that a being, though it be a part of a whole, derive its being from itself and not from its frontiers (not from its definition), exist independently, depend neither on relations that designate its place within Being nor on the recognition that the Other would bring it. The myth of Gyges is the very myth of the I and interiority, which exist non-recognized. They are, to be sure, the eventuality of all unpunished crimes, but such is the price of interiority, which is the price of separation. The inner life, the I, separation are uprootedness itself, non-participation, and consequently the ambivalent possibility of error and of truth. The knowing subject is not a part of a whole, for it is limitrophe of nothing. Its aspiration to truth is not the hollowed-out outline of the being it lacks. Truth presupposes a being autonomous in separation; the quest for a truth is precisely a relation that does not rest on the privation of need. To seek and to obtain truth is to be in a relation not because one is defined by something other than oneself, but because in a certain sense one lacks nothing.

But the quest for truth is an event more fundamental than theory, even though theoretical research is a privileged mode of the relation with exteriority we name truth. Because the separation of the separated being has not been relative, has not been a movement away from the other, but was produced as psychism, the relation with the other does not consist in repeating the movement apart in a reverse direction, but in going toward the other in Desire. Theory itself derives the exteriority of its term from this movement, for the idea of exteriority which guides the quest for truth is possible only as the idea of Infinity. The conversion of the soul to exteriority, to the absolutely other, to Infinity, is not deducible from the very identity of the soul, for it is not commensurate with the soul. The idea of infinity hence does not proceed from the I, nor from a need in the I gauging exactly its own voids; here the movement proceeds from what is thought and not from the thinker. It is the unique knowledge that presents this inversion—a knowledge without

---

[6] By contrast the things may poetically be called "blind persons." Cf. J. Wahl, "Dictionnaire subjectif," in *Poésie, pensée, perception* (Paris, 1948).

a priori. The idea of Infinity *is revealed,* in the strong sense of the term. There is no natural religion. But this exceptional knowledge is thus no longer objective. Infinity is not the "object" of a cognition (which would be to reduce it to the measure of the gaze that contemplates), but is the desirable, that which arouses Desire, that is, that which is approachable by a thought that at each instant *thinks more than it thinks.* The infinite is not thereby an immense object, exceeding the horizons of the look. It is Desire that measures the infinity of the infinite, for it is a measure through the very impossibility of measure. The inordinateness [démesure] measured by Desire is the face. Thus we again meet with the distinction between Desire and need: desire is an aspiration that the Desirable animates; it originates from its "object"; it is revelation—whereas need is a void of the Soul; it proceeds from the subject.

Truth is sought in the other, but by him who lacks nothing. The distance is untraversable, and at the same time traversed. The separated being is satisfied, autonomous, and nonetheless searches after the other with a search that is not incited by the lack proper to need nor by the memory of a lost good. Such a situation is language. Truth arises where a being separated from the other is not engulfed in him, but speaks to him. Language, which does not touch the other, even tangentially, reaches the other by calling upon him or by commanding him or by obeying him, with all the straightforwardness* of these relations. Separation and interiority, truth and language constitute the categories of the idea of infinity or metaphysics.

In separation—which is produced in the psychism of enjoyment, in egoism, in happiness, where the I identifies itself—the I is ignorant of the Other. But the Desire for the other, above happiness, requires this happiness, this autonomy of the sensible in the world, even though this separation is deducible neither analytically nor dialectically from the other. The I endowed with personal life, the atheist I whose atheism is without wants and is integrated in no destiny, surpasses itself in the Desire that comes to it from the presence of the other. This Desire is a desire in a being already happy: desire is the misfortune of the happy, a luxurious need.

Already the I exists in an eminent sense: for one cannot imagine it as

---

* *"Droiture":* we are translating this term sometimes by "straightforwardness," sometimes by "uprightness."—Trans.

first existing and in addition endowed with happiness as an attribute added to this existence. The I exists as separated in its enjoyment, that is, as happy; and it can sacrifice its pure and simple being to happiness. It *exists* in an eminent sense; it exists above being. But in Desire the being of the I appears still higher, since it can sacrifice to its Desire its very happiness. It thus finds itself above, or at the apex, at the apogee of being by enjoying (happiness) and by desiring (truth and justice). Above being. Desire marks a sort of inversion with regard to the classical notion of substance. In it being becomes goodness: at the apogee of its being, expanded into happiness, in egoism, positing itself as *ego*, here it is, beating its own record, preoccupied with another being! This represents a fundamental inversion not of some one of the functions of being, a function turned from its goal, but an inversion of its very exercise of being, which suspends its spontaneous movement of existing and gives another direction to its unsurpassable apology.

Insatiable Desire—not because it corresponds to an infinite hunger, but because it is not an appeal for food. This Desire is insatiable, but not because of our finitude. Might the Platonic myth of love as offspring of abundance and poverty be interpreted as the indigence of wealth itself, as the desire not of what one has lost, but absolute Desire, produced in a being in possession of itself and consequently already absolutely "on its own feet"? Has not Plato, rejecting the myth of the androgynous being presented by Aristophanes, caught sight of the non-nostalgic character of Desire and of philosophy, implying autochthonous existence and not exile—desire as erosion of the absoluteness of being by the presence of the Desirable, which is consequently a revealed presence, opening Desire in a being that in separation experiences itself as autonomous?

But love as analyzed by Plato does not coincide with what we have called Desire. Immortality is not the objective of the first movement of Desire, but the other, the Stranger. It is absolutely non-egoist; its name is justice. It does not link up beings already akin. The great force of the idea of creation such as it was contributed by monotheism is that this creation is *ex nihilo*—not because this represents a work more miraculous than the demiurgic informing of matter, but because the separated and created being is thereby not simply issued forth from the father, but is absolutely other than him. Filiality itself can not appear as essential to the destiny of the I unless man retains this memory of the creation *ex nihilo,* without which the son is not a true other.

Finally, the distance that separates happiness from desire separates politics from religion. Politics tends toward reciprocal recognition, that is, toward equality; it ensures happiness. And political law concludes and sanctions the struggle for recognition. Religion is Desire and not struggle for recognition. It is the surplus possible in a society of equals, that of glorious humility, responsibility, and sacrifice, which are the condition for equality itself.

3. *Discourse*

In affirming truth to be a modality of the relation between the same and the other we do not oppose intellectualism, but rather ensure its fundamental aspiration, the respect for being illuminating the intellect. The originality of separation has appeared to us to consist in the autonomy of the separated being. Whence in knowledge, or more exactly in the claim to it, the knower neither participates in nor unites with the known being. The relation of truth thus involves a dimension of interiority, a psychism, in which the metaphysician, while being in relation with the Metaphysical, maintains himself apart. But we have also indicated that this relation of truth, which at the same time spans and does not span the distance—does not form a totality with the "other shore"—rests on language: a relation in which the terms *absolve* themselves from the relation, remain absolute within the relation. Without this absolution the absolute distance of metaphysics would be illusory.

The knowledge of objects does not secure a relation whose terms would absolve themselves from the relation. Though objective knowledge remain disinterested, it is nevertheless marked by the way the knowing being has approached the Real. To recognize truth to be disclosure is to refer it to the horizon of him who discloses. Plato, who identifies knowledge with vision, stresses, in the myth of the chariot of the *Phaedrus,* the movement of the soul that contemplates truth and the relativeness of truth to that course. The disclosed being is relative to us and not καθ'αὐτό. According to the classical terminology, sensibility— a pretension to pure experience, a receptivity of being—becomes knowledge only after having been modeled by the understanding. According to the modern terminology, we disclose only with respect to a project. In labor we approach the Real with a view to a goal conceived by us. This modification that knowledge brings to bear on the One, which in cognition loses its unity, is evoked by Plato in the *Parmenides.* Knowledge in the absolute sense of the term, the pure experience of the other being, would have to maintain the other being καθ'αὐτό.

If the object thus refers to the project and labor of the knower, it is because objective cognition is a relation with the being that one always goes beyond and that always is to be interpreted. The "what is it?" approaches "this" qua "that." For to know objectively is to know the historical, the *fact,* the *already happened,* the already passed by.* The historical is not defined by the past; both the historical and the past are defined as themes of which one can speak. They are thematized precisely because they no longer speak. The historical is forever absent from its very presence. This means that it disappears behind its manifestations; its apparition is always superficial and equivocal; its origin, its principle, always elsewhere. It is a phenomenon—a reality without reality. The flow of time in which, according to the Kantian schema, the world is constituted is without origin. This world that has lost its principle, an-archical, a world of phenomena, does not answer to the quest for the true; it suffices for enjoyment, which is self-sufficiency itself, nowise disturbed by the evasion that exteriority opposes to the quest for the true. This world of enjoyment does not suffice for the metaphysical claim. The knowledge of the thematized is only a recommencing struggle against the always possible mystification of facts—at the same time an idolatry of facts, that is, an invocation of what does not speak, and an insurmountable plurality of significations and mystifications. Or else this knowledge invites the knower to an interminable psychoanalysis, to the desperate search for a true origin at least in oneself, to the effort to awaken.

The manifestation of the καθ'αὐτό in which a being concerns us without slipping away and without betraying itself does not consist in its being disclosed, its being exposed to the gaze that would take it as a theme for interpretation, and would command an absolute position dominating the object. Manifestation καθ'αὐτό consists in a being telling itself to us independently of every position we would have taken in its regard, *expressing itself.* Here, contrary to all the conditions for the visibility of objects, a being is not placed in the light of another but presents itself in the manifestation that should only announce it; it is present as directing this very manifestation—present before the manifestation, which only manifests it. *The absolute experience is not disclosure but*

---

* ". . . le *fait,* le *déjà fait,* le déjà dépassé."

revelation: a coinciding of the expressed with him who expresses, which is the privileged manifestation of the Other, the manifestation of a face over and beyond form. Form—incessantly betraying its own manifestation, congealing into a plastic form, for it is adequate to the same— alienates the exteriority of the other. The face is a living presence; it is expression. The life of expression consists in undoing the form in which the existent, exposed as a theme, is thereby dissimulated. The face speaks. The manifestation of the face is already discourse. He who manifests himself comes, according to Plato's expression, to his own assistance. He at each instant undoes the form he presents.

This way of undoing the form adequate to the Same so as to present oneself as other is to signify or to have a meaning. To present oneself by signifying is to speak. This presence, affirmed in the presence of the image as the focus of the gaze that is fixed on you, is said. Signification or expression thus contrasts with every intuitive datum precisely because to signify is not to give. Signification is not an ideal essence or a relation open to intellectual intuition, thus still analogous to the sensation presented to the eye. It is preeminently the presence of exteriority. Discourse is not simply a modification of intuition (or of thought), but an original relation with exterior being. It is not a regretable defect of a being deprived of intellectual intuition—as though intuition, which is a solitary thought, were the model for all straightforwardness in relations. It is the production of meaning. Meaning is not produced as an ideal essence; it is said and taught by presence, and teaching is not reducible to sensible or intellectual intuition, which is the thought of the same. To give meaning to one's presence is an event irreducible to evidence. It does not enter into an intuition; it is a presence more direct than visible manifestation, and at the same time a remote presence—that of the other. This presence dominates him who welcomes it, comes from the heights, unforeseen, and consequently teaches its very novelty. It is the frank presence of an existent that can lie, that is, disposes of the theme he offers, without being able to dissimulate his frankness as interlocutor, always struggling openly [à visage découvert]. The eyes break through the mask—the language of the eyes, impossible to dissemble. The eye does not shine; it speaks. The alternative of truth and lying, of sincerity and dissimulation, is the prerogative of him who abides in the relation of absolute frankness, in the absolute frankness which cannot hide itself.

Action does not express. It has meaning, but leads us to the agent in his absence. To approach someone from works is to enter into his interiority as though by burglary; the other is surprised in his intimacy, where, like the personages of history, he is, to be sure, exposed, but does not express himself.[7] Works signify their author, but indirectly, in the third person.

One can, to be sure, conceive of language as an act, as a gesture of behavior. But then one omits the essential of language: the coinciding of the revealer and the revealed in the face, which is accomplished in being situated in height with respect to us—in teaching. And, conversely, gestures and acts produced can become, like words, a revelation, that is, as we will see, a teaching. But the reconstitution of the personage on the basis of his behavior is the work of our already acquired science.

Absolute experience is not disclosure; to disclose, on the basis of a subjective horizon, is already to miss the noumenon. The interlocutor alone is the term of pure experience, where the Other enters into relation while remaining καθ'αὐτό, where he expresses himself without our having to disclose him from a "point of view," in a borrowed light. The "objectivity" sought by the knowledge that is fully knowledge is realized beyond the objectivity of the object. What presents itself as independent of every subjective movement is the interlocutor, whose *way* consists in starting from himself, foreign and yet presenting himself to me.

But the relationship with this "thing in itself" does not lie at the limit of a cognition that begins as a constitution of a "living body," as according to Husserl's celebrated analysis in the fifth of his *Cartesian Meditations*. The constitution of the Other's body in what Husserl calls "the primordial sphere," the transcendental "coupling" of the object thus constituted with my own body itself experienced from within as an "I can," the comprehension of this body of the Other as an *alter ego*—this analysis dissimulates, in each of its stages which are taken as a description of constitution, mutations of object constitution into a relation with the Other—which is as primordial as the constitution from which it is to be derived. The primordial sphere, which corresponds to what we call the same, turns to the absolutely other only on call from the Other. *Revelation* constitutes a veritable inversion *objectifying cognition*. In Heidegger coexistence is, to be sure, taken as a relationship with the Other irreducible to objective cognition; but in the final analysis it also rests on the relationship with *being in general,* on comprehension, on ontology. Heidegger posits in advance this ground of being as the

---

[7] See below [pp. 177–178, 226–232.—Trans.].

horizon on which every existent arises, as though the horizon, and the idea of limit it includes and which is proper to vision, were the ultimate structure of relationship. Moreover, for Heidegger intersubjectivity is a coexistence, a *we* prior to the I and the other, a neutral intersubjectivity. The face to face both announces a society, and permits the maintaining of a separated I.

Durkheim already in one respect went beyond this optical interpretation of the relation with the other in characterizing society by religion. I relate to the Other only across Society, which is not simply a multiplicity of individuals or objects; I relate to the Other who is not simply a part of a Whole, nor a singular instance of a concept. To reach the Other through the social is to reach him through the religious. Durkheim thus gives an indication of a transcendence other than that of the objective. And yet for him the religious is immediately reducible to collective representation: the structure of representation, and consequently of the objectifying intentionality that subtends it, serves as an ultimate interpretation of the religious itself.

Because of a current of ideas appearing independently in Gabriel Marcel's *Metaphysical Journal* and Martin Buber's *I and Thou,* the relationship with the Other as irreducible to objective knowledge has lost its unwonted character, whatever be the attitude one adopts with regard to the accompanying systematic expositions. Buber distinguished the relation with Objects, which would be guided by the practical, from the dialogic relation, which reaches the other as Thou, as partner and friend. This idea, central in his work, he modestly claims to have found in Feuerbach.[8] In reality it acquires all its force only in Buber's analyses, and it is in them that it figures as an essential contribution to contemporary thought. One may, however, ask if the *thou-saying* [*tutoiement*] does not place the other in a reciprocal relation, and if this reciprocity is primordial. On the other hand, the I-Thou relation in Buber retains a formal character: it can unite man to things as much as man to man. The I-Thou formalism does not determine any concrete structure. The I-Thou is an event (*Geschehen*), a shock, a comprehension, but does not

---

[8] Cf. M. Buber, "Das Problem des Menschen," *Dialogisches Leben,* p. 366. Concerning the influences upon Buber, cf. Maurice S. Friedman, "Martin Buber's Theory of Knowledge," *The Review of Metaphysics,* Vol. VIII, n. 2 (December, 1954), p. 264, note.

enable us to account for (except as an aberration, a fall, or a sickness) a life other than friendship: economy, the search for happiness, the representational relation with things. They remain, in a sort of disdainful spiritualism, unexplored and unexplained. This work does not have the ridiculous pretension of "correcting" Buber on these points. It is placed in a different perspective, by starting with the idea of the Infinite.

The claim to know and to reach the other is realized in the relationship with the Other that is cast in the relation of language, where the essential is the interpellation, the vocative. The other is maintained and confirmed in his heterogeneity as soon as one calls upon him, be it only to say to him that one cannot speak to him, to classify him as sick, to announce to him his death sentence; at the same time as grasped, wounded, outraged, he is "respected." The invoked is not what I comprehend: *he is not under a category*. He is the one to whom I speak —he has only a reference to himself; he has no quiddity. But the formal structure of interpellation has to be worked out.

The object of knowledge is always a fact, already happened and passed through. The interpellated one is called upon to speak; his speech consists in "coming to the assistance" of his word—in being *present*. This present is not made of instants mysteriously immobilized in duration, but of an *incessant* recapture of instants that flow by by a presence that comes to their assistance, that answers for them. This *incessance* produces the present, is the presentation, the life, of the present. It is as though the presence of him who speaks inverted the inevitable movement that bears the spoken word to the past state of the written word. Expression is this actualization of the actual. The present is produced in this struggle against the past (if one may so speak), in this actualization. The unique actuality of speech tears it from the situation in which it appears and which it seems to prolong. It brings what the written word is already deprived of: mastery. Speech, better than a simple sign, is essentially magisterial. It first of all teaches this teaching itself, by virtue of which alone it can teach (and not, like maieutics, *awaken* in me) things and ideas. Ideas instruct me coming from the master who *presents* them to me: who puts them in question; the objectification and theme upon which objective knowledge opens already rest on teaching. The calling into question of things in a dialectic is not a modifying of the perception of them; it coincides with their *objectification*. The object is *presented* when we have welcomed an interlocutor. The master, the coinciding of the teaching and the teacher, is not in turn a fact among others. The present of the manifestation of the master who teaches overcomes the anarchy of facts.

We must not say that language conditions consciousness, under the pretext that it provides self-consciousness with an incarnation in the objective work language would be (as the Hegelians would say). The exteriority that language, the relation with the Other, delineates is unlike the exteriority of a work, for the objective exteriority of works is already situated in the world established by language—by transcendence.

4. Rhetoric and Injustice

Not every discourse is a relation with exteriority.

It is not the interlocutor our master whom we most often approach in our conversations, but an object or an infant, or a man of the multitude, as Plato says.[9] Our pedagogical or psychagogical discourse is rhetoric, taking the position of him who approaches his neighbor with ruse. And this is why the art of the sophist is a theme with reference to which the true conversation concerning truth, or philosophical discourse, is defined. Rhetoric, absent from no discourse, and which philosophical discourse seeks to overcome, resists discourse (or leads to it: pedagogy, demagogy, psychagogy). It approaches the other not to face him, but obliquely— not, to be sure, as a thing, since rhetoric remains conversation, and across all its artifices goes unto the Other, solicits his yes. But the specific nature of rhetoric (of propaganda, flattery, diplomacy, etc.) consists in corrupting this freedom. It is for this that it is preeminently violence, that is, injustice—not violence exercised on an inertia (which would not be a violence), but on a freedom, which, precisely as freedom, should be incorruptible. To freedom it manages to apply a category; it seems to judge of it as of a nature; it asks the question, contradictory in its terms, "what is the nature of this freedom?"

To renounce the psychagogy, demagogy, pedagogy rhetoric involves is to face the Other, in a veritable conversation. Then this being is nowise an object, is outside of all emprise. This disengagement from all objectivity means, positively, this being's presentation in the face, his

---

[9] *Phaedrus,* 273d.

expression, his language. *The other qua other is the Other.** To "let him be" the relationship of discourse is required; pure "disclosure," where he is proposed as a theme, does not respect him enough for that. *We call justice this face to face approach, in conversation.* If truth arises in the absolute *experience* in which being gleams with its own light, then truth is produced only in veritable conversation or in justice.

This absolute experience in the face to face, in which the interlocutor presents himself as absolute being (that is, as being withdrawn from the categories), would for Plato be inconceivable without the inter-position of the Ideas. The impersonal relation and discourse seem to refer to solitary discourse, or reason, to the soul conversing with itself. But is the Platonic idea attended to by the thinker equivalent to a sublimated and perfected *object?* Is the kinship between the Soul and the Ideas, emphasized in the *Phaedo,* but an idealist metaphor expressing the permeability of being to thought? Is the ideality of the ideal reducible to a superlative extension of qualities, or does it lead us to a region where beings have a face, that is, are present in their own message? Herman Cohen (in this a Platonist) maintained that one can love only ideas; but the notion of an Idea is in the last analysis tantamount to the transmutation of the other into the Other. For Plato true discourse can come to its own assistance: the content that is pre-sented to me is inseparable from him who has thought it—which means that the author of the discourse responds to questions. Thought, for Plato, is not reducible to an impersonal concatenation of true relations, but implies persons and interpersonal relations. Socrates' daemon inter-venes in the maieutic art itself, which, however, refers to what is common to men.[10] Community through the interposition of the ideas does not establish pure and simple equality among the interlocutors. The philoso-pher who, in the *Phaedo,* is compared with the caretaker assigned to his post, is under the magistrature of the gods; he is not their equal. Can the hierarchy of beings, at whose summit is found rational being, be transcended? To what new purity does the elevation of a god corre-spond? To the words and actions that are addressed to me, and which are always still to a certain extent rhetoric and negociation ("where we deal with them"), words addressed to men who are the multitude,[11] Plato opposes the utterances with which we please the gods. The

---

* *"L'Autre en tant qu'autre est Autrui."*
[10] *Theaetetus,* 151a.
[11] *Phaedrus,* 273e.

interlocutors are not equals; when it has reached truth discourse is conversation with a god who is not our "fellow-servant."[12] Society does not proceed from the contemplation of the true; truth is made possible by relation with the Other our master.   Truth is thus bound up with the social relation, which is justice. Justice consists in recognizing in the Other my master. Equality among persons means nothing of itself; it has an economic meaning and presupposes money, and already rests on justice—which, when well-ordered, begins with the Other. Justice is the recognition of his privilege qua Other and his mastery, is access to the Other outside of rhetoric, which is ruse, emprise, and exploitation. And in this sense justice coincides with the overcoming of rhetoric.

5. Discourse and Ethics

Can objectivity and the universality of thought be founded on discourse? Is not universal thought of itself prior to discourse? Does not a mind in speaking evoke what the other mind already thinks, both of them participating in common ideas? But the community of thought ought to have made language as a relation between beings impossible. Coherent discourse is one. A universal thought dispenses with communication. A reason cannot be other for a reason. How can a reason be an I or an other, since its very being consists in renouncing singularity?

European thought has always combated, as skeptical, the idea of man as measure of all things, although this idea contributes the idea of atheist separation and one of the foundations of discourse. For it the sentient I could not found Reason; the I was defined by reason. Reason speaking in the first person is not addressed to the other, conducts a monologue. And, conversely, it would attain to veritable personality, would recover the sovereignty characteristic of the autonomous person, only by becoming universal. Separated thinkers become rational only in the measure that their personal and particular acts of thinking figure as moments of this unique and universal discourse. There would be reason in the thinking individual only in the measure that he would himself enter into his own discourse, that thought would, in the etymological sense of the term, comprehend the thinker—that it would include him.

But to make of the thinker a moment of thought is to limit the revealing function of language to its coherence, conveying the coher-

---

[12] Ibid.

ence of concepts. In this coherence the unique I of the thinker volatilizes. The function of language would amount to suppressing "the other," who breaks this coherence and is hence essentially irrational. A curious result: language would consist in suppressing the other, in making the other agree with the same! But in its expressive function language precisely maintains the other—to whom it is addressed, whom it calls upon or invokes. To be sure, language does not consist in invoking him as a being represented and thought. But this is why language institutes a relation irreducible to the subject-object relation: the *revelation* of the other. In this revelation only can language as a system of signs be constituted. The other called upon is not something represented, is not a given, is not a particular, through one side already open to generalization. Language, far from presupposing universality and generality, first makes them possible. Language presupposes interlocutors, a plurality. Their commerce is not a representation of the one by the other, nor a participation in universality, on the common plane of language. Their commerce, as we shall show shortly, is ethical.

Plato maintains the difference between the objective order of truth, that which doubtlessly is established in writings, impersonally, and reason *in* a living being, "a living and animated discourse," a discourse "which can defend itself, and knows when to speak and when to be silent."[13] This discourse is therefore not the unfolding of a prefabricated internal logic, but the constitution of truth in a struggle between thinkers, with all the risks of freedom. The relationship of language implies transcendence, radical separation, the strangeness of the interlocutors, the revelation of the other to me. In other words, language is spoken where community between the terms of the relationship is wanting, where the common plane is wanting or is yet to be constituted. It takes place in this transcendence. Discourse is thus the experience of something absolutely foreign, a *pure* "knowledge" or "experience," a *traumatism of astonishment.*

The absolutely foreign alone can instruct us. And it is only man who could be absolutely foreign to me—refractory to every typology, to every genus, to every characterology, to every classification—and consequently the term of a "knowledge" finally penetrating beyond the object. The strangeness of the Other, his very freedom! Free beings alone can be strangers to one another. Their freedom which is "common" to them

---

[13] *Phaedrus*, 276a.

is precisely what separates them. As a "pure knowledge" language consists in the relationship with a being that in a certain sense is not by relation to me, or, if one likes, that is in a relationship with me only inasmuch as he is wholly by relation to himself,* καθ'αὐτό, a being that stands beyond every attribute, which would precisely have as its effect to qualify him, that is, to reduce him to what is common to him and other beings—a being, consequently, completely naked.

The things are naked, by metaphor, only when they are without adornments: bare walls, naked landscapes. They have no need of adornment when they are absorbed in the accomplishment of the function for which they are made: when they are subordinated to their own finality so radically that they disappear in it. They disappear beneath their form. The perception of individual things is the fact that they are not entirely absorbed in their form; they then stand out in themselves, breaking through, rending their forms, are not resolved into the relations that link them up to the totality. They are always in some respect like those industrial cities where everything is adapted to a goal of production, but which, full of smoke, full of wastes and sadness, exist also for themselves. For a thing nudity is the surplus of its being over its finality. It is its absurdity, its uselessness, which itself appears only relative to the form against which it contrasts and of which it is deficient. The thing is always an opacity, a resistance, a ugliness. Thus the Platonic conception of the intelligible sun situated outside of the eye that sees and the object it illuminates describes with precision the perception of things. Objects have no light of their own; they receive a borrowed light.

Beauty then introduces a new finality, an internal finality, into this naked world. To disclose by science and by art is essentially to clothe the elements with signification, to go beyond perception. To disclose a thing is to clarify it by forms: to find for it a place in the whole by apperceiving its function or its beauty.

The work of language is entirely different: it consists in entering into relationship with a nudity disengaged from every form, but having meaning by itself, καθ'αὐτό, signifying before we have projected light upon it, appearing not as a privation on the ground of an ambivalence of values (as good or evil, as beauty or ugliness), but as an *always positive value*. Such a nudity is the face. The nakedness of the face is not

---

* ". . . consist dans le rapport avec un être qui dans un certain sens, n'est pas par rapport à moi; ou, si l'on veut, qui n'est en rapport avec moi que dans la mesure où il est entièrement par rapport à soi, . . ."

what is presented to me because I disclose it, what would therefore be presented to me, to my powers, to my eyes, to my perceptions, in a light exterior to it. The face has turned to me—and this is its very nudity. It *is* by itself and not by reference to a system.

To be sure nakedness can have still a third meaning, outside of the absurdity of the thing losing its system or the signification of the face breaking through all form: the nudity of the body felt in modesty, appearing to the Other in repulsion and desire. But this nudity always refers in one way or other to the nakedness of the face. Only a being absolutely naked by his face can also denude himself immodestly.

But the difference between the nakedness of the face that turns to me and the disclosure of the thing illuminated by its form does not simply separate two modes of "knowledge." The relation with the face is not an object-cognition. The transcendence of the face is at the same time its absence from this world into which it enters, the exiling [depaysement] of a being, his condition of being stranger, destitute, or proletarian. The strangeness that is freedom is also strangeness-destitution [étrangeté-misère]. Freedom presents itself as the other to the same, who is always the autochthon of being, always privileged in his own residence. The other, the free one, is also the stranger. The nakedness of his face extends into the nakedness of the body that is cold and that is ashamed of its nakedness. Existence $\kappa\alpha\theta'\alpha\dot{\nu}\tau\acute{o}$ is, in the world, a destitution. There is here a relation between me and the other beyond rhetoric.

This gaze that supplicates and demands, that can supplicate only because it demands, deprived of everything because entitled to every-thing, and which one recognizes in giving (as one "puts the things in question in giving")—this gaze is precisely the epiphany of the face as a face. The nakedness of the face is destituteness.* To recognize the Other is to recognize a hunger. To recognize the Other is to give. But it is to give to the master, to the lord, to him whom one approaches as "You"** in a dimension of height.

It is in generosity that the world possessed by me—the world open to enjoyment—is apperceived from a point of view independent of the egoist position. The "objective" is not simply the object of an impassive contemplation. Or rather impassive contemplation is defined by gift, by the abolition of inalienable property. The presence of the Other is

---

* "La nudité du visage est dénûment."
** "Vous"—the "you" of majesty, in contrast with the "thou" of intimacy (cf. pp. 87-88).—Trans.

equivalent to this calling into question of my joyous possession of the world. The conceptualization of the sensible arises already from this incision in the living flesh of my own substance, my home, in this suitability of the mine for the Other, which prepares the descent of the things to the rank of possible merchandise. This initial dispossession conditions the subsequent generalization by money. Conceptualization is the first generalization and the condition for objectivity. Objectivity coincides with the abolition of inalienable property—which presupposes the epiphany of the other. The whole problem of generalization is thus posed as a problem of objectivity. The problem of the general and abstract idea cannot presuppose objectivity as constituted: the general object is not a sensible object that would, however, be thought in an intention of generality and ideality. For the nominalist critique of the general and abstract idea is not yet overcome thereby; it is still necessary to say what this intention of ideality and generality signifies. The passage from perception to the concept belongs to the constitution of the objectivity of the perceived object. We must not speak of an intention of ideality investing perception, an intention in which the solitary being of the subject, identifying itself in the same, directs itself toward the transcendent world of the ideas. The generality of the Object is correlative with the generosity of the subject going to the Other, beyond the egoist and solitary enjoyment, and hence making the community of the goods of this world break forth from the exclusive property of enjoyment.

To recognize the Other is therefore to come to him across the world of possessed things, but at the same time to establish, by gift, community and universality. Language is universal because it is the very passage from the individual to the general, because it offers things which are mine to the Other. To speak is to make the world common, to create commonplaces. Language does not refer to the generality of concepts, but lays the foundations for a possession in common. It abolishes the inalienable property of enjoyment. The world in discourse is no longer what it is in separation, in the being at home with oneself where everything is given to me; it is what I give: the communicable, the thought, the universal.

Thus conversation is not a pathetic confrontation of two beings absenting themselves from the things and from the others. Discourse is not love. The transcendence of the Other, which is his eminence, his height, his lordship, in its concrete meaning includes his destitution, his exile [dépaysement], and his rights as a stranger. I can recognize the gaze of the stranger, the widow, and the orphan only in giving or in refusing; I am free to give or to refuse, but my recognition passes necessarily through the interposition of things. Things are not, as in Heidegger, the foundation of the site, the quintessence of all the relations that constitute our presence on the earth (and "under the heavens, in company with men, and in the expectation of the gods"). The relationship between the same and the other, my welcoming of the other, is the ultimate fact, and in it the things figure not as what one builds but as what one gives.

6. The Metaphysical and the Human

To relate to the absolute as an atheist is to welcome the absolute purified of the violence of the sacred. In the dimension of height in which his sanctity, that is, his separation, is presented, the infinite does not burn the eyes that are lifted unto him. He speaks; he does not have the mythical format that is impossible to confront and would hold the I in its invisible meshes. He is not numinous: the I who approaches him is neither annihilated on contact nor transported outside of itself, but remains separated and keeps its as-for-me. Only an atheist being can relate himself to the other and already *absolve himself* from this relation. Transcendence is to be distinguished from a union with the transcendent by participation. The metaphysical relation, the idea of infinity, connects with the noumenon which is not a numen. This noumenon is to be distinguished from the concept of God possessed by the believers of positive religions ill disengaged from the bonds of participation, who accept being immersed in a myth unbeknown to themselves. The idea of infinity, the metaphysical relation, is the dawn of a humanity without myths. But faith purged of myths, the monotheist faith, itself implies metaphysical atheism. Revelation is discourse; in order to welcome revelation a being apt for this role of interlocutor, a separated being, is required. Atheism conditions a veritable relationship with a true God καθ'αὐτό. But this relationship is as distinct from objectification as from participation. To hear the divine word does not amount to knowing an object; it is to be in relation with a substance overflowing its own idea in me, overflowing what Descartes calls its "objective existence." When simply known, thematized, the substance no longer is "according to itself." Discourse, in which it is at the same time foreign and present, suspends participation and, beyond object-cognition, institutes the pure experience of the social relation, where a being does not draw its existence from its contact with the other.

To posit the transcendent as stranger and poor one is to prohibit the metaphysical relation with God from being accomplished in the ignorance of men and things. The dimension of the divine opens forth from the human face. A relation with the Transcendent free from all captivation by the Transcendent is a social relation. It is here that the Transcendent, infinitely other, solicits us and appeals to us. The proximity of the Other, the proximity of the neighbor, is in being an ineluctable moment of the revelation of an absolute presence (that is, disengaged from every relation), which expresses itself. His very epiphany consists in soliciting us by his destitution in the face of the Stranger, the widow, and the orphan. The atheism of the metaphysician means, positively, that our relation with the Metaphysical is an ethical behavior and not theology, not a thematization, be it a knowledge by analogy, of the attributes of God. God rises to his supreme and ultimate presence as correlative to the justice rendered unto men. The direct comprehension of God is impossible for a look directed upon him, not because our intelligence is limited, but because the relation with infinity respects the total Transcendence of the other without being bewitched by it, and because our possibility of welcoming him in man goes further than the comprehension that thematizes and encompasses its object. It goes further, for precisely it thus goes into Infinity. The comprehension of God taken as a participation in his sacred life, an allegedly direct comprehension, is impossible, because participation is a denial of the divine, and because nothing is more direct than the face to face, which is straightforwardness itself. A God invisible means not only a God unimaginable, but a God accessible in justice. Ethics is the spiritual optics. The subject-object relation does not reflect it; in the impersonal relation that leads to it the invisible but personal God is not approached outside of all human presence. The ideal is not only a being superlatively being, a sublimation of the objective, or, in the solitude of love, a sublimation of a Thou. The work of justice—the uprightness of the face to face—is necessary in order that the breach that leads to God be produced—and "vision" here coincides with this work of justice. Hence metaphysics is enacted where the social relation is enacted—in our relations with men. There can be no "knowledge" of God separated from the relationship with men. The Other is the very locus of metaphysical truth, and is indispensable for my relation with God. He does not play the role of a mediator. The Other is not the incarnation of God, but precisely by his face, in which he is disincarnate, is the manifestation of the height in which God is revealed. It is our relations with men, which describe a field of research hardly glimpsed at (where more often than not we confine ourselves to a few formal categories whose content would be but "psychology"), that give to theological concepts the sole signification they admit of. The establishing of this primacy of the ethical, that is, of the relationship of man to man—signification, teaching, and justice—a primacy of an irreducible structure upon which all the other structures rest (and in particular all those which seem to put us primordially in contact with an impersonal sublimity, aesthetic or ontological), is one of the objectives of the present work.

Metaphysics is enacted in ethical relations. Without the signification they draw from ethics theological concepts remain empty and formal frameworks. The role Kant attributed to sensible experience in the domain of the understanding belongs in metaphysics to interhuman relations. It is from moral relationships that every metaphysical affirmation takes on a "spiritual" meaning, is purified of everything with which an imagination captive of things and victim of participation charges our concepts. The ethical relation is defined, in contrast with every relation with the sacred, by excluding every signification it would take on *unbeknown* to him who maintains that relation. When I maintain an ethical relation I refuse to recognize the role I would play in a drama of which I would not be the author or whose outcome another would know before me; I refuse to figure in a drama of salvation or of damnation that would be enacted in spite of me and that would make game of me. This is not equivalent to a diabolical pride, for it does not exclude obedience. But obedience precisely is to be distinguished from an involuntary participation in mysterious designs in which one figures or which one prefigures. Everything that cannot be reduced to an interhuman relation represents not the superior form but the forever primitive form of religion.

7. The Face to Face—An Irreducible Relation

Our analyses are guided by a formal structure: the idea of Infinity in us. To have the idea of Infinity it is necessary to exist as separated. This separation cannot be produced as only echoing the transcendence of Infinity, for then the separation would be maintained within a correlation that would restore totality and render transcendence illusory. But the idea of Infinity is transcendence itself, the overflowing of an adequate idea. If totality can not be constituted it is because Infinity does not permit itself to be integrated. It is not the insufficiency of the I that prevents totalization, but the Infinity of the Other.

In metaphysics a being separated from the Infinite nonetheless relates to it, with a relation that does not nullify the infinite interval of the separation—which thus differs from every interval. In metaphysics a being is in a relation with what it cannot absorb, with what it cannot, in the etymological sense of the term, comprehend. In the concrete the positive face of the formal structure, having the idea of infinity, is discourse, specified as an ethical relation. For the relation between the being here below and the transcendent being that results in no community of concept or totality—a relation without relation—we reserve the term religion.

The negative description of transcendence as the impossibility for the transcendent being and the being that is separated from it to participate in the same concept also comes from Descartes. For he affirms that the term being is applied to God and to creation in an equivocal sense. Across the theology of the analogous attributes of the Middle Ages this thesis goes back to the conception of the only analogical unity of being in Aristotle. In Plato it is found in the transcendence of the Good with respect to being. It should have served as a foundation for a pluralist philosophy in which the plurality of being would not disappear into the unity of number nor be integrated into a totality. Totality and the embrace of being, or ontology, do not contain the final secret of being. Religion, where relationship subsists between the same and the other despite the impossibility of the Whole—the idea of Infinity—is the ultimate structure.

The same and the other can not enter into a cognition that would encompass them; the relations that the separated being maintains with what transcends it are not produced on the ground of totality, do not crystallize into a system. Yet do we not name them together? The *formal* synthesis of the word that names them together is already part of a discourse, that is, of a conjuncture of transcendence, breaking the totality. The conjuncture of the same and the other, in which even their verbal proximity is maintained, is the *direct* and *full face* welcome of the other by me. This conjuncture is irreducible to totality; the "face to face" position is not a modification of the "along side of. . . ." Even when I shall have linked the Other to myself with the conjunction "and" the Other continues to face me, to reveal himself in his face. *Religion* subtends this formal totality. And if I set forth, as in a final and absolute vision, the separation and transcendence which are the themes of this book, these relations, which I claim form the fabric of being itself, first come together in my discourse presently addressed to my interlocutors: inevitably across my idea of the Infinite the other faces me—hostile, friend, my master, my student. Reflection can, to be sure, become aware of this face to face, but the "unnatural" position of reflection is not an accident in the life of consciousness. It involves a calling into question of oneself, a critical attitude which is itself produced in face of the other and under his authority. We shall show this further. The face to face remains an ultimate situation.

C. TRUTH AND JUSTICE

1. Freedom Called into Question

Metaphysics or transcendence is recognized in the work of the intellect that aspires after exteriority, that is Desire. But the Desire for exteriority has appeared to us to move not in objective cognition but in Discourse, which in turn has presented itself as justice, in the uprightness of the welcome made to the face. Is not the vocation to truth to which traditionally the intellect answers belied by this analysis? What is the relation between justice and truth?

Truth is in effect not separable from intelligibility; to know is not simply to record, but always to comprehend. We also say that to know is to justify, making intervene, by analogy with the moral order, the notion of justice. The justification of a fact consists in lifting from it its character of being a fact, accomplished, past, and hence irrevocable, which as such obstructs our spontaneity. But to say that as an obstacle to our spontaneity a fact is unjust is to suppose that spontaneity is not to be put in question, that free exercise is not subject to norms, but is the norm. And yet the concern for intelligibility is fundamentally different from an attitude that engenders an action without regard for obstacles. It signifies on the contrary a certain respect for objects. For an obstacle to become a fact that requires a theoretical justification or a reason the spontaneity of the action that surmounts it had to be inhibited, that is, itself put into question. It is then that we move from an activity without regard for anything to a *consideration* of the fact. The famous suspension of action that is said to make theory possible depends on a reserve of freedom, which does not abandon itself to its drives, to its impulsive movements, and keeps its distances. Theory, in which truth arises, is the attitude of a being that distrusts itself. Knowing becomes knowing of a fact only if it is at the same time critical, if it puts itself into question, goes back beyond its origin—in an unnatural move-

82

ment to seek higher than one's own origin, a movement which evinces or describes a created freedom.

This self-criticism can be understood as a discovery of one's weakness or a discovery of one's unworthiness—either as a consciousness of failure or as a consciousness of guilt. In the latter case to justify freedom is not to prove it but to render it just.

The predominance of a tradition that subordinates unworthiness to failure, moral generosity itself to the necessities of objective thought, is perceivable in European thought. The spontaneity of freedom is not called in question; its limitation alone is held to be tragic and to constitute a scandal. Freedom is called in question only inasmuch as it somehow finds itself imposed upon itself: if I could have freely chosen my own existence everything would be justified. The failure of my spontaneity still bereft of reason awakens reason and theory; there would have been a suffering that would be the mother of wisdom. From failure alone would come the necessity of curbing violence and introducing order into human relations. Political theory derives justice from the undiscussed value of spontaneity; its problem is to ensure, by way of knowledge of the world, the most complete exercise of spontaneity by reconciling my freedom with the freedom of the others.

This position admits not only the undiscussed value of spontaneity but also the possibility of a rational being being situated within the totality. The critique of spontaneity engendered by failure, which calls in question the central place the I occupies in the world, implies then a power to reflect on its failure and on the totality, an uprooting of the I torn up from itself and living in the universal. It founds neither theory nor truth; it presupposes them: it proceeds from knowledge of the world, is already born from a knowledge, the knowledge of failure. The consciousness of failure is already theoretical.

The critique of spontaneity engendered by the consciousness of moral unworthiness, on the contrary, precedes truth, precedes the consideration of the whole, and does not imply the sublimation of the I in the universal. The consciousness of unworthiness is not in its turn a truth, is not a consideration of facts. The first consciousness of my immorality is not my subordination to facts, but to the Other, to the Infinite. The idea of totality and the idea of infinity differ precisely in that the first is purely theoretical, while the second is moral. The freedom that can be ashamed of itself founds truth (and thus truth is not deduced from truth). The Other is not initially a *fact,* is not an *obstacle,* does not threaten me with death; he is desired in my shame. To discover the unjustified facticity of power and freedom one must not consider it as an object, nor consider the Other as an object; one must measure oneself against infinity, that is, desire him. It is necessary to have the idea of infinity, the idea of the perfect, as Descartes would say, in order to know one's own imperfection. The idea of the perfect is not an idea but desire; it is the welcoming of the Other, the commencement of moral consciousness, which calls in question my freedom. Thus this way of measuring oneself against the perfection of infinity is not a theoretical consideration; it is accomplished as shame, where freedom discovers itself murderous in its very exercise. It is accomplished in shame where freedom at the same time is *discovered* in the consciousness of shame and is *concealed* in the shame itself. Shame does not have the structure of consciousness and clarity. It is oriented in the inverse direction; its subject is exterior to me. Discourse and Desire, where the Other presents himself as interlocutor, as him over whom I *can*not have power [je *ne peux* pas pouvoir], whom I cannot kill, condition this shame, where, qua I, I am not innocent spontaneity but usurper and murderer. Contrariwise, a theoretical idea of another myself is not adequate to the infinite, to the other as other, already for the simple reason that he provokes my shame and presents himself as dominating me. His justified existence is the primary fact, the synonym of his very perfection. And if the other can invest me and invest my freedom, of itself arbitrary, this is in the last analysis because I myself can feel myself to be the other of the other. But this comes about only across very complex structures.

Conscience welcomes the Other. It is the revelation of a resistance to my powers that does not counter them as a greater force, but calls in question the naïve right of my powers, my glorious spontaneity as a living being. Morality begins when freedom, instead of being justified by itself, feels itself to be arbitrary and violent. The search for the intelligible and the manifestation of the *critical* essence of knowing, the movement of a being back to what precedes its condition, begin together.

2. The Investiture of Freedom, or Critique

Existence is not in reality condemned to freedom, but is *invested* as freedom. Freedom is not bare. To philosophize is to trace freedom back to what lies before it, to disclose the investiture that liberates freedom from the arbitrary. Knowledge as a critique, as a tracing back to what precedes freedom, can arise only in a being that has an origin prior to its origin—that is created.*

Critique or philosophy is the essence of knowing. But what is proper to knowing is not its possibility of going unto an object, a movement by which it is akin to other acts; its prerogative consists in being able to put itself in question, in penetrating beneath its own condition. It is not drawn back from the world because it has the world as its object; it can have the world as its theme, make of it an object, because its exercise consists, as it were, in taking charge of the very condition that supports it and that supports even this very act of taking charge.

What is the meaning of this taking charge, this penetration beneath one's condition first dissimulated by the naïve movement that conducts cognition as an act toward its object? What is the meaning of this calling in question? It cannot be reduced to the repetition with regard to cognition as a whole of the questions that are raised for the understanding of the things aimed at in the naïve act of cognition. In that case to know knowledge would amount to elaborating a psychology, which has its place among the other sciences that bear upon objects. The critical question raised in psychology or in theory of knowledge would amount to asking, for example, from what certain principle cognition is derived, or what is its cause. Infinite regression would here be indeed inevitable, and it is to this sterile course that the proceeding back beneath one's condition, the power to pose the problem of the foundation, would be reduced. To identify the problem of the foundation with an objective knowledge of knowledge is to suppose in advance that freedom can be founded only on itself, for freedom, the determination of the other by the same, is the very movement of representation and of its evidence. To identify the problem of foundation with the knowledge of knowledge is to forget the arbitrariness of freedom, which is precisely what has to be grounded. The knowing whose essence is critique cannot be reduced to objective cognition; it leads to the Other. To welcome the Other is to put in question my freedom.

But the critical essence of knowing also leads us beyond the knowledge of the *cogito,* which we may wish to distinguish from objective knowledge. The evidence of the *cogito*—where knowledge and the known

---

* "Le savoir comme critique, comme remontée en deçà de la liberté—ne peut surgir que dans un être qui a une origine en deçà de son origine—qui est créé."

coincide without knowledge having had to be already in operation, where knowledge thus involves no commitment prior to its present commitment, is at each instant at the beginning, is not in *situation* (which, moreover, is what is proper to all *evidence,* a pure experience of the present without condition or past)—cannot satisfy the critical exigency, for the commencement of the *cogito* remains antecedent to it. It does indeed mark commencement, because it is the awakening of an existence that takes charge of its own condition. But this awakening comes from the Other. Before the *cogito* existence dreams itself, as though it remained foreign to itself. It is because it suspects that it is dreaming itself that it awakens. The doubt makes it seek certainty. But this suspicion, this consciousness of doubt, implies the idea of the Perfect. The knowing of the *cogito* thus refers to a relation with the Master—with the idea of infinity or of the Perfect. The idea of Infinity is neither the immanence of the *I think* nor the transcendence of the object. The *cogito* in Descartes rests on the other who is God and who has put the idea of infinity in the soul, who had taught it, and has not, like the Platonic master, simply aroused the reminiscence of former visions.

As the act unsettling its own condition, knowing comes into play above all action. And if the tracing back from a condition to what precedes that condition describes the status of the creature, in which the uncertainty of freedom and its recourse to justification are bound up, if knowing is a creature activity, this unsettling of the condition and this justification come from the Other. The Other alone eludes thematization. Thematization cannot serve to found thematization, for it supposes it to be already founded; it is the exercise of a freedom sure of itself in its naïve spontaneity—whereas the presence of the Other is not equivalent to his thematization and consequently does not require this naïve and self-sure spontaneity. The welcoming of the Other is ipso facto the consciousness of my own injustice—the shame that freedom feels for itself. If philosophy consists in knowing critically, that is, in seeking a foundation for its freedom, in justifying it, it begins with conscience, to which the other is presented as the Other, and where the movement of thematization is inverted. But this inversion does not amount to "knowing oneself" as a theme attended to by the Other, but rather in submitting oneself to an exigency, to a morality. The Other measures me with a gaze incomparable to the gaze by which I discover him. The dimension of *height* in which the Other is placed is as it were the primary curvature of being from which the privilege of the Other results, the gradient [dénivellement] of transcendence. The Other is metaphysical. The Other is not transcendent because he would be free as I am; on the contrary his freedom is a superiority that comes from his very transcendence. What does this inversion of critique consist in? The subject is "for itself"—it represents itself and knows itself as long as it is. But in knowing or representing itself it possesses itself, dominates itself, extends its identity to what of itself comes to refute this identity. This imperialism of the same is the whole essence of freedom. The "for itself" as a mode of existence designates an attachment to oneself as radical as a naïve will to live. But if freedom situates me effrontedly before the non-me in myself and outside of myself, if it consists in negating or possessing the non-me, before the Other it retreats. The relationship with the Other does not move (as does cognition) into enjoyment and possession, into freedom; the Other imposes himself as an exigency that dominates this freedom, and hence as more primordial than everything that takes place in me. The Other, whose exceptional presence is inscribed in the ethical impossibility of killing him in which I stand, marks the end of powers. If I can no longer have power over him it is because he overflows absolutely every *idea* I can have of him.

The I can indeed, to justify itself, enter upon a different course: it can endeavor to apprehend itself within a totality. This seems to us to be the justification of freedom aspired after by the philosophy that, from Spinoza to Hegel, identifies will and reason, that, contrary to Descartes, removes from truth its character of being a free work so as to situate it where the opposition between the I and the non-I disappears, in an impersonal reason. Freedom is not maintained but reduced to being the reflection of a universal order which maintains itself and justifies itself all by itself, like the God of the ontological argument. This privilege of the universal order, that it sustains itself and justifies itself (which situates it beyond the still subjective work of the Cartesian will), constitutes the divine dignity of this order. Knowing would be the way by which freedom would denounce its own contingency, by which it would vanish into the totality. In reality this way dissimulates the ancient triumph of the same over the other. If freedom thus ceases to maintain itself in the arbitrariness of the solitary certitude of evidence, and if the solitary is united to the impersonal reality of the divine, the I disappears in this sublimation. For the philosophical tradition of the West every relation between the same and the other, when it is no longer an affirmation of the supremacy of the same, reduces itself to an impersonal relation within a universal order. Philosophy itself is identified with the substitution of ideas for persons, the theme for the interlocutor, the interiority of the logical relation for the exteriority of interpellation. Existents are reduced to the neuter state of the idea, Being, the concept. It was to escape the arbitrariness of freedom, its disappearance into the Neuter, that we have approached the I as atheist and created— free, but capable of tracing back beneath its condition—before the Other, who does not deliver himself in the "thematization" or "conceptual- ization" of the Other. To wish to escape dissolution into the Neuter, to posit knowing as a welcoming of the Other, is not a pious attempt to maintain the spiritualism of a personal God, but is the condition for language, without which philosophical discourse itself is but an abortive act, a pretext for an unintermitting psychoanalysis or philology or sociol- ogy, in which the appearance of a discourse vanishes in the Whole. Speaking implies a possibility of breaking off and beginning.

To posit knowing as the very *existing* of the creature, as the tracing back beyond the condition to the other that founds, is to separate oneself from a whole philosophical tradition that sought the foundation of the self in the self, outside of heteronomous opinions. We think that exist- ence *for itself* is not the ultimate meaning of knowing, but rather the putting back into question of the self, the turning back to what is prior to oneself, in the presence of the Other. The presence of the Other, a privileged heteronomy, does not clash with freedom but invests it. The shame for oneself, the presence of and desire for the other are not the negation of knowing: knowing is their very articulation. The essence of reason consists not in securing for man a foundation and powers, but in calling him in question and in inviting him to justice.

Metaphysics therefore does not consist in bending over the "for itself" of the I to seek in it the solid ground for an absolute approach to being. It is not in the "know thyself" that its ultimate movement is pursued— not that the "for itself" be limited or be of bad faith, but because by itself it is only freedom, that is, arbitrary and unjustified, and in this sense detestable; it is I, egoism. To be sure, the atheism of the *I* marks the break with participation and consequently the possibility of seeking a justification for oneself, that is, a dependence upon an exteriority without this dependence absorbing the dependent being, held in invisible meshes. This dependence, consequently, *at the same time* maintains independence; such is the face to face relation. In the quest for truth, a work eminently individual, which always, as Descartes saw, comes back to the freedom of the individual, atheism affirms itself as atheism. But its critical power takes it beneath its freedom. The unity of spontaneous freedom, working on straight ahead, and critique, where freedom is capable of being called in question and thus preceding itself, is what is termed a creature. The marvel of creation does not only consist in being a creation *ex nihilo,* but in that it results in a being capable of receiving a revelation, learning that it is created, and putting itself in question. The miracle of creation lies in creating a moral being. And this implies precisely atheism, but at the same time, beyond atheism, shame for the arbitrariness of the freedom that constitutes it.

We therefore are also radically opposed to Heidegger who subordinates the relation with the Other to ontology (which, moreover, he determines as though the relation with the interlocutor and the Master could be reduced to it) rather than seeing in justice and injustice a primordial access to the Other beyond all ontology. The existence of the Other does not concern us in the collectivity by reason of his participation in the being that is already familiar to us all, nor by reason of his power and freedom which we should have to subjugate and utilize for ourselves, nor by virtue of the difference of his attributes which we would have to surmount in the process of cognition or in a movement of sympathy merging us with him, as though his existence were an embarrassment. The Other does not affect us as what must be surmounted, enveloped, dominated, but as other, independent of us: behind every relation we could sustain with him, an absolute upsurge. It is this way of welcoming an absolute existent that we discover in justice and injustice, and that discourse, essentially teaching, effectuates. The term welcome of the Other expresses a simultaneity of activity and passivity which places the relation with the other outside of the dichotomies valid for things: the a priori and the a posteriori, activity and passivity.

But we wish to show also how, starting from knowing identified with thematization, the truth of this knowing leads back to the relation with the Other, that is, to justice. For the sense of our whole effort is to contest the ineradicable conviction of every philosophy that objective knowledge is the ultimate relation of transcendence, that the Other (though he be different from the things) must be known objectively, even if his freedom should deceive this nostalgia for knowledge. The sense of our whole effort lies in affirming not that the Other forever escapes knowing, but that there is no meaning in speaking here of knowledge or ignorance, for justice, the preeminent transcendence and the condition for knowing, is nowise, as one would like, a noesis correlative of a noema.

3. *Truth Presupposes Justice*

The spontaneous freedom of the I unconcerned with its justification is an eventuality inscribed in the essence of the separated being: a being *no longer participating* and hence drawing from itself its own existence, coming forth from a dimension of interiority, a being conformable to the fate of Gyges who sees those who look at him without seeing him, and who knows that he is not seen.

But does not Gyges's position involve the impunity of a being alone in the world, that is, a being for whom the world is a spectacle? And is not this the very condition for solitary, and hence uncontested and unpunished, freedom, and for certitude?

Is not this silent world, that is, this pure spectacle, accessible to true knowledge? Who can punish the exercise of the freedom of knowing? Or, more exactly, how can the spontaneity of the freedom that is manifested in certitude be called in question? Is not truth correlative with a freedom that is this side of justice, since it is the freedom of a being that is alone?

a) THE ANARCHY OF THE SPECTACLE: THE EVIL GENIUS

But a world absolutely silent that would not come to us from the word, be it mendacious, would be an-archic, without principle, without a beginning. Thought would strike nothing substantial. On first contact the *phenomenon* would degrade into *appearance* and in this sense would remain in equivocation, under suspicion of an evil genius. The evil genius does not manifest himself to *state* his lie; he remains, as possible, behind things which all seem to manifest themselves for good. The possibility of their fall to the state of images or veils codetermines their apparition as a pure spectacle, and betrays the recess that harbors the evil genius; whence the possibility of universal doubt, which is not a personal adventure that happened to Descartes. This possibility is constitutive of *apparition* as such, whether produced in sensible experience or in mathematical evidence. Husserl, who nonetheless admitted the possibility of an autopresentation of things, found this equivocation again in the *essential* incompletion of that autopresentation, and in the always possible break-up of the "synthesis" that sums up the sequence of its "aspects."

The equivocation here is not due to the confusion of two notions, two substances, or two properties. It is not to be counted among the confusions produced within a world that has already appeared. Nor is it the confusion of being and nothingness. What appears is not degraded into a nothing. But the appearance, which is not a nothing, is not a being either—not even an interior being, for it is nowise *in itself*. It proceeds as though from a mocking intention. He to whom the real had just presented itself, with an appearance that shone forth as the very *skin* of being, is being made game of. For already the *primordial* or the *ultimate* abandons the very skin in which it shone in its nudity, as a covering that announces, dissimulates, imitates, or deforms it. The doubt that arises from this ever renewed equivocation that constitutes the very apparition of the phenomenon does not implicate the acuity of the gaze that might erroneously confuse quite distinct beings in a world fully univocal, nor does the doubt question the constancy of forms of this world, which in fact may be borne by an unremitting becoming; it concerns the sincerity of what appears. It is as though in this silent and indecisive apparition a lie were perpetrated, as though the danger of error arose from an imposture, as though the silence were but the modality of an utterance.

The silent world is a world that comes to us from the Other, be he an evil genius. Its equivocation is insinuated in a mockery. Thus silence is not a simple absence of speech; speech lies in the depths of silence like a laughter perfidiously held back. It is the inverse of language: the interlocutor has given a sign, but has declined every interpretation; this is the silence that terrifies. Speech consists in the Other coming to the assistance of the sign given forth, attending his own manifestation in signs, redressing the equivocal by this attendance.

The evil genius' lie is not an utterance opposed to the veridical word; it is in that interspace between the illusory and the serious in which a subject who doubts breathes. The evil genius' lie is beyond every lie; in the ordinary lie the speaker dissimulates himself, to be sure, but in the dissimulating word does not evade speech, and hence can be refuted. The inverse of language is like a laughter that seeks to destroy language, a laughter infinitely reverberated where mystification interlocks in mystification without ever resting on a real speech, without ever commencing. The spectacle of the silent world of facts is bewitched: every phenomenon masks, mystifies ad infinitum, making actuality impossible. It is the situation created by those derisive beings communicating across a labyrinth of innuendos which Shakespeare and Goethe have appear in their scenes of sorcerers where speech is antilanguage and where to respond would be to cover oneself with ridicule.

b) EXPRESSION IS THE PRINCIPLE

The ambivalence of apparition is surmounted by expression, the presentation of the Other to me, the primordial event of signification. To comprehend a signification is not to go from one term of relationship to another, apperceiving relations within the given. To receive the given is already to receive it as taught—as an expression of the Other. Not that it would be necessary to mythically presuppose a god who signals himself by his world: the world becomes our theme, and hence our object, as proposed to us; it comes from a primordial teaching, in which scientific work itself is established and which it requires. The world is offered in the language of the Other; it is borne by propositions. The Other is the principle of phenomena. The phenomenon is not deduced from him; one does not rediscover him by tracing back from the sign the thing would be to the interlocutor giving this sign, in a movement analogous to that leading from the appearance to things in themselves. For deduction is a mode of thinking that applies to objects already given. The interlocutor can not be deduced, for the relationship between him and me is presupposed by every proof. It is presupposed by every symbolism, and not only because it is necessary to agree on that symbolism, establish its conventions—which, according to Plato in the *Cratylus,* cannot be laid down arbitrarily. This relationship is already necessary for a given to appear as a sign, a sign signaling a speaker, whatever be signified by the sign and though it be forever undecipherable. And it is necessary that the given function as a sign for it to be even given. He who signals himself by a sign qua signifying that sign is not the signified of the sign—but delivers the sign and gives it. The given refers to the giver, but this reference is not causality, as it is not the relation of a sign to its signification. We shall speak of it at greater length presently.

c) THE "COGITO" AND THE OTHER

The *cogito* does not provide a commencement to this iteration of dreaming. In the Cartesian *cogito,* taken as the first certitude (but which, for Descartes, already rests on the existence of God), there is an arbitrary halt which is not justified of itself. Doubt with regard to objects implies the evidence of the exercise of doubt itself. To deny this exercise would be again to affirm this exercise. In the *cogito* the thinking subject which denies its evidences ends up at the evidence of this work of negation, although in fact at a different level from that at which it had denied. But it ends up at the affirmation of an evidence that is not a final or initial affirmation, for it can be cast into doubt in its turn. The truth of the second negation, then, is affirmed at a still deeper level —but, once again, one not impervious to negation. This is not purely and simply a Sisyphean labor, since the distance traversed each time is not the same; it is a movement of descent toward an ever more profound abyss which we elsewhere* have called *there is,* beyond affirmation and negation. It is by reason of this operation of vertiginous descent unto the abyss, by reason of this change of level, that the Cartesian *cogito* is not a reasoning in the ordinary sense of the term nor an intuition. Descartes enters into a work of infinite negation, which is indeed the work of the atheist subject that has broken with participation and that remains incapable of an affirmation (although, by the sensibility, disposed for agreeableness**)—enters into a movement unto the abyss, vertiginously sweeping along the subject incapable of stopping itself.

The I in the negativity manifested by doubt breaks with participation, but does not find in the *cogito* itself a stopping place. It is not I, it is the other that can say *yes.* From him comes affirmation; he is at the commencement of experience. Descartes seeks a certitude, and stops at the first change of level in this vertiginous descent; in fact he possesses the idea of infinity, and can gauge in advance the return of affirmation behind the negation. But to possess the idea of infinity is to have already welcomed the Other.

d) OBJECTIVITY AND LANGUAGE

Thus the silent world would be an-archic. Knowing could not commence in it. But already as an-archic, at the limit of non-sense, its presence to consciousness lies in its expectation for a word that does not come. Thus it appears within a relation with the Other, as the sign the Other delivers, even if he dissimulates his face, that is, declines the assistance he would have to bring to the signs he delivers, and which he

---

* *De l'existence à l'existant* (Paris, 1947), pp. 93-105.—Trans.
** *"Agrément."* The sensibility, which does not "affirm," does "agree to" the agreeableness, or pleasure, of the element enjoyed.

delivers, consequently, in equivocation. A world absolutely silent, indifferent to the word never uttered, silent in a silence that does not permit the divining, behind the appearances, of anyone that signals this world and signals himself by signaling this world—be it to lie through the appearances, as an evil genius—a world so silent could not even present itself as a spectacle.

In fact, a spectacle is contemplated only in the measure that it has a meaning. The meaningful [sensé] is not posterior to the "seen," to the "sensible," of themselves meaningless, which our thought would work over or modify in a certain way in accordance with a priori categories.

Once the indissoluble bond that connects apparition with signification was understood, an effort was made to render the apparition posterior to signification by situating it within the finality of our practical behavior. What only appears, "pure objectivity," the "nothing but objective" would be only a residue of this practical finality from which it would derive its meaning. Whence the priority of care over contemplation, the enrootedness of cognition in a comprehension that opens upon the "worldhood" of the world, and opens the horizon for the apparition of the object.

The objectivity of the object is thereby being underestimated. The ancient thesis that puts representation at the basis of every practical behavior—taxed with intellectualism—is too hastily discredited. The most penetrating gaze can not discover in the thing its function as an implement; does a simple suspension of action suffice to apperceive the tool as a thing?

Moreover, is practical significance the primordial domain of meaning? Does it not presuppose the presence of a thought to which it appears and before which it acquires this meaning? Does it suffice, by its own operation, to make this thought arise?

Qua practical, signification refers ultimately to the being that exists in view of this very existence. It is thus derived from a term that is of itself an end. Thus he who comprehends the signification is indispensible for the series in which the things acquire a meaning, as the end of the series. The reference that signification implies would terminate where the reference is made from self to self—in enjoyment. The process from which beings would derive their meaning would not only in fact be finite, but as a finality it would *by essence* consist in proceeding to a term, in coming to an end [à finir]. But the outcome is the point at which every signification is precisely lost. Enjoyment, the satisfaction and egoism of the I, is an outcome in function of which beings take on or lose their signification as means according as they are situated on the way that leads to it or away from it. But the means themselves lose their signification in the outcome. The end is unconscious as soon as it is reached. By what right could the innocence of unconscious satisfaction be said to illuminate things with signification, while it itself is assuagement?

In fact signification has always been envisaged on the level of relations. A relation did not appear to be an intelligible content, which could be fixed intuitively; it was signifying by virtue of the system of relations into which it itself entered. Thus throughout the whole of Western philosophy, since the late philosophy of Plato, the comprehension of the intelligible appears as a movement and never as an intuition. It is Husserl who transforms relations into correlatives of a gaze that fixes them and takes them as contents. He brings forward the idea of a signification and an intelligibility intrinsic to the content as such, of the luminosity of a content (in clarity yet more than in distinction, which is relativity, since it detaches the object from something other than itself). But it is not certain that this autopresentation in the light could have meaning of itself. And idealism, the *Sinngebung* by the subject, concludes all this realism of meaning.

In fact signification is maintained only in the breach of the ultimate unity of the satisfied being. Things begin to take on signification in the care of the being that is still "on the way." Thus consciousness itself has been derived from this breach. The intelligible would result from the non-satisfaction, the provisional indigence of this being, its remaining short of its accomplishment. But by what miracle is this possible—if the outcome is the completed being, if the act is more than the potency?

Must we not rather think that the calling in question of satisfaction, which is a becoming aware of it, does not come from its failing, but from an event for which the process of finality cannot serve as the prototype? The consciousness that spoils happiness goes beyond happiness and does not lead us back over the paths that led to it. The consciousness that spoils happiness and gives signification to happiness and to finality, and to the finalist concatenation of implements and their users, does not come out of finality. Objectivity, where being is proposed to consciousness, is not a residue of finality. The objects are not objects when they offer themselves to the hand that uses them, to the mouth and the nose, the eyes and the ears that enjoy them. Objectivity is not what remains of an implement or a food when separated from the world in which their being comes into play. It is *posited* in a discourse, in a *conversation* [*entre-tien*] which *proposes* the world. This *proposition* is held between [se tient entre] two points which do not constitute a system, a cosmos, a totality.

The objectivity of the object and its signification comes from language. This way the object is posited as a theme offered envelops the instance of signifying—not the referring of the thinker who fixes it to what is signified (and is part of the same system), but the manifesting of the signifier, the issuer of the sign, an absolute alterity which nonetheless speaks to him and thereby thematizes, that is, proposes a world. The world precisely qua proposed, qua expression, has a meaning, but for this very reason is never in the original. For a signification to be given *leibhaft,* to exhaust its being in an exhaustive apparition, is an absurdity. But the non-originality of what has a meaning is not a lesser being, a reference to a reality it imitates, reverberates, or symbolizes. The meaningful refers to a signifier. The sign does not signify the signifier as it signifies the signified. The signified is never a complete presence; always a sign in its turn, it does not come in a straightforward frankness. The signifier, he who emits the sign, *faces,* despite the interposition of the sign, without proposing himself as a theme. He can, to be sure, speak of himself—but then he would announce himself as signified and consequently as a sign in his turn. The Other, the signifier, manifests himself in speech by speaking of the world and not of himself; he manifests himself by proposing the world, by *thematizing* it.

Thematization manifests the Other because the proposition that posits and offers the world does not float in the air, but promises a response to him who receives this proposition, who directs himself toward the Other because in his proposition he receives the possibility of questioning. Questioning is not explained by astonishment only, but by the presence of him to whom it is addressed. A proposition is maintained in the outstretched field of questions and answers. A proposition is a sign which is already interpreted, which provides its own key. The presence of the interpretative key in the sign to be interpreted is precisely the presence of the other in the proposition, the presence of him who can come to the assistance of his discourse, the teaching quality of all speech. Oral discourse is the plenitude of discourse.

Signification or intelligibility does not arise from the identity of the same who remains in himself, but from the face of the other who calls upon the same. Signification does not arise because the same has needs, because he lacks something, and hence all that is susceptible of filling this lack takes on meaning. Signification is in the absolute surplus of the other with respect to the same who desires him, who desires what he does not lack, who welcomes the other across themes which the other proposes to him or receives from him, without absenting himself from the signs thus given. Signification arises from the other stating or understanding the world, which precisely is thematized in his language or his understanding. Signification starts with the speech in which the world is at the same time thematized and interpreted, in which the signifier never separates himself from the sign he delivers, but takes it up again always while he exposes. For this assistance always given to the word which posits the things is the unique essence of language.

The signification of beings is manifested not in the perspective of finality, but in that of language. A relation between terms that resist totalization, that absolve themselves from the relation or that specify it, is possible only as language. The resistance of one term to the other is not due to the obscure and hostile residue of alterity, but, on the contrary, to the inexhaustible surplus of attention which speech, ever teaching, brings me. For speech is always a taking up again of what was a simple sign cast forth by it, an ever renewed promise to clarify what was obscure in the utterance.

To have meaning is to be situated relative to an absolute, that is, to come from that alterity that is not absorbed in its being perceived. Such an alterity is possible only as a miraculous abundance, an inexhaustible surplus of attention arising in the ever recommenced effort of language to clarify its own manifestation. To have meaning is to teach or to be taught, to speak or to be able to be stated.

In the perspective of finality and enjoyment signification appears only in labor, which implies enjoyment impeded. But enjoyment impeded would by itself engender no signification but only suffering did it not occur in a world of objects, that is, in a world where speech has already resounded.

The function of being origin does not fall to an *end* that, within a referential system, would refer to itself (such as the being for itself characteristic of consciousness). Commencement and end are not ultimate concepts in the same sense. The "for itself" closes in upon itself and, satisfied, loses all signification; to him who approaches it it appears as enigmatic as any other apparition. The origin is what provides the key to its own enigma—what provides the word for it. Language is exceptional in that it attends its own manifestation. Speech consists in explaining oneself with respect to speech; it is a teaching. Apparition is a congealed form from which someone has already withdrawn, whereas in language there is accomplished the unintermittent afflux of a presence that rends the inevitable veil of its own apparition, which is plastic like every apparition. Apparition reveals and conceals; speech consists in surmounting, in a total frankness ever renewed, the dissimulation inevitable in every apparition. Thereby a sense—an orientation— is given to every phenomenon.

The commencement of knowing is itself possible only if the bewitchment and the permanent equivocation of a world in which every apparition is a possible dissimulation, where commencement is wanting, is dispelled. Speech introduces a principle into this anarchy. Speech disenchants, for the speaking being guarantees his own apparition and comes to the assistance of himself, attends his own manifestation. His being is brought about in this *attendance.* The speech which already dawns in the face that looks at me looking introduces the primary frankness of revelation. In function of it the world is oriented, that is, takes on signification. In function of the word the world commences, which is not equivalent to the formula: the world issues in speech. The world is *said* and hence can be a theme, can be proposed. The entry of beings into a proposition constitutes the original event of their *taking on signification;* the possibility of their algorithmic expression itself will be established on this basis. Speech is thus the origin of all signification—of tools and all human works—for through it the referential system from which every signification arises receives the very principle of its functioning, its key. Language is not one modality of symbolism; every symbolism refers already to language.

e) LANGUAGE AND ATTENTION

As an attendance of being at its own presence, speech is a teaching. Teaching does not simply transmit an abstract and general content already common to me and the Other. It does not merely assume an after all subsidiary function of being midwife to a mind already pregnant with its fruit. Speech first founds community by *giving,* by presenting the phenomenon as given; and it gives by thematizing. The given is the

---

* The French *sens* means both "meaning" and "direction."

work of a sentence. In the sentence the apparition loses its phenomenality in being fixed as a theme; in contrast with the silent world, ambiguity infinitely magnified, stagnant water, water stilled with mystification that passes for mystery, the proposition relates the phenomenon to the existent, to exteriority, to the Infinity of the other uncontained by my thought. It defines. The definition that situates the object within its genus presupposes the definition that consists in disengaging the amorphous phenomenon from its confusion to orient it in function of the Absolute, its origin, to thematize it. Every logical definition—*per genesim* or *per genus et differentiam specificam*—already presupposes this thematization, this entry into a world in which sentences resound.

The very objectification of truth refers to language. The infinite, against which every definition stands out, is not defined, does not offer itself to the gaze, but signals itself, not as a theme but as thematizing, as him starting from *whom* everything can be fixed in its identity. But also he signals himself by attending the work that signals him; he does not only signal himself, but speaks, is a face.

Teaching, the end of equivocation or confusion, is a thematization of phenomena. It is because phenomena have been taught to me by him who presents himself—by reviving the acts of this thematization which are the signs—by speaking—that henceforth I am not the plaything of a mystification, but consider objects. The presence of the Other dispels the anarchic sorcery of the facts: the world becomes an object. To be an object, to be a theme, is to be what I can speak of with someone who has broken through the screen of phenomena and has associated me with himself. We shall speak later of the structure of this association, a structure which, as we have intimated, can only be moral, such that truth is founded on my relationship with the other, or justice. To put speech at the origin of truth is to abandon the thesis that disclosure, which implies the solitude of vision, is the first work of truth.

Thematization as the work of language, as an *action* exercised by the Master on me, is not a mysterious information, but the appeal addressed to my attention. Attention and the explicit thought it makes possible are not a refinement of consciousness, but consciousness itself. But the eminently sovereign attention in me is what *essentially* responds to an appeal. Attention is attention to something because it is attention to someone. The exteriority of its point of departure is essential to it: it is the very tension of the I. The school, without which no thought is explicit, conditions science. It is there that is affirmed the exteriority that accomplishes freedom and does not offend it: the exteriority of the Master. Thought can become explicit only among two; explicitation is not limited to finding what one already possessed. But the first teaching of the teacher is his very presence as teacher from which representation comes.

f) LANGUAGE AND JUSTICE

But what can it mean that the teacher who calls forth attention exceeds the consciousness? How is the teacher outside of the consciousness he teaches? He is not exterior to it as the content thought is exterior to the thought that thinks it; this exteriority is assumed by thought, and in this sense does not *overflow* the consciousness. Nothing that concerns thought can overflow it; everything is freely assumed. *Nothing—except the judge judging the very freedom of thought.* The presence of the Master who by his word gives meaning to phenomena and permits them to be thematized is not open to an objective knowing; this presence is in society with me. The presence of being in the phenomenon, which breaks the charm of the bewitched world, which utters the *yes* of which the I is incapable, which brings the preeminent positivity of the Other, is ipso facto as-sociation. But the reference to commencement is not a knowing of the commencement; quite the contrary: every objectification already refers to this reference. Association, a preeminent experience of being, does not disclose. One may call it a disclosure of what is revealed —the experience of a face; but one thus conjures away the originality of this disclosure. In this disclosure there disappears precisely the consciousness of solitary certitude in which every knowing is enacted, even that one can have of a face. Certitude rests, in fact, on my freedom, and is in this sense solitary. Whether it be through a priori concepts which enable me to assume the given, or whether it be by adherence of the will (as in Descartes), it is finally my freedom alone that takes the responsibility for the true. As-sociation, the welcoming of the master, is the opposite course: in it the exercise of my freedom is called in question. If we call a situation where my freedom is called in question conscience, association or the welcoming of the Other is conscience. The originality of this situation does not only lie in the formal antithesis it represents with regard to the cognitive consciousness. The calling in question of oneself is all the more severe the more rigorously the self is in control of itself. This receding of the goal in the very measure one approaches it is the life of conscience. The increase of my exigencies with regard to myself aggravates the judgment that is borne upon me, increases my responsibility. It is in this very concrete sense that the judgment that is borne upon me is never assumed by me. This inability to assume is the very life, the essence, of conscience. My freedom does not have the last word; I am not alone. And we shall say then that conscience alone leaves itself. In other words again, in conscience I have an experience that is not commensurate with any a priori framework—a conceptless experience. Every other experience is conceptual, that is, becomes my own or arises from my freedom. We have just described the essential insatiability of conscience, which does not belong to the order of hunger or satiety. It is thus that above we defined desire. Conscience and desire are not modalities of consciousness among others, but its condition. Concretely they are the welcoming of the Other across his judgment.

The transitivity of teaching, and not the interiority of reminiscence, manifests being; the locus of truth is society. The *moral* relation with the Master who judges me subtends the freedom of my adherence to the true. Thus language commences. He who speaks to me and across the words proposes himself to me retains the fundamental foreignness of the Other who judges me; our relations are never reversible. This supremacy posits him in himself, outside of my knowing, and it is by relation to this absolute that the *given* takes on meaning.

The "communication" of ideas, the reciprocity of dialogue, already hide the profound essence of language. It resides in the irreversibility of the relation between me and the other, in the Mastery of the Master coinciding with his position as other and as exterior. For language can be spoken only if the interlocutor is the commencement of his discourse, if, consequently, he remains beyond the system, if he is not *on the same plane* as myself. The interlocutor is not a Thou, he is a You;* he reveals himself in his lordship. Thus exteriority coincides with a mastery. My freedom is thus challenged by a Master who can invest it. Truth, the sovereign exercise of freedom, becomes henceforth possible.

---

* ". . . pas un Toi, il est un Vous."

D. SEPARATION AND ABSOLUTENESS

The same and the other at the same time maintain themselves in relationship and *absolve* themselves from this relation, remain absolutely separated. The idea of Infinity requires this separation. It was posited as the ultimate structure of being, as the *production* of its very infinitude. Society accomplishes it *concretely*. But is not to broach being on the level of separation to broach it in its fallenness? The positions we have outlined oppose the ancient privilege of unity which is affirmed from Parmenides to Spinoza and Hegel. Separation and interiority were held to be incomprehensible and irrational. The metaphysical knowledge which puts the same in touch with the other then would reflect this fallenness. Metaphysics would endeavor to suppress separation, to unite; the metaphysical being should absorb the being of the metaphysician. The de facto separation with which metaphysics begins would result from an illusion or a fault. As a stage the separated being traverses on the way of its return to its metaphysical source, a moment of a history that will be concluded by union, metaphysics would be an Odyssey, and its disquietude nostalgia. But the philosophy of unity has never been able to say whence came this accidental illusion and fall, inconceivable in the Infinite, the Absolute, and the Perfect.

To conceive separation as a fall or privation or provisional rupture of the totality is to know no other separation than that evinced by *need*. Need indicates void and lack in the needy one, its dependence on the exterior, the insufficiency of the needy being precisely in that it does not entirely possess its being and consequently is not strictly speaking *separate*. One of the ways of Greek metaphysics consisted in seeking the return to and the fusion with Unity. But Greek metaphysics conceived the Good as separate from the totality of essences, and in this way (without any contribution from an alleged Oriental thought) it caught sight of a structure such that the totality could admit of a beyond. The

Good is Good *in itself* and not by relation to the need to which it is wanting; it is a luxury with respect to needs. It is precisely in this that it is beyond being. When, above, disclosure was contrasted with revelation, in which truth is expressed and illuminates us before we sought it, the notion of the Good in itself was already being taken up anew. Plotinus returns to Parmenides when he represents the apparition of the essence from the One by emanation and by *descent*. Plato nowise deduces being from the Good: he posits transcendence as surpassing the totality. Alongside of needs whose satisfaction amounts to filling a void, Plato catches sight also of aspirations that are not preceded by suffering and lack, and in which we recognize the pattern of Desire: the need of him who lacks nothing, the aspiration of him who possesses his being entirely, who goes beyond his plenitude, who has the idea of Infinity. The Place of the Good above every essence is the most profound teaching, the definitive teaching, not of theology, but of philosophy. The paradox of an Infinity admitting a being outside of itself which it does not encompass, and accomplishing its very infinitude by virtue of this proximity of a separated being—in a word, the paradox of creation—thenceforth loses something of its audacity.

But then it is necessary to cease interpreting separation as pure and simple diminution of the Infinite, a degradation. Separation with regard to the Infinite, compatible with the Infinite, is not a simple "fall" of the Infinite. Though being *better* than the relations connecting the finite to the infinite formally, in the abstract, the relations with the Good are announced through an apparent diminution. The diminution counts only if, by abstract thought, one retains from separation (and from the creature) its finitude, instead of situating finitude within the transcendence by which it opens to Desire and goodness. The ontology of human existence, philosophical anthropology, endlessly paraphrases this abstract thought by insisting, with pathos, on finitude. In reality what is at issue is an order where the very notion of the Good first takes on meaning; what is at issue is society. Here the relation connects not terms that complete one another and consequently are reciprocally lacking to one another, but terms that suffice to themselves. This relation is Desire, the life of beings that have arrived at self-possession. Infinity thought concretely, that is, starting with the separated being turned toward it, *surpasses* itself. In other words, it opens to itself the order of the Good. In saying that infinity is *thought* concretely starting with the separated being turned toward it we are nowise taking a thought that starts with the separated being to be relative. Separation is the very constitution of thought and interiority, that is, a relationship within independence.

Infinity is produced by withstanding the invasion of a totality, in a contraction that leaves a place for the separated being. Thus relationships that open up a way outside of being take form. An infinity that does not close in upon itself in a circle but withdraws from the ontological extension so as to leave a place for a separated being exists divinely. Over and beyond the totality it inaugurates a society. The relations that are established between the separated being and Infinity redeem what diminution there was in the contraction creative of Infinity. Man redeems creation. Society with God is not an addition to God nor a disappearance of the interval that separates God from the creature. By contrast with totalization we have called it religion. Multiplicity and the limitation of the creative Infinite are compatible with the perfection of the Infinite; they articulate the meaning of this perfection.

Infinity opens the order of the Good. It is an order that does not contradict, but goes beyond the rules of formal logic. The distinction between need and Desire can not be reflected in formal logic, where desire is always forced into the forms of need. From this purely formal necessity comes the force of Parmenidean philosophy. But the order of Desire, the relationship between strangers who are not wanting to one another —desire in its positivity—is affirmed across the idea of creation *ex nihilo*. Then the plane of the needy being, avid for its complements, vanishes, and the possibility of a sabbatical existence, where existence suspends the necessities of existence, is inaugurated. For an existent is an existent only in the measure that it is free, that is, outside of any system, which implies dependence. Every restriction put on freedom is a restriction put on being. For this reason multiplicity is taken to be the ontological fallenness of beings mutually limiting one another in their proximity. Since Parmenides across Plotinus we have not succeeded in thinking otherwise. For multiplicity seemed to us to be united in a totality, of which the multiplicity could be but an appearance—moreover inexplicable. But the idea of creation *ex nihilo* expresses a multiplicity not united into a totality; the creature is an existence which indeed does depend on an other, but not as a part that is separated from it. Creation *ex nihilo* breaks with system, posits a being outside of every system, that is, there where its freedom is possible. Creation leaves to the creature a trace of dependence, but it is an unparalleled dependence: the dependent being draws from this exceptional dependence, from this relationship, its very independence, its exteriority to the system. What is essential to created existence is not the limited character of its being, and the concrete structure of the creature is not deducible from this finitude. What is essential to created existence is its separation with regard to the Infinite. This separation is not simply a negation. Accomplished as psychism, it precisely opens upon the idea of Infinity.

Thought and freedom come to us from separation and from the consideration of the Other—this thesis is at the antipodes of Spinozism.

SECTION II

INTERIORITY AND ECONOMY

A. SEPARATION AS LIFE

1. Intentionality and the Social Relation

In describing the metaphysical relation as disinterested, as disengaged from all participation, we would be wrong to recognize in it intentionality, the consciousness of . . . , simultaneously proximity and distance. For this Husserlian term evokes the relation with the object, the posited, the *thematic,* whereas the metaphysical relation does not link up a subject with an object. It is not that our intent be anti-intellectualist. In contradistinction to the philosophers of existence we will not found the relation with the existent respected in its being, and in this sense absolutely exterior, that is, metaphysical, on being in the world, the *care* and *doing* characteristic of the Heideggerian *Dasein.* Doing, labor, already implies the relation with the transcendent. If cognition in the form of the objectifying act does not seem to us to be at the level of the metaphysical relation, this is not because the exteriority contemplated as an object, the theme, would withdraw from the subject as fast as the abstractions proceed; on the contrary it does not withdraw enough. The contemplation of objects remains close to action; it disposes of its theme, and consequently comes into play on a plane where one being limits another. Metaphysics approaches without touching. Its *way* is not an action, but is the social relation. But we maintain that the social relation is experience preeminently, for it takes place before the existent that expresses himself, that is, remains in himself. In distinguishing between the objectifying act and the metaphysical we are on our way not to the denunciation of intellectualism but to its very strict development—if it is true that the intellect desires being in itself. It will therefore be necessary to show the difference that separates the relations analogous to transcendence from those of transcendence itself. The relations of transcendence lead to the other, whose mode the idea of Infinity has enabled us to specify. Even if they rest on transcendence, the relations analogous to transcendence, and the objectifying act among them, remain within the same.

109

The analysis of the relations that are produced within the same, to which the present section is devoted, will in reality describe the interval of separation. The formal pattern of separation is not that of every relation—a simultaneity of distance between the terms and their union. In the case of separation the union of the terms maintains separation in an eminent sense. The being that is in relation absolves itself from the relation, is absolute within relationship. Its concrete analysis as it is undertaken by a being who accomplishes it (and who does not cease to accomplish it while analyzing it) will, we have indicated, recognize separation as inner life, or as psychism. But in turn this interiority will appear as a presence at home with oneself, which means inhabitation and economy. The psychism and the perspectives it opens maintain the distance that separates the metaphysician from the metaphysical, and their resistance to totalization.

2. Living from . . .* (Enjoyment) The Notion of Accomplishment

We live from "good soup," air, light, spectacles, work, ideas, sleep, etc. . . . These are not objects of representations. We live from them. Nor is what we live from a "means of life," as the pen is a means with respect to the letter it permits us to write—nor a goal of life, as communication is the goal of the letter. The things we live from are not tools, nor even implements, in the Heideggerian sense of the term. Their existence is not exhausted by the utilitarian schematism that delineates them as having the existence of hammers, needles, or machines. They are always in a certain measure—and even the hammers, needles, and machines are—objects of enjoyment, presenting themselves to "taste," already adorned, embellished. Moreover, whereas the recourse to the instrument implies finality and indicates a dependence with regard to the other, living from . . . delineates independence itself, the independence of enjoyment and of its happiness, which is the original pattern of all independence.

Conversely, the independence of happiness always depends on a content: it is the joy or the pain of breathing, looking, eating, working, handling the hammer and the machine, etc. But the dependence of

---

* "Vivre de. . . ." While we are uniformedly translating this as "living from . . . ," sometimes "living on . . ." would be more appropriate.—Trans.

happiness on the content is not that of the effect on a cause. The contents from which life lives are not always indispensable to it for the maintenance of that life, as means or as the fuel [carburant] necessary for the "functioning" of existence. Or at least they are not lived as such. With them we die, and sometimes prefer to die rather than be without them. Still the "moment" of restoration, for example, is phenomenologically included in the nourishing of oneself, and it is even the essential, though, in order to account for it, we do not have to resort to any of the knowledge a physiologist or economist possesses. Nourishment, as a means of invigoration, is the transmutation of the other into the same, which is in the essence of enjoyment: an energy that is other, recognized as other, recognized, we will see, as sustaining the very act that is directed upon it, becomes, in enjoyment, my own energy, my strength, me. All enjoyment is in this sense alimentation. Hunger is need, is privation in the primal sense of the word, and thus precisely *living from* . . . is not a simple becoming conscious of what fills life. These contents are lived: they feed life. One lives one's life: to live is a sort of transitive verb, and the contents of life are its direct objects. And the act of living these contents is ipso facto a content of life. The relation with the direct object of the verb to exist (which, since the philosophers of existence, has become transitive) in fact resembles the relation with nourishment, where there is a relation with an object and at the same time a relation with this relation which also nourishes and fills life. One does not only exist one's pain or one's joy; one exists from pains and joys. Enjoyment is precisely this way the act nourishes itself with its own activity. To live from bread is therefore neither to represent bread to oneself nor to act on it nor to act by means of it. To be sure, it is necessary to earn one's bread, and it is necessary to nourish oneself in order to earn one's bread; thus the bread I eat is also that with which I earn my bread and my life. But if I eat my bread in order to labor and to live, I live *from* my labor and *from* my bread. Bread and labor do not, in the Pascalian sense, divert me from the bare fact of existence or occupy the emptiness of my time: enjoyment is the ultimate consciousness of all the contents that fill my life—it embraces them. The life that I earn is not a *bare* existence; it is a life of labor and nourishments; these are contents which do not preoccupy it only, but which "occupy" it, which "entertain" it, of which it is enjoyment. Even if the content of life ensures my life, the means is immediately sought as an end, and the pursuit of this end becomes an end in its turn. Thus things are always more than the strictly necessary; they make up the grace of life. We live from our labor which ensures our subsistence; but we also live from our labor because it fills (delights or saddens) life. The first meaning of "to live from one's labor" reverts to the second—if the things are in place. Qua object the object seen occupies life; but the vision of the object makes up the "joy" of life.

This does not mean that there is here a vision of vision: life's relation with its own dependence on the things is enjoyment—which, as happiness, is independence. The acts of life are not straightforward [droits] and as it were strained toward their finality. We live in the consciousness of consciousness, but this consciousness of consciousness is not reflection. It is not knowing but enjoyment, and, as we shall say, the very egoism of life.

To say that we live from contents is therefore not to affirm that we resort to them as to conditions for ensuring our life, taken as the bare fact of existing. The bare fact of life is never bare. Life is not the naked will to be, an ontological *Sorge* for this life. Life's relation with the very conditions of its life becomes the nourishment and content of that life. Life is *love of life,* a relation with contents that are not my being but more dear than my being: thinking, eating, sleeping, reading, working, warming oneself in the sun. Distinct from my substance but constituting it, these contents make up the worth [prix] of my life. When reduced to pure and naked existence, like the existence of the shades Ulysses visits in Hades, life dissolves into a shadow. Life is an existence that does not precede its essence. Its essence makes up its worth [prix]; and here value [valeur] constitutes being. The reality of life is already on the level of happiness, and in this sense beyond ontology. Happiness is not an accident of being, since being is risked for happiness.

If "living *from* . . ." is not simply a representation of something, "living from . . ." also does not fit into the categories of activity and potency, determinative for Aristotelian ontology. The Aristotelian act was equivalent to being. Placed within a system of ends and means, man actualized himself in exceeding his apparent limits *by action.* Like every other nature, human nature accomplished itself, that is, became entirely itself, by functioning, by entering into relations. Every being is an exercise of being, and the identification of thought with action then is non-metaphorical. If living from . . . , enjoyment, likewise consists in entering into relation with something other, this relation does not take form on the plane of *pure being*. Moreover, action itself, which unfolds on the plane of being, enters into our happiness. We live from acts—and from the very act of being, just as we live from ideas and sentiments. What I do and what I am is at the same time that *from which* I live. We relate ourselves to it with a relation that is neither theoretical nor practical. Behind theory and practice there is enjoyment of theory and of practice: the egoism of life. The final relation is enjoyment, *happiness*.

Enjoyment is not a psychological state among others, the affective tonality of empiricist psychology, but the very pulsation of the I. In enjoyment we maintain ourselves always at the second power, which, however, is not yet the level of reflection. For happiness, in which we move already by the simple fact of living, is always beyond being, in which the things are hewn. It is an outcome, but one where the memory of the aspiration confers upon the outcome the character of an accomplishment, which is worth *more* than ataraxy. Pure existing is ataraxy; happiness is accomplishment. Enjoyment is made of the memory of its thirst; it is a quenching. It is the act that remembers its "potency." It does not express (as Heidegger would have it) the mode of my implantation—my *disposition*—in being, the tonus of my bearing. It is not my bearing in being, but already the exceeding of being; being itself "befalls" him who can seek happiness as a new glory above substantiality; being itself is a content which makes up the happiness or unhappiness of him who does not simply realize his nature but seeks in being a triumph inconceivable in the order of substances. Substances are only what they are. The independence of happiness is therefore to be distinguished from the independence that, for philosophers, substance possesses. It is as though the existent could aspire to a new triumph above and beyond the plenitude of being. To be sure, the objection can be brought against us that the imperfection of the existing an existent disposes of alone renders this triumph possible and precious, and that the triumph can coincide only with the plenitude of existing. But we shall then say that the strange possibility of an incomplete being is already the opening of the order of happiness and the ransom paid for this promise of an independence higher than substantiality.

Happiness is a condition for activity, if activity means a commencement occurring in duration, which nevertheless is continuous. Action implies being, to be sure, but it marks a beginning and an end in an anonymous being—where end and beginning have no meaning. But within this continuity enjoyment realizes independence with regard to continuity: each happiness comes for the first time. Subjectivity originates in the independence and sovereignty of enjoyment.

Plato speaks of the soul that feasts on truths.[1] He discerns in rational thought, in which the sovereignty of the soul is manifested, a relation with the object that is not only contemplative but confirms the same (characteristic of the thinker) in its sovereignty. In the meadow that lies in the plain of truth "that pasturage is found which is suited to the highest part of the soul; and the wing on which the soul soars is nourished with this."[2] What enables the soul to rise to truth is nourished with truth. Throughout this book we are opposing the full analogy drawn between truth and nourishment, because metaphysical Desire is above life, and with regard to it one cannot speak of satiety. But the Platonic image describes, with regard to thought, the very relationship that will be accomplished by life, where the attachment to the contents that fill it provides it with a supreme content. The consumption of foods is the food of life.

3. Enjoyment and Independence

We have said that to *live from something* does not amount to drawing vital energy from somewhere. Life does not consist in seeking and consuming the fuel furnished by breathing and nourishment, but, if we may so speak, in consummating terrestrial and celestial nourishments. Though it thus depends on what is not itself, this dependence is not without a counterpart which in the final analysis nullifies it. What we live from does not enslave us; we enjoy it. Need cannot be interpreted as a simple lack, despite the psychology of need given by Plato, nor as pure passivity, despite Kantian ethics. The human being thrives on his needs; he is happy for his needs. The paradox of "living from something," or, as Plato would say, the folly of these pleasures, is precisely in a complacency with regard to what life depends on—not a mastery on the one hand and a dependence on the other, but a mastery in this dependence. This is perhaps the very definition of complacency and pleasure. *Living from* . . . is the dependency that turns into sovereignty, into happiness—essentially egoist. Need—the vulgar Venus—is also, in a certain sense, the child of πόρος and of πενία; it is πενία as

---

[1] *Phaedrus*, 246e.
[2] *Phaedrus*, 248b-c.

source of πόρος, in contrast with desire, which is the πενία of πόρος. What it lacks is its source of plenitude and wealth. Need, a happy dependence, is capable of satisfaction, like a void, which gets filled. Physiology, from the exterior, teaches us that need is a lack. That man could be happy for his needs indicates that in human need the physiological plane is transcended, that as soon as there is need we are outside the categories of being—even though in formal logic the structures of happiness—independence through dependence, or I, or human creature—cannot show through without contradiction.

Need and enjoyment can not be covered by the notions of activity and passivity, though they be merged in the notion of finite freedom, Enjoyment, in relation with nourishment, which is the *other* of life, is an independence *sui generis,* the independence of happiness. The life that is life *from* something is happiness. Life is affectivity and sentiment; to live is to enjoy life. To despair of life makes sense only because originally life is happiness. Suffering is a failing of happiness; it is not correct to say that happiness is an absence of suffering. Happiness is made up not of an absence of needs, whose tyranny and imposed character one denounces, but of the satisfaction of all needs. For the privation of need is not just a privation, but is privation in a being that knows the surplus of happiness, privation in a being gratified. Happiness is accomplishment: it exists in a soul satisfied and not in a soul that has extirpated its needs, a castrated soul. And because life is happiness it is personal. The personality of the person, the ipseity of the I, which is more than the particularity of the atom and of the individual, is the particularity of the happiness of enjoyment. Enjoyment accomplishes the atheist separation; it deformalizes the notion of separation, which is not a cleavage made in the abstract, but the existence at home with itself of an autochthonous I. The soul is not, as in Plato, what "has the care of inanimate being everywhere"[3]; it to be sure dwells in what is not itself, but it acquires its own identity by this dwelling in the "other" (and not logically, by opposition to the other).

4. Need and Corporeity

If enjoyment is the very eddy of the same, it is not ignorance but exploitation of the other. The alterity of the other the world is is

---

[3] *Phaedrus,* 246b.

surmounted by need, which enjoyment remembers and is enkindled by; need is the primary movement of the same.   To be sure, need is also a dependence with regard to the other, but it is a dependence across time, a dependence that is not an instantaneous betraying of the same but a suspension or postponement of dependence, and thus the possibility to break, by labor and by economy, the very thrust of the alterity upon which need depends.

In denouncing as illusory the pleasures that accompany the satisfaction of needs Plato has fixed the negative notion of need: it would be a *less,* a lack that satisfaction would make good. The essence of need would be visible in the need to scratch oneself in scabies, in sickness.* Must we remain at a philosophy of need that apprehends it in poverty? Poverty is one of the dangers the liberation of man breaking with the animal and vegetable condition risks. In need the essential is in this rupture, despite this risk. To conceive of need as a simple privation is to apprehend it in the midst of a disorganized society which leaves it neither time nor consciousness. The distance intercalated between man and the world on which he depends constitutes the essence of need. A being has detached itself from the world from which it still nourishes itself! The part of being that has detached itself from the whole in which it was enrooted disposes of its own being, and its relation with the world is henceforth only need. It frees itself from all the weight of the world, from immediate and incessant contacts; it is at a distance. This distance can be converted into time, and subordinate a world to the liberated but needy being. There is here an ambiguity of which the body is the very articulation. Animal need is liberated from vegetable dependence, but this liberation is itself dependence and uncertainty. An animal's need is inseparable from struggle and fear; the exterior world from which it is liberated remains a threat. But need is also the time of labor: a relation with an other yielding its alterity. To be cold, hungry, thirsty, naked, to seek shelter—all these dependencies with regard to the world, having become needs, save the instinctive being from anonymous menaces and constitute a being independent of the world, a veritable *subject* capable of ensuring the satisfaction of its needs, which are recognized as material, that is, as admitting of satisfaction. Needs are in my power; they constitute me as the same and not as dependent on the other. My body is not only a way for the subject to be reduced to slavery, to de-

---

* Cf. *Philebus* 46a.

pend on what is not itself, but is also a way of possessing and of working, of having time, of overcoming the very alterity of what I have to live from. The body is the very self-possession by which the I, liberated from the world by need, succeeds in overcoming the very destitution of this liberation. We shall return to this further.

Having recognized its needs as material needs, as capable of being satisfied, the I can henceforth turn to what it does not lack. It distinguishes the material from the spiritual, opens to Desire. Labor, however, already requires discourse and consequently the height of the other irreducible to the same, the presence of the Other. There is no natural religion; but already human egoism leaves pure nature *by virtue of the human body raised upwards,* committed in the *direction of height. This is not its empirical illusion but its ontological production and its ineffaceable testimony.* The "I can" proceeds from this height.

Let us again note the difference between need and Desire: in need I can sink my teeth into the real and satisfy myself in assimilating the other; in Desire there is no sinking one's teeth into being, no satiety, but an uncharted future before me. Indeed the time presupposed by need is provided me by Desire; human need already rests on Desire. Need has thus the time to convert this *other* into *the same* by labor. I exist as a body, that is, as raised up, an organ that will be able to grasp and consequently place itself, in this world on which I depend, before ends technically realizable. For a body that labors everything is not already accomplished, already done; thus to be a body is to have time in the midst of the facts, to be *me* though living in the *other.*

This revelation of distance is an ambiguous revelation, for time both destroys the security of instantaneous happiness, and permits the fragility thus discovered to be overcome. And it is the relation with the other, inscribed in the body as its elevation, that makes possible the transformation of enjoyment into consciousness and labor.

5. *Affectivity as the Ipseity of the I*

We are catching sight of a possibility of rendering the unicity of the I intelligible. The unicity of the I conveys separation. Separation in the strictest sense is solitude, and enjoyment—happiness or unhappiness—is isolation itself.

The I is not unique like the Eiffel Tower or the Mona Lisa. The unicity of the I does not merely consist in being found in one sample only, but in existing without having a genus, without being the individuation of a concept. The ipseity of the I consists in remaining outside the distinction between the individual and the general. The refusal of the concept is not a resistance to generalization by the τόδε τι, which is on the same plane of the concept—and by which the concept is defined, as by an antithetical term. Here the refusal of the concept is not only one of the aspects of its being, but its whole content; it is interiority. This refusal of the concept drives the being that refuses it into the dimension of interiority. It is at home with itself. The I is thus the mode in which the break-up of totality, which leads to the presence of the absolutely other, is concretely accomplished. It is solitude par excellence. The secrecy of the I guarantees the discretion of the totality.

This logically absurd structure of unicity, this non-participation in genus, is the very egoism of happiness. Happiness, in its relation with the "other" of nutriments, suffices to itself; it even suffices to itself *because* of this relation with the other: it consists in satisfying its needs and not in suppressing them. Happiness suffices to itself through the "not sufficing to oneself" proper to need. The lack in enjoyment, which Plato denounced, does not compromise the instant of sufficiency. The opposition between the ephemeral and the eternal does not convey the true meaning of sufficiency, which is the very contraction of the ego. It is an existence *for itself*—but not, initially, in view of its own existence. Nor is it a representation of self by self. It is for itself as in the expression "each for himself"; for itself as the "famished stomach that has no ears," capable of killing for a crust of bread, is for itself; for itself as the surfeited one who does not understand the starving and approaches him as an alien species, as the philanthropist approaches the destitute. The self-sufficiency of *enjoying* measures the egoism or the ipseity of the Ego and the same. Enjoyment is a withdrawal into oneself, an involution. What is termed an affective state does not have the dull monotony of a state, but is a vibrant exaltation in which dawns the self. For the I is not the *support* of enjoyment. The "intentional" structure is here wholly different; the I is the very contraction of sentiment, the pole of a spiral whose coiling and involution is drawn by enjoyment: the focus of the curve is a part of the curve. It is precisely as a "coiling," as a movement toward oneself, that enjoyment comes into play. And now one can understand in what sense we were able to say above that the I is an apology: whatever be the transfigurations this egoism will receive from speech, it is for the happiness constitutive of its very egoism that the I who speaks pleads.

The breach of the totality that is accomplished by the enjoyment of solitude—or the solitude of enjoyment—is radical. When the critical presence of the Other will call in question this egoism it will not destroy its solitude. Solitude will be recognized in the concern for *knowing,* which is formulated as a problem of origin—inconceivable in a totality. To this problem the notion of causality can bring no solution, since it is precisely a question of a *self,* a being absolutely isolated, whose isolation causality would compromise by reinstating it in a series. The notion of creation alone will be commensurate with such a question, respecting at the same time the absolute novelty of the I and its attachment to a principle, its having been called in question. The solitude of the subject will be recognized also in the goodness in which the apology issues.

The upsurge of the self beginning in enjoyment, where the substantiality of the I is apperceived not as the subject of the verb to be, but as implicated in happiness (not belonging to ontology, but to axiology) is the exaltation of the *existent* as such. The existent would then not be justiciable to the "comprehension of being," or ontology. One becomes a subject of being not by assuming being but in enjoying happiness, by the interiorization of enjoyment which is also an exaltation, an "above being." The existent is "autonomous" with respect to being; it designates not a participation in being, but happiness. The existent par excellence is man.

When the I is identified with reason, taken as the power of thematization and objectification, it loses its very ipseity. To represent to oneself is to empty oneself of one's subjective substance and to insensibilize enjoyment. By imagining this anaesthesia limitless Spinoza conjures away separation. But the joy of this intellectual coincidence and the freedom of this obedience mark a cleavage line in the unity won in this way. Reason makes human society possible; but a society whose members would be only reasons would vanish as a society. What could a being entirely rational speak of with another entirely rational being? Reason has no plural; how could numerous reasons be distinguished? How could the Kantian kingdom of ends be possible, had not the rational beings that compose it retained, as the principle of individuation, their exigency for happiness, miraculously saved from the shipwreck of sensible nature? In Kant the I is met with again in this need for happiness.

To be I is to exist in such a way as to be already beyond being, in happiness. For the I to be means neither to oppose nor to represent something to itself, nor to use something, nor to aspire to something, but to enjoy something.

6. The I of Enjoyment Is Neither Biological Nor Sociological

Individuation through happiness individuates a "concept" whose comprehension and extension coincide; the individuation of the concept by self-identification constitutes the content of this concept. The notion of the separated person which we have approached in the description of enjoyment, which is posited in the independence of happiness, is to be distinguished from the notion of person such as it is fabricated by the philosophy of life or of race. In the exaltation of biological life the person arises as a product of the species or of impersonal life, which has recourse to the individual so as to ensure its impersonal triumph.[4] The unicity of the I, its status as a conceptless individual, would disappear in this *participation* in what exceeds it.

The pathos of liberalism, which we rejoin on one side, lies in the promotion of a person inasmuch as he represents nothing further, that is, is precisely a self. Then multiplicity can be produced only if the individuals retain their secrecy, if the relation that unites them into a multiplicity is not visible from the outside, but proceeds from one unto the other. If it were entirely visible from the outside, if the exterior point of view would open upon its ultimate reality, the multiplicity would form a totality in which the individuals would participate; the bond between persons would not have preserved the multiplicity from addition. In order that multiplicity be maintained, the relation proceeding from me to the Other—the attitude of one person with regard to another—must

---

[4] Cf. for example Kurt Schilling, "Einführung in die Staats- und Rechtsphilosophie," in *Rechtswissenschaftliche Grundrisse,* ed. by Otto Korellreuter (Berlin, 1939). According to this book, typical of racist philosophy, individuality and sociality would be events of life that proceed individuals and create them for better adaptation, in order to ensure life. The concept of happiness, with the individualness it evokes, is lacking in this philosophy. Want—*Not*— is what threatens life. The State is but an organization of this multiplicity, in view of making life possible. To the end the person—even the person of the leader—remains at the service of life and of the creation of life. The principle of personality proper is never an end.

be stronger than the formal signification of conjunction, to which every relation risks being degraded. This greater force is concretely affirmed in the fact that the relation proceeding from me to the other cannot be included within a network of relations visible to a third party. If this bond between me and the other could be entirely apprehended from the outside it would suppress, under the gaze that encompassed it, the very multiplicity bound with this bond. The individuals would appear as participants in the totality: the Other would amount to a second copy of the I—both included in the same concept. Pluralism is not a numerical multiplicity. In order that a pluralism in itself (which cannot be reflected in formal logic) be realized there must be produced in depth the movement from me to the other, an attitude of an I with regard to the Other (an attitude already *specified* as love or hatred, obedience or command, learning or teaching, etc. . . .), that would not be a species of relationship in general; this means that the movement from me to the other could not present itself as a theme to an objective gaze freed from this confrontation with the other, to a reflection. Pluralism implies a radical alterity of the other, whom I do not simply *conceive* by relation to myself, but *confront* out of my egoism. The alterity of the Other is in him and is not relative to me; it *reveals* itself. But I have access to it proceeding from myself and not through a comparison of myself with the other. I have access to the alterity of the Other from the society I maintain with him, and not by quitting this relation in order to reflect on its terms. Sexuality supplies the example of this relation, accomplished before being reflected on: the other sex is an alterity borne by a being as an essence and not as the reverse of his identity; but it could not affect an unsexed me. The Other as master can also serve us as an example of an alterity that is not only *by relation* to me, an alterity that, belonging to the essence of the other, is nevertheless visible only from an I.

B. ENJOYMENT AND REPRESENTATION

What we live from and enjoy is not the same as that life itself. I eat bread, listen to music, follow the course of my ideas. Though I live my life, the life I live and the fact of living it nonetheless remain distinct, even though it is true that this life itself continually and essentially becomes its own content.

Can this relationship be specified? Is not enjoyment, as the way life relates to its contents, a form of intentionality in the Husserlian sense, taken very broadly, as the universal fact of human existence? Every moment of life (conscious and even unconscious, such as consciousness divines it) is in relation with an *other* than that moment itself. We know the rhythm with which this thesis is exposed: every perception is a perception of the perceived, every idea an idea of an ideate, every desire a desire of a desired, every emotion an emotion of something moving . . . ; but every obscure thought of our being is also oriented toward *something*. Every present in its temporal nudity tends toward the future and returns upon the past or resumes that past—is prospection and retrospection. Yet already with the first exposition of intentionality as a philosophical thesis there appeared the privilege of representation. The thesis that every intentionality is either a representation or founded on a representation dominates the *Logische Untersuchungen* and returns as an obsession in all of Husserl's subsequent work. What is the relation between the theoretical intentionality of the objectifying act, as Husserl calls it, and enjoyment?

1. Representation and Constitution

In order to find an answer we shall try to follow the movement proper to objectifying intentionality.

This intentionality is a necessary moment of the event of separation in itself, to whose description this section is devoted, and which is articulated starting with enjoyment in dwelling and in possession.[1] The possibility of representing to oneself and the resultant temptation to idealism do indeed profit already from the metaphysical relation and the relationship with the absolutely other, but they attest separation in the midst of this very transcendence (although the separation is not reducible to an echo of transcendence). We shall first describe it detached from its sources. Taken in itself, as it were uprooted, representation seems to be oriented in an opposite direction from enjoyment and will permit us to show by contrast the "intentional" pattern of enjoyment and sensibility (although representation is in fact woven of it and repeats its event, which is separation).

The Husserlian thesis of the primacy of the objectifying act—in which was seen Husserl's excessive attachment to theoretical consciousness, and which has served as a pretext to accuse Husserl of intellectualism (as though that were an accusation!)—leads to transcendental philosophy, to the affirmation (so surprising after the realist themes the idea of intentionality seemed to approach) that the object of consciousness, while distinct from consciousness, is as it were a product of consciousness, being a "meaning" endowed by consciousness, the result of *Sinngebung*. The object of representation is to be distinguished from the act of representation—this is the fundamental and most fecund affirmation of Husserl's phenomenology, to which a realist import is hastily given. But does the theory of mental images, betraying a confusion of the act with the object of consciousness, rest uniquely on a false description of consciousness inspired by the prejudices of a psychological atomism? In a sense the object of representation is indeed interior to thought: despite its independence it falls under the power of thought. We are not alluding to the Berkeleyan ambiguity between the sentient and the sensed within sensation, and we are not limiting our reflection to objects called sensible; it is rather a question of what in Cartesian terminology becomes the clear and distinct idea. In clarity an object which is first exterior *is given* that is, is delivered over to him who encounters it as though it had been entirely determined by him. In clarity the exterior being presents itself as the work of the thought that receives it. Intelligibility, characterized by clarity, is a total adequation of the thinker with what is thought, in the precise sense of a mastery exercised

---

[1] See pp. 152 ff.

by the thinker upon what is thought in which the object's resistance as an exterior being vanishes. This mastery is total and as though creative; it is accomplished as a giving of meaning: the object of representation is reducible to noemata. The intelligible is precisely what is entirely reducible to noemata and all of whose relations with the understanding reducible to those established by the light. In the intelligibility of representation the distinction between me and the object, between interior and exterior, is effaced. Descartes's clear and distinct idea manifests itself as true and as entirely immanent to thought: entirely present, without anything clandestine; its very novelty is without mystery. Intelligibility and representation are equivalent notions: an exteriority surrendering in clarity and without immodesty its whole being to thought, that is, totally present without in principle anything shocking thought, without thought ever feeling itself to be indiscreet. Clarity is the disappearance of what could shock. Intelligibility, the very occurrence of representation, is the possibility for the other to be determined by the same without determining the same, without introducing alterity into it; it is a free exercise of the same. It is the disappearance, within the same, of the I opposed to the non-I.

Thus, within the work of intentionality, representation occupies the place of a privileged event. The intentional relation of representation is to be distinguished from every other relation—from mechanical causality, from the analytic or synthetic relation of logical formalism, from every intentionality other than representational—in that in it the same is in relation with the other but in such a way that the other does not determine the same; it is always the same that determines the other. To be sure, representation is the seat of truth: the movement proper to truth consists in the thinker being determined by the object presented to him. But it determines him without touching him, without weighing on him—such that the thinker who submits to what is thought does so "gracefully," as though the object, even in the surprises it has in store for cognition, had been anticipated by the subject.

While every activity is in one way or other illuminated by a representation, hence advances on a terrain already familiar, representation is a movement proceeding from the same with no searchlight preceding it. "The soul is something divinatory,"[2] according to Plato's expression. There is an absolute, creative freedom, prior to the venturesome course

---

[2] *Phaedrus,* 242c.

of the hand[3] which chances on to the goal it seeks—for at least the vision of that goal had cleared a passage for it, had been already projected forth. Representation is this very projection, inventing the goal that will be presented to the still groping acts as won a priori. The "act" of representation discovers, properly speaking, nothing before itself.

Representation is pure spontaneity, though prior to all activity. Thus the exteriority of the object represented appears to reflection to be a meaning ascribed by the representing subject to an object that is itself reducible to a work of thought.

The I that thinks the sum of the angles of a triangle is, to be sure, also determined by this object; it is precisely the one that thinks of this sum, and not the one that thinks of atomic weight. Whether it remembers or has forgotten, it is determined by the fact of having passed through the thought of the sum of the angles. This is what will be visible to the historian for whom the I representing to itself is already something represented. At the very moment of representation the I is not *marked* by the past but *utilizes* it as a represented and objective element. Illusion? Ignorance of its own involvements? Representation is the force of such an illusion and of such forgettings. Representation is a pure present. The positing of a pure present without even tangential ties with time is the marvel of representation. It is a void of time, interpreted as eternity. To be sure the I who conducts his thoughts *becomes* (or more exactly ages) in time, in which his successive thoughts, across which he thinks in the present, are spread forth. But this becoming in time does not appear on the plane of representation: representation involves no passivity. The same in relating itself to the other refuses what is exterior to its own instant, to its own identity, only to find again in this instant, which owes itself to nothing, which is pure gratuity, everything that had been refused—as "meaning given," as noema. Its first movement is negative: it consists in finding and exhausting in itself the meaning of an exteriority, precisely convertible into noemata. Such is the movement of the Husserlian ἐποχή, which, strictly speaking, is characteristic of representation. Its very possibility defines representation.

The fact that in representation the same defines the other without being determined by the other justifies the Kantian conception according to which the unity of transcendental appreception remains an empty form

---

[3] Cf. p. 167-168.

in the midst of its synthetic work. But we are far from thinking that one
starts with representation as a non-conditioned condition! Representation is *bound* to a very different "intentionality," which we are endeavoring to approach throughout this analysis. And its marvelous work of
constitution is especially possible in reflection. It is the "uprooted"
representation that we have analyzed. The way representation is bound
to a "wholly other" intentionality is different from the way the object is
bound to the subject or the subject to history.

The total freedom of the same in representation has a positive condition in the other that is not something represented, but is the Other.
For the moment let us note that the structure of representation as a
non-reciprocal determination of the other by the same is precisely for the
same to be present and for the other to be present to the same. We call
it "the same" because in representation the I precisely loses its opposition
to its object; the opposition fades, bringing out the identity of the I
despite the multiplicity of its objects, that is, precisely the unalterable
character of the I. To remain the same is to represent to oneself. The
"I think" is the pulsation of rational thought. The identity of the same
unaltered and unalterable in its relations with the other is in fact the I of
representation.   The subject that thinks by representation is a subject
that hearkens to its own thought: one has to think of thought as in an
element analogous to sound and not to light.   Its own spontaneity is a
surprise for the subject, as though despite its full mastery qua I the I
surprised what was taking place.   This *inspiration* [*génialité*] is the
very structure of representation: a return in the present thought to the
thought's past, an assuming of this past in the present, a going beyond
this past and this present—as in the Platonic reminiscence, in which
the subject hoists himself up to the eternal.   The particular I is one
with the same, coincides with the "daemon" that speaks to it in thought,
and is universal thought.   The I of representation is the natural passage
from the particular to the universal.   Universal thought is a thought in
the first person.   This is why the constitution that for idealism remakes
the universe starting from the subject is not the freedom of an I that
would survive this constitution free and above the laws it will have constituted. The I that constitutes dissolves into the work it comprehends,
and enters into the eternal.   The idealist creation is representation.

But this is true only of the I proper to representation—detached from
the conditions of its latent birth.   And enjoyment, likewise detached
from concrete conditions, presents a totally different structure, as we

shall show shortly. For the moment let us note the essential correlation of intelligibility and representation. To be intelligible is to be represented and hence to be a priori. To reduce a reality to its content thought is to reduce it to the same. The thinking thought is the locus where a total identity and a reality that ought to negate it are reconciled, without contradiction. The most ponderous reality envisaged as an object of a thought is engendered in the gratuitous spontaneity of a thought that thinks it. Every anteriority of the given is reducible to the instantaneity of thought and, simultaneous with it, arises in the present. It thereby takes on meaning. To represent is not only to render present "anew"; it is to reduce to the present an actual perception which flows on. To represent is not to reduce a past fact to an actual image but to reduce to the instantaneousness of thought everything that seems independent of it; it is in this that representation is constitutive. The value of the transcendental method and its share of eternal truth lies in the universal possibility of reducing the represented to its meaning, the existent to the noema, the most astonishing possibility of reducing to a noema the very being of the existent.

2. *Enjoyment and Nourishment*

The intentionality of enjoyment can be described by contrast with the intentionality of representation; it consists in holding on to the exteriority which the transcendental method involved in representation suspends. To hold on to exteriority is not simply equivalent to affirming the world, but is to posit oneself in it corporeally. The body is the elevation, but also the whole weight of position. The body naked and indigent identifies the *center* of the world it perceives, but, *conditioned* by its own representation of the world, it is thereby as it were torn up from the center from which it proceeded, as water gushing forth from rock washes away that rock. The body indigent and naked is not a thing among things which I "constitute" or see in God to be in a relation with a thought, nor is it the instrument of a gestural thought, of which theory would be simply the ultimate development. The body naked and indigent is the very reverting, irreducible to a thought, of representation into life, of the subjectivity that represents into life which is sustained by these representations and *lives of them;* its indigence—its needs—affirm "exteriority" as non-constituted, prior to all affirmation.

To doubt that the form that stands out in profiles on the horizon or in the darkness exists, to impose on a chunk of iron that presents itself a given form so as to make of it a knife, to overcome an obstacle, or to do away with an enemy: to doubt, to labor, to destroy, to kill—these negating acts assume objective exteriority rather than constitute it. To assume exteriority is to enter into a relation with it such that the same determines the other while being determined by it. But the way it is determined does not simply bring us back to the reciprocity designated by the third Kantian category of relation. The way in which the same is determined by the other, and which delineates the plane in which the negating acts themselves are situated, is precisely the *way* designated above as "living from. . . ." It is brought about by the body whose essence is to *accomplish* my position on the earth, that is, to give me as it were a vision already and henceforth borne by the very image that I see. To posit oneself corporeally is to touch an earth, but to do so in such a way that the touching finds itself already conditioned by the position, the foot settles into a real which this very action outlines or constitutes—, as though a painter would notice that he is descending from the picture he is painting.

Representation consists in the possibility of accounting for the object as though it were constituted by a thought, as though it were a noema. And this reduces the world to the unconditioned instant of thought. In "living from . . ." the process of constitution which comes into play wherever there is representation is reversed. What I live from is not in my life as the represented is within representation in the eternity of the same or in the unconditioned present of cogitation. If we could still speak of constitution here we would have to say that the constituted, reduced to its meaning, here overflows its meaning, becomes within constitution the condition of the constituting, or, more exactly, the nourishment of the constituting. This overflowing of meaning can be fixed by the term alimentation. The surplus over meaning is not a meaning in its turn, simply thought as a condition—which would be to reduce the aliment to a correlate represented. The aliment conditions the very thought that would think it as a condition. It is not that this conditioning is only noticed after the event: the originality of the situation lies in that the conditioning is produced in the midst of the relation between representing and represented, constituting and constituted—a relation which we find first in every case of consciousness. Eating, for example, is to be sure not reducible to the chemistry of alimentation. But eating also does not reduce itself to the set of

gustative, olfactory, kinesthetic, and other sensations that would constitute the consciousness of eating. This sinking one's teeth into the things
which the act of eating involves above all measures the surplus of the reality of the aliment over every represented reality, a surplus that is not
quantitative, but is the way the I, the absolute commencement, is suspended on the non-I. The corporeity of the living being and its indigence as a naked and hungry body is the accomplishment of these structures (described in abstract terms as an affirmation of exteriority which is
not a theoretical affirmation, and as a position on the earth which
is not the positing of one mass on another). To be sure, in the
satisfaction of need the alienness of the world that founds me loses its
alterity: in satiety the real I sank my teeth into is assimilated, the forces
that were in the other become *my* forces, become me (and every satisfaction of need is in some respect nourishment). Through labor and
possession the alterity of nutriments enters into the same. Yet it remains
true that this relationship differs fundamentally from the inspiration
[génialité] of representation we spoke of above. Here the relation is
reversed, as though the constitutive thought were stimulated by its own
game, by its free play, as though freedom as a present absolute commencement found its condition in its own product, as though this product
did not receive its meaning from a consciousness that ascribes meaning to
being. The body is a permanent contestation of the prerogative attributed to consciousness of "giving meaning" to each thing; it lives as this
contestation. The world I live in is not simply the counterpart or the
contemporary of thought and its constitutive freedom, but a conditioning and an antecedence. The world I constitute nourishes me and
bathes me. It is aliment and "medium" ["milieu"]. The intentionality
aiming at the exterior changes direction in the course of its very aim by
becoming interior to the exteriority it constitutes, somehow comes from
the point to which it goes, recognizing itself past in its future, lives from
what it thinks.

If the intentionality of "living from . . ." which is properly enjoyment is not constitutive, this is therefore not because an elusive,
inconceivable content, inconvertible into a meaning of thought, irreducible to the present and consequently unrepresentable, would compromise
the universality of representation and the transcendental method; it is
the very movement of constitution that is reversed. It is not the
encounter with the irrational that stops the play of constitution; the play
changes its sense. The body indigent and naked is this very changing

of sense. This is the profound insight Descartes had when he refused to sense data the status of clear and distinct ideas, ascribed them to the body, and relegated them to the useful. This is his superiority over Husserlian phenomenology which puts no limit on noematization. A movement radically different from thought is manifested when the constitution by thought finds its condition in what it has freely welcomed or refused, when the represented turns into a past that had not traversed the *present* of representation, as an absolute past not receiving its meaning from memory.

The world I live from is not simply constituted at a second level after representation would have spread before us a backdrop of a reality simply given, and after "axiological" intentions would have ascribed to this world a value that renders it apt for habitation. The "turning" of the constituted into a condition is accomplished as soon as I open my eyes: I but open my eyes and already enjoy the spectacle. Objectification proceeding somehow from the center of a thinking being manifests, upon its contact with the earth, an eccentricity. What the subject contains represented is also what supports and nourishes its activity as a subject. The represented, the present, is a *fact,* already belonging to the past.

3. Element and Things, Implements

But in what does the world of enjoyment resist the effort to describe it as correlative to representation? Would that universally possible reversal of the lived into the known, which feeds philosophical idealism, miscarry for enjoyment? In what respect does the sojourn of man in the world he enjoys remain irreducible and anterior to the knowledge of that world? Why declare the interiority of man to the world that conditions him—sustains and contains him? Does not this amount to affirming the exteriority of the things with respect to man?

In order to answer we have to analyze more closely the way the things we enjoy come to us. Enjoyment precisely does not reach them qua things. Things come to representation from a background from which they emerge and to which they return in the enjoyment we can have of them.

In enjoyment the things are not absorbed in the technical finality that organizes them into a system. They take form within a medium [milieu] in which we take hold of them. They are found in space, in the air, on the earth, in the street, along the road. The medium remains essential to things, even when they refer to *property,* whose intent we shall show further, and which constitutes the things qua things. This medium is not reducible to a system of operational references and is not equivalent to the totality of such a system, nor to a totality in which the look or the hand would have the possibility of choosing, a virtuality of things which choice would each time actualize. The medium has its own density. Things refer to possession, can be carried off, are *furnishings**; the medium from which they come to me lies escheat, a common fund or terrain, essentially non-possessable, "nobody's": earth, sea, light, city. Every relation or possession is situated within the non-possessable which envelops or contains without being able to be contained or enveloped. We shall call it the elemental.

The navigator who makes use of the sea and the wind dominates these elements but does not thereby transform them into things. They retain the indetermination of elements despite the precision of the laws that govern them, which can be known and taught. The element has no forms containing it; it is content without form. Or rather it has but a side: the surface of the sea and of the field, the edge of the wind; the medium upon which this side** takes form is not composed of things. It unfolds in its own dimension: depth, which is inconvertible into the breadth and length in which the side of the element extends. To be sure, a thing likewise presents itself by but one unique side; but we can circle round it, and the reverse is equivalent to the obverse; all the points of view are equivalent. The depth of the element prolongs it till it is lost in the earth and in the heavens. "Nothing ends, nothing begins."

To tell the truth the element has no side at all. One does not approach it. The relation adequate to its essence discovers it precisely as a medium: one is steeped in it; I am always within the element. Man has overcome the elements only by surmounting this interiority without issue by the domicile, which confers upon him an extraterritoriality. He gets a foothold in the elemental by a side already appropriated: a field cultivated by me, the sea in which I fish and moor my boats, the forest in which I cut wood; and all these acts, all this labor, refer to the domicile. Man plunges into the elemental from the domicile, the primary appropri-

---

* "Meubles." Furnishings are, in French, "moveables"; this root subsists in the usage Levinas makes of this term.—Trans.

** "Face"—it is in order to reserve the English word "face" to translate "visage"—the countenance of the Other—that we are using the term "side" to translate "face" in this context.—Trans.

ation, of which we shall speak further. He is *within* what he possesses, such that we shall be able to say that the domicile, condition for all property, renders the inner life possibe. The I is thus at home with itself. Through the home our relation with space as distance and extension is substituted for the simple "bathing in the element." But the adequate relation with the element is precisely bathing. The interiority of immersion is not convertible into exteriority. The pure quality of the element does not cling to a substance that would support it. To bathe in the element is to be in an inside-out world, and here the reverse is not equivalent to the obverse. A thing offers itself to us by its side, as a solicitation coming from its substantiality, from a solidity (already suspended by possession). We can, to be sure, represent the liquid or the gaseous to ourselves as a multiplicity of solids, but we then are abstracting from our presence in the midst of the element. The liquid manifests its liquidity, its qualities without support, its adjectives without substantive, to the immersion of the bather. The element presents us as it were the reverse of reality, without origin in a being, although presenting itself in familiarity—of enjoyment—as though we were in the bowels of being. Hence we can say that the element comes to us from nowhere; the side it presents to us does not determine an object, remains entirely anonymous. It is wind, earth, sea, sky, air.* Indetermination here is not equivalent to the infinite surpassing limits; it precedes the distinction between the finite and the infinite. It is not a quesion of a *something,* an existent manifesting itself as refractory to qualitative determination. Quality manifests itself in the element as determining nothing.

Thus thought does not fix the element as an object. As pure quality it lies outside the distinction between the finite and the infinite. The question what is the "other side" of what offers us one side does not arise in the relation maintained with the element. The sky, the earth, the sea, the wind—suffice to themselves. The element as it were stops up the infinite by relation to which it should have had to have been thought, and by relation to which scientific thought, which has received from elsewhere the idea of infinity, does in fact situate it. The element separates us from the infinite.

Every object offers itself to enjoyment, a universal category of the

---

* "Wind" designates neither a singular object nor a plurality; the partitive construction renders this in the French: "C'est du vent, de la terre, de la mer, du ciel, de l'air."—Trans.

empirical—even if I lay hold of an object-implement, if I handle it as a *Zeug*. The handling and utilization of tools, the recourse to all the instrumental gear of a life, whether to fabricate other tools or to render things accessible, concludes in enjoyment. As material or gear the objects of everyday use are subordinated to enjoyment—the lighter to the cigarette one smokes, the fork to the food, the cup to the lips. Things refer to my enjoyment. This is an observation as commonplace as could be, which the analyses of *Zeughaftigkeit* do not succeed in effacing. Possession itself and all the relations with abstract notions are inverted into enjoyment. Pushkin's greedy knight enjoys possessing the possession of the world.

Enjoyment—an ultimate relation with the substantial plenitude of being, with its materiality—embraces all relations with things. The structure of the *Zeug* as *Zeug* and the system of references in which it has its place do indeed manifest themselves, in concerned handling, as irreducible to vision, but do not encompass the substantiality of objects, which is always there in addition. Moreover furnishings, the home, food, clothing are not *Zeuge* in the proper sense of the term: clothing serves to protect the body or to adorn it, the home to shelter it, food to restore it, but we enjoy them or suffer from them; they are ends. Tools themselves, which are-in-view-of . . . , become objects of enjoyment. The enjoyment of a thing, be it a tool, does not consist simply in bringing this thing to the usage for which it is fabricated—the pen to the writing, the hammer to the nail to be driven in—but also in suffering or rejoicing over this operation. The things that are not tools —the crust of bread, the flame in the fireplace, the cigarette—offer themselves to enjoyment. But this enjoyment accompanies every utilization of things, even in a complex enterprise where the end of a labor alone absorbs the research. The utilization of a thing in view of . . . , this reference to the whole, remains on the level of its attributes. One can like one's job, enjoy these material gestures and the things that permit the accomplishing of them. One can transform the curse of labor into sport. Activity does not derive its meaning and its value from an ultimate and unique goal, as though the world formed one system of use-references whose term touches our very existence. The world answers to a set of autonomous finalities which ignore one another. To enjoy without utility, in pure loss, gratuitously, without referring to anything else, in pure expenditure—this is the human. There is a non-systematic accumulation of occupations and tastes, equidistant from the system of reason, where the encounter with the Other opens the infinite, and from the system of the instinct, anterior to separated being, anterior to the being veritably born, separated from its cause, nature.

Will it be said that this accumulation has as its condition the apperception of utility, reducible to the care for existence? But the care for nutriments is not bound to a care for existence. The inversion of the instincts of nutrition, which have lost their biological finality, marks the very disinterestedness of man. The suspension or absence of the ultimate finality has a positive face—the disinterested joy of play. To live is to play, despite the finality and tension of instinct to live from something without this something having the sense of a goal or an ontological means—simply play or enjoyment of life. It is carefreeness with regard to existence, which has a positive meaning: it consists in sinking one's teeth fully into the nutriments of the world, agreeing to [agréer] the world as wealth, releasing its elemental essence. In enjoyment the things revert to their elemental qualities. Enjoyment, the sensibility (whose essence it exhibits), is produced as a possibility of being precisely by ignoring the prolongation of hunger into the concern for self-preservation. Here lies the permanent truth of hedonist moralities: to not seek, behind the satisfaction of need, an order relative to which alone satisfaction would acquire a value; to take satisfaction, which is the very meaning of pleasure, as a term. The need for food does not have existence as its goal, but food. Biology teaches the prolongation of nourishment into existence; need is naïve. In enjoyment I am absolutely for myself. Egoist without reference to the Other, I am alone without solitude, innocently egoist and alone. Not against the Others, not "as for me . . ."—but entirely deaf to the Other, outside of all communication and all refusal to communicate—without ears, like a hungry stomach.

The world as a set of implements forming a system and suspended on the care of an existence anxious for its being interpreted as an onto-logy, attests labor, habitation, the home, and economy; but in addition, it bears witness to a particular organization of labor in which "foods" take on the signification of fuel in the economic machinery. It is interesting to observe that Heidegger does not take the relation of enjoyment into consideration. The implement has entirely masked the usage and the issuance at the term—the satisfaction. *Dasein* in Heidegger is never hungry. Food can be interpreted as an implement only in a world of exploitation.

4. Sensibility

But to posit the element as a quality without substance does not amount to admitting the existence of a mutilated or still stammering "thought" correlative of such phenomena. To-be-in-the-element does indeed disengage a being from blind and deaf participation in a whole, but differs from a thought making its way outward. Here on the contrary the movement comes incessantly upon me, as the wave that engulfs and submerges and drowns—an incessant movement of afflux without respite, a total contact without fissure nor gap from which the reflected movement of a thought could arise. It is to be within, to be inside of. . . . This situation is not reducible to a representation, not even an inarticulate representation; it belongs to sensibility, which is the *mode* of enjoyment. It is when sensibility is interpreted as representation and mutilated thought that the finitude of our thought has to be invoked so as to account for these "obscure" thoughts. The sensibility we are describing starting with enjoyment of the element does not belong to the order of thought but to that of sentiment, that is, the affectivity wherein the egoism of the I pulsates. One does not know, one lives sensible qualities: the green of these leaves, the red of this sunset. Objects *content* me in their finitude, without appearing to me on a ground of infinity. The finite without the infinite is possible only as contentment. The finite as contentment is sensibility. Sensibility does not constitute the world, because the world called sensible does not have as its function to constitute a representation—but constitutes the very contentment of existence, because its rational insufficiency does not even appear in the enjoyment it procures me. To sense is to be within, without the conditioned, and consequently of itself inconsistent, character of this ambience, which troubles rational thought, being in any way included in the sensation. Sensibility, essentially naïve, suffices to itself in a world insufficient for thought. The objects of the world, which for thought lie in the void, for sensibility—or for life—spread forth on a horizon which entirely hides that void. The sensibility touches the reverse, without wondering about the obverse; this is produced precisely in contentment.

The profundity of the Cartesian philosophy of the sensible consists, we have said, in affirming the irrational character of sensation, an idea forever without clarity or distinctness, belonging to the order of the useful and not of the true. The strength of the Kantian philosophy of the sensible likewise consists in separating sensibility and understanding, in affirming, though only negatively, the independence of the "matter" of cognition with regard to the synthetic power of representation. In postulating things in themselves so as to avoid the absurdity of apparitions without there being anything that is appearing, Kant does indeed go beyond the phenomenology of the sensible. But at least he does recognize thereby that of itself the sensible is an apparition without there being anything that appears.

Sensibility establishes a relation with a pure quality without support, with the element. Sensibility is enjoyment. The sensitive being, the body, concretizes this *way of being,* which consists in finding a condition in what, in other respects, can appear as an object of thought, as simply constituted.

The sensibility is therefore to be described not as a moment of representation, but as the instance of enjoyment. Its intention (if we may resort to this term) does not go in the direction of representation. It does not suffice to say that sensation lacks clarity and distinctness, as though it were situated on the plane of representation. Sensibility is not an inferior theoretical knowledge bound however intimately to affective states: in its very *gnosis* sensibility is enjoyment; it is satisfied with the given, it is contented. Sensible "knowledge" does not have to surmount infinite regression, that vertigo of the understanding; it does not even experience it. It finds itself immediately at the term; it concludes, it finishes without referring to the infinite. Finition* without reference to the infinite, finition without limitation, is the relation with the end [fin] as a goal. The sense datum with which sensibility is nourished always comes to gratify a need, responds to a tendency. It is not that at the beginning there was hunger; the simultaneity of hunger and food constitutes the paradisal initial condition of enjoyment. Thus the Platonic theory of negative pleasures confines itself to the formal pattern of enjoyment only, and fails to recognize the originality of a structure which does not show through in the formal, but concretely weaves the living from. . . . An existence that has this mode is the body—both separated from its end (that is, need), but already proceeding toward that end without having to know the means necessary for its obtainment, an action released by the end, accomplished without knowledge of means, that is, without tools. Pure finality, irreducible to

---

* "Finition." We retain this form, to correspond with the form "infinition" introduced earlier (cf. p. xiii).—Trans.

a result, is produced only by corporeal action ignorant of the mechanism of its own physiology. But the body is not only what is steeped in the element, but what *dwells,* that is, inhabits and possesses. In sensibility itself and independently of all thought there is announced an insecurity which throws back in question this quasi-eternal immemoriality of the element, which will disturb it as the *other,* and which it will appropriate by recollecting [se recueillant] in a dwelling.

Enjoyment seems to be in touch with an "other" inasmuch as a future is announced within the element and menaces it with insecurity. We will speak further of this insecurity belonging to the order of enjoyment; for the moment what is important for us is to show that sensibility is of the order of enjoyment and not of the order of experience. Sensibility thus understood is not to be confused with still vacillating forms of "consciousness of." It is not separated from thought by a simple difference of degree, nor even by a difference in the nobility or the extent of expansion of their objects. Sensibility does not aim at an object, however rudimentary. It concerns even the elaborated forms of consciousness, but its proper work consists in enjoyment, through which every object is dissolved into the element in which enjoyment is steeped. For in fact the sensible objects we enjoy have already undergone labor. The sensible quality already clings to a substance. And we shall have to analyze further the signification of the sensible object qua thing. But contentment, in its naïveté, lurks behind the relation with things. This earth upon which I find myself and from which I welcome sensible objects or make my way to them suffices for me. The earth which upholds me does so without my troubling myself about knowing what upholds the earth. I am content with the aspect this corner of the world, universe of my daily behavior, this city or this neighborhood or this street in which I move, this horizon within which I live, turn to me; I do not ground them in a more vast system. It is they that ground me. I welcome them without thinking them. I enjoy this world of things as pure elements, as qualities without support, without substance.

But does not this "for me" presuppose a representation of oneself in the idealist sense of the term? The world is for me—this does not mean that I represent the world to myself as being for me, and represent this me in its turn to myself. This relation of myself with myself is accomplished when I *stand* [me tiens]* in the world which precedes me as an absolute of an unrepresentable antiquity. To be sure, I cannot

---

* Cf. p. 37, note.

think the horizon in which I find myself to be an absolute, but I *stand* in it as in an absolute. Standing there is precisely different from "thinking." The bit of earth that supports me is not only my object; it supports my experience of objects. Well-trampled places do not resist me but support me. The relation with my site in this "stance" ["tenue"] precedes thought and labor. The body, position, the fact of standing—patterns of the primary relation with myself, of my coincidence with myself—nowise resemble idealist representation. I am myself, I am here, at home with myself, inhabitation, immanence in the world. My sensibility is here. In my position there is not the sentiment of localization, but the localization of my sensibility. Position, absolutely without transcendence, does not resemble the comprehension of the world by the Heideggerian *Da*. It is not a care for Being, nor a relation with existents, nor even a negation of the world, but its accessibility in enjoyment. Sensibility is the very narrowness of life, the naïveté of the unreflected I, beyond instinct, beneath reason.

But does not the "side of things" offered as an element refer implicitly to the other side? Implicitly, to be sure. And in the eyes of reason the contentment of sensibility is ridiculous. But sensibility is not a blind reason and folly. It is prior to reason; the sensible is not to be ascribed to the totality to which it is closed. Sensibility enacts the very separation of being—separated and independent. The aptitude to keep [se tenir] to the immediate is not reducible to anything else; it does not signify the lapse of the power that would dialectically render explicit the presuppositions of the immediate, set them in movement, and suppress them in sublimating them. Sensibility is not a thought unaware of itself. To pass from the implicit to the explicit a master who evokes attention is necessary. To evoke attention is not a subsidiary work; in attention the I transcends itself. But a relation with the exteriority of the master was necessary to engage attention. Explicitation presupposes this transcendence.

The limitation of contentment without reference to the unlimited precedes the distinction between the finite and the infinite such as it is incumbent upon thought. The descriptions of contemporary psychology that make of sensation an islet that emerges from an obscure viscous ground of the unconscious—relative to which the consciousness of the sensible would already have lost its sincerity—fail to recognize the fundamental and irreducible self-sufficience of sensibility, due to its keeping [se tenir] within its horizon. To sense is precisely to be sincerely content with what is sensed, to enjoy, to refuse the unconscious prolongations, to be thoughtless, that is, without ulterior motives,* unequivocal, to break with all the implications—to maintain oneself at home with oneself. Torn up from all the implications, from all the prolongations thought offers, all the instants of our life can reach completion, precisely because life dispenses with the intellectual search for the unconditioned. To reflect on each of one's acts is, to be sure, to situate them with respect to infinity, but the unreflected and naïve consciousness constitutes the originality of enjoyment. The naïveté of consciousness was described as a torpid thought, but from this somnolence thought can nowise be extracted. It is life, in the sense that we speak of relishing life. We enjoy the world before referring to its prolongations; we breathe, walk, see, stroll, ...

The description of enjoyment as it has been conducted to this point assuredly does not render the concrete man. In reality man has already the idea of infinity, that is, lives in society and represents things to himself. The separation accomplished as enjoyment, that is, as interiority, becomes a consciousness of objects. The things are fixed by the word which gives them, which communicates them and thematizes them. And the new fixity things acquire due to language presupposes much more than the adjunction of a sound to a thing. Over and above enjoyment —with dwelling, possession, the making common—a discourse about the world takes form. Appropriation and representation add a new event to enjoyment. They are founded on language as a relation among men. Things have a name and an identity. Transformations occur to things which remain the same: the stone crumbles but remains the same stone; I rediscover my pen and armchair the same; it is in the selfsame palace of Louis XIV that the Treaty of Versailles was signed; the same train is the train that leaves at the same hour. The world of perception is thus a world where things have identity. The subsistence of this world is visibly possible only through memory. The identity of persons and the continuity of their labors project over the things the grill through which they find again identical things. An earth inhabited by men endowed with language is peopled with stable things.

But this identity of things remains unstable and does not close off the return of things to the element. A thing exists in the midst of its wastes. When the kindling wood becomes smoke and ashes the identity

---

* ". . . être sans pensée, c'est à dire sans arrière-pensées . . ."

of my table disappears. The wastes become indiscernible; the smoke drifts off anywhere. If my thought follows the transformation of things I lose the trace of their identity very quickly—as soon as they quit their container. Descartes's reasoning about the piece of wax indicates the itinerary by which each thing loses its identity. In things the distinction between matter and form is essential, as also the dissolution of form in the matter. It imposes a quantitative physics in place of the world of perception.

The distinction between form and matter does not characterize all experience. The face has no form added to it, but does not present itself as the formless, as matter that lacks and calls for form. Things have a form, are seen *in* the light—silhouettes or profiles; the face signifies *itself*. As silhouette and profile a thing owes its nature to a perspective, remains relative to a point of view; a thing's situation thus constitutes its being. Strictly speaking it has no identity; convertible into another thing, it can become money. Things have no face; convertible, "realizable," they have a price. They represent money because they are of elemental nature, are wealth. Their rootedness in the elemental, their accessibility to physics, and their signification as tools are thus confirmed. The aesthetic orientation man gives to the whole of his world represents a return to enjoyment and to the elemental on a higher plane. The world of things calls for art, in which intellectual accession to being moves into enjoyment, in which the Infinity of the idea is idolized in the finite, but sufficient, image. All art is plastic. Tools and implements, which themselves presuppose enjoyment, offer themselves to enjoyment in their turn. They are playthings [jouets]: the fine cigarette lighter, the fine car. They are adorned by the decorative arts; they are immersed in the beautiful, where every going beyond enjoyment reverts to enjoyment.

5. The Mythical Format of the Element

The sensible world, overflowing the freedom of representation, does not betoken the failure of freedom, but the enjoyment of a world, a world "for me," which already contents me. The elements do not receive man as a land of exile, humiliating and limiting his freedom. The human being does not find himself in an absurd world in which he would be *geworfen*. And this is true absolutely. The disquietude that manifests itself within the enjoyment of the element, in the overflowing of the instant that escapes the gentle mastery of enjoyment, is, we shall see further, recouped by labor. Labor recoups the lag between the element and the sensation.

But this overflowing of sensation by the element, which appears in the indetermination with which it offers itself to my enjoyment, takes on a temporal meaning. In enjoyment quality is not a quality of something. The solidity of the earth that supports me, the blue of the sky above my head, the breath of the wind, the undulation of the sea, the sparkle of the light do not cling to a substance. They come from nowhere. This coming from nowhere, from "something" that is not, appearing without there being anything that appears—and consequently *coming always,* without my being able to *possess* the source—delineates the future of sensibility and enjoyment. This is not yet a representation of the future, in which the threat allows for respite and liberation. By representation the enjoyment that has recourse to labor becomes again absolutely mistress of the world, interiorizing it with respect to its dwelling. The future, as insecurity, is already in the pure quality which lacks the category of substance, of something. It is not that the source escapes me *in fact:* in enjoyment quality is lost in the nowhere. It is the *apeiron* distinct from the infinite, and which, by contrast with things, presents itself as a quality refractory to identification. Quality does not withstand identification because it would represent a flux and a duration; rather its elemental character, its coming forth from nothing, constitutes its fragility, the disintegration of becoming, that time prior to representation—which is menace and destruction.

The element suits me—I enjoy it; the need to which it responds is the very *mode* of this conformity or of this happiness. The indetermination of the future alone brings insecurity to need, indigence: the perfidious elemental gives itself while escaping. Hence it is not the relation of need with a radical alterity that would indicate the non-freedom of need. The resistance of matter does not block like the absolute. As a resistance already overcome, open to labor, it opens up an abyss within enjoyment itself. Enjoyment does not refer to an infinity beyond what nourishes it, but to the virtual vanishing of what presents itself, to the instability of happiness. Nourishment comes as a happy chance. This ambivalence of nourishment, which on the one hand offers itself and contents, but which already withdraws, losing itself in the *nowhere,* is to be distinguished from the presence of the infinite in the finite and from the structure of the thing.

This coming forth from nowhere opposes the element to what we will describe under the name of face [visage], where precisely an existent presents itself personally. To be affected by a side [face] of being while its whole depth remains undetermined and comes upon me from nowhere is to be bent toward the insecurity of the morrow. The future of the element as insecurity is lived concretely as the mythical divinity of the element. Faceless gods, impersonal gods to whom one does not speak, mark the nothingness that bounds the egoism of enjoyment in the midst of its familiarity with the element. But it is thus that enjoyment accomplishes separation. The separated being must run the risk of the paganism which evinces its separation and in which this separation is accomplished, until the moment that the death of these gods will lead it back to atheism and to the true transcendence.

The nothingness of the future ensures separation: the element we enjoy issues in the nothingness which separates. The element I inhabit is at the frontier of a night. What the side of the element that is turned toward me conceals is not a "something" susceptible of being revealed, but an ever-new depth of absence, an existence without existent, the impersonal par excellence. This way of existing without revealing itself, outside of being and the world, must be called mythical. The nocturnal prolongation of the element is the reign of mythical gods. Enjoyment is without security. But this future does not take on the character of a *Geworfenheit,* for insecurity menaces an enjoyment already happy in the element, rendered sensitive to disquietude only by this happiness.

We have described this nocturnal dimension of the future under the title *there is.** The element extends into the there is. Enjoyment, as interiorization, runs up against the very strangeness of the earth.

But it has the recourse of labor and possession.

Existence and Existents, trans. A. F. Lingis, The Hague, Nijhoff, 1978, pp. 57–64.—Trans.

C. I AND DEPENDENCE

1. Joy and Its Morrows

The movement to self in enjoyment and happiness marks the sufficiency of the I, although the image we have used of the spiral that coils over itself does not enable us to depict also the enrootedness of this sufficiency in the insufficiency of living from. . . . The I is, to be sure, happiness, presence at home with itself. But, as sufficiency in its non-sufficiency, it remains in the non-I; it is enjoyment of "something else," never of itself. Autochthonous, that is, enrooted in what it is not, it is nevertheless, within this enrootedness, independent and separated. The relationship of the I with the non-I produced as happiness which promotes the I consists neither in assuming nor in refusing the non-I. Between the I and *what it lives from* there does not extend the absolute distance that separates the same from the other. The acceptance or refusal of what we live from implies a prior *agreement* [agrément]*, both given and received, the agreement of happiness. The primary agreement, to live, does not alienate the I but maintains it, constitutes its *being at home with itself.* The dwelling, inhabitation, belongs to the essence—to the egoism—of the I. Against the anonymous *there is,* horror, trembling, and vertigo, perturbation of the I that does not coincide with itself, the happiness of enjoyment affirms the I at home with itself. But if, in the relation with the non-I of the world it inhabits, the I is produced as self-sufficiency and is maintained in an instant torn up from the continuity of time, dispensed from assuming or refusing a past, it does not benefit from this dispensation by virtue of a privilege enjoyed from eternity. The veritable position of the I in time consists in interrupting time by punctuating it with beginnings. This is produced in the form of action. Commencement within a continuity is possible only as action. But time, in which the I can commence its action, portends the lability of its independence. The uncertainties of the future that mar happiness

---

* To be taken in the double sense of "assent" and also "agreeableness" or pleasure.—Trans

143

remind enjoyment that its independence envelops a dependence. Happiness does not succeed in dissimulating this fault in its sovereignty —which is exposed as "subjective," "psychic," and "merely inward." The reversion of all the modes of being to the I, to the inevitable subjectivity constituting itself in the happiness of enjoyment, does not institute an absolute subjectivity, independent of the non-I. The non-I feeds enjoyment; the I needs the world, which exalts it. The freedom of enjoyment thus is experienced as limited. Limitation is not due to the fact that the I has not chosen its birth and thus is already and henceforth in situation, but to the fact that the plenitude of its instant of enjoyment is not ensured against the unknown that lurks in the very element it enjoys, the fact that joy remains a chance and a stroke of luck. The fact that enjoyment would be but a void that fills can nowise throw suspicion on the qualitative plenitude of enjoyment. Enjoyment and happiness are not calculated by the quantities of being and nothingness which compensate or fail to compensate for one another; enjoyment is an exaltation, a peak that exceeds the pure exercise of being. But the happiness of enjoyment, a satisfaction of needs which is not compromised by the need-satisfaction rhythm, can be tarnished by the concern for the morrow involved in the fathomless depth of the element in which enjoyment is steeped. The happiness of enjoyment flourishes on the "pain" of need and thus depends on an "other"; it is a stroke of good fortune, a chance. But this conjuncture justifies neither the denunciation of pleasure as illusory nor the characterizing of man in the world as dereliction. The indigence that *menaces* living as *living from* . . .— because what life lives from can come to be wanting—cannot be confounded with the void of appetite already settled in enjoyment, which in satisfaction makes possible, beyond simple being, its jubilation. On the other hand, the "pain" of need nowise evinces an alleged irrationality of the sensible, as though the sensible offended the autonomy of the rational person. In the pain of needs reason does not revolt against the scandal of a *given* pre-existing freedom. For one cannot first posit an I and then ask if enjoyment and need run counter to it, limit it, injure it, or negate it: only in enjoyment does the I crystallize.

2. The Love of Life

At the origin there is a being gratified, a citizen of paradise. The "emptiness" felt implies that the need which becomes aware of it abides already in the midst of an enjoyment—be it that of the air one breathes. It anticipates the joy of satisfaction, which is *better* than ataraxy. Far from putting the sensible life into question, pain takes place within its horizons and refers to the joy of living. Already and henceforth life is loved. The I can, to be sure, revolt against the givens of its situation, for it does not lose itself in living at home, and remains distinct from what it lives from. But this interval between the I and what nourishes it does not allow of the negation of nourishment as such. If in this interval an opposition can come into play, it is maintained within the limits of the very situation it refuses and from which it is nourished. Every opposition to life takes refuge in life and refers to its values. This is the *love of life,* a pre-established harmony with what is yet to come to us.

The love of life does not resemble the care for Being, reducible to the comprehension of Being, or ontology. The love of life does not love Being, but loves the happiness of being. Life loved is the very enjoyment of life, contentment—already appreciated in the refusal I bear against it, where contentment is refused in the name of contentment itself. The love of life, a relation of life with life, is neither a representation of life nor a reflection on life. The lag between me and my joy does not leave room for a total refusal. There is in revolt no radical refusal, just as in life's joyous access to life there is no assumption. The famous passivity of feeling is such that it leaves no play for the movement of a freedom that would assume it. *The gnosis of the sensible is already enjoyment.* What one might be tempted to present as negated or consumed in enjoyment is not affirmed for itself, but is given from the first. Enjoyment reaches a world that has neither secrecy nor veritable foreignness. The primordial positivity of enjoyment, perfectly innocent, is opposed to nothing and in this sense suffices to itself from the first. An instant or a standstill, it is the success of the *carpe diem,* the sovereignty of the "after us the deluge." These pretensions would be pure nonsense and not eternal temptations could not enjoyment tear itself absolutely from the disintegration characteristic of duration.

Need therefore can be characterized neither as freedom, since it is dependence, nor as passivity, since it lives from what, already familiar and without secret, does not subjugate it but gladdens it. The philosophers of existence who emphasize dereliction misconstrue the opposition arising between the I and its joy—an opposition due to the disquietude that insinuates itself into enjoyment, menaced with the indetermination of the future essential to sensibility, or due to the pain inherent in labor. Being is here nowise refused in its totality. In its opposition to being the I seeks refuge in being itself. Suicide is tragic, for death does not bring a resolution to all the problems to which birth gave rise, and is powerless to humiliate the values of the earth—whence Macbeth's final cry in confronting death, defeated because the universe is not destroyed at the same time as his life. Suffering at the same time despairs for being riveted to being—and loves the being to which it is riveted. It knows the impossibility of quitting life: what tragedy! what comedy . . . The *taedium vitae* is steeped in the love of the life it rejects; despair does not break with the ideal of joy. In reality this pessimism has an economic infrastructure; it expresses the anxiety for the morrow and the pain of labor, whose role in metaphysical desire we shall show later. The Marxist views retain here their whole force, even in a different perspective. The suffering of need is not assuaged in anorexy, but in satisfaction. Need is loved; man is happy to have needs. A being without needs would not be happier than a needy being, but outside of happiness and unhappiness. That indigence could mark the pleasure of satisfaction, that instead of possessing plenitude pure and simple we would reach enjoyment through need and labor—this conjuncture is due to the very structure of separation. The separation that is accomplished by egoism would be but a word if the ego, the separated and self-sufficient being, did not hear the muffled rustling of nothingness back unto which the elements flow and are lost.

Labor can surmount the indigence with which not need, but the uncertainty of the future affects being.

The nothingness of the future, we shall see, turns into an interval of time in which possession and labor are inserted. The passage from instantaneous enjoyment to the fabrication of things refers to habitation, to economy, which presupposes the welcoming of the Other. The pessimism of dereliction is hence not irremediable—man holds in his hands the remedy for his ills, and the remedies preexist the ills.

But labor itself, by virtue of which I live freely, ensuring myself against life's uncertainty, does not bring life its final signification. It also becomes that *from which* I live. I live from the whole content of life—even from the labor which ensures the future; I live from my labor as I live from air, light, and bread. The limit case in which need prevails over enjoyment, the proletarian condition condemning to accursed labor in which the indigence of corporeal existence finds neither refuge nor leisure at home with itself, is the absurd world of *Geworfen-heit.*

3. Enjoyment and Separation

In enjoyment throbs egoist being. Enjoyment separates by engaging in the contents from which it lives. Separation comes to pass as the positive work of this engagement; it does not result from a simple split, like a spatial removal. To be separated is to be at home with oneself. But to be at home with oneself . . . is to live from . . . , to enjoy the elemental. The "failure" of the constitution of the objects from which one lives is not due to the irrationality or the obscurity of those objects, but to their function as nutriments. Food is not unrepresentable; it subtends its own representation, but in it the I again finds itself. The ambiguity of a constitution in which the world represented conditions the act of representing is the *way of being* of him who is not simply posited but posits *himself.* The absolute void, the "nowhere" in which the element loses itself and from which it arises, on all sides beats against the islet of the I who lives interiorly. The interiority which enjoyment opens up is not added as an attribute to the subject "endowed" with conscious life, as one psychological property among others. The interiority of enjoyment is separation in itself, is the mode according to which such an event as separation can be produced in the economy of being.

Happiness is a principle of individuation, but individuation in itself is conceivable only from within, through interiority. In the happiness of enjoyment is enacted the individuation, the auto-personification, the sub-stantialization, and the independence of the self, a forgetting of the infinite depths of the past and the instinct that resumes them. Enjoyment is the very production of a being that is *born,* that breaks the tranquil eternity of its seminal or uterine existence to enclose itself in a person, who in living from the world lives at home with itself. The incessant turning of ecstatic representation into enjoyment, which we have brought to light, in each instant restores the antecedence of what I constitute to this very constitution. It is the living and lived past, not in the sense we thus speak of a very vivid or close memory, nor even a past that marks us and has a hold on us and thereby subjugates us, but a past that founds what separates and frees itself from that past. This libera-tion flashes in the light of happiness, in separation. Its free flight and its grace are felt—and are produced—as the very ease of good time. It is freedom referring to happiness, made of happiness, and consequently compatible with a being that is not *causa sui,* that is created.

We have sought to elaborate the notion of enjoyment in which the I arises and pulsates: we have not determined the I by freedom. Freedom as the possibility of commencement, referring to happiness, to the marvel of the good time standing out from the continuity of the hours, is the production of the I and not one experience among others that "happens" to the I. Separation and atheism, these negative notions, are produced by positive events. To be I, atheist, at home with oneself, separated, happy, created—these are synonyms.

Egoism, enjoyment, sensibility, and the whole dimension of interiority —the articulations of separation—are necessary for the idea of Infinity, the relation with the Other which opens forth from the separated and finite being. Metaphysical Desire, which can be produced only in a separated, that is, enjoying, egoist, and satisfied being, is then not derived from enjoyment. But if the separated, that is, sentient being is necessary for the production of infinity and exteriority in metaphysics, its constitution as thesis or as antithesis, within a dialectical play, would destroy this exteriority. The infinite does not raise up the finite by opposition. Just as the interiority of enjoyment is not deducible from the transcendental relation, the transcendental relation is not deducible from the separated being as a dialectical antithesis forming a counterpart to the subjectivity, as union forms the counterpart of distinction among two terms of any relation. The movement of separation is not on the same plane as the movement of transcendence. We are outside of the dialectical conciliation of the I and the non-I, in the eternal sphere proper to representation (or in the identity of the I).

Neither the separated being nor the infinite being is produced as an antithetical term. The interiority that ensures separation (but not as an abstract rejoinder to the notion of relation) must produce a being absolutely closed over upon itself, not deriving its isolation dialectically from its opposition to the Other. And this closedness must not prevent egress from interiority, so that exteriority could speak to it, reveal itself to it, in an unforeseeable movement which the isolation of the separated being could not provoke by simple contrast. In the separated being the door to the outside must hence be at the same time open and closed. The closedness of the separated being must be ambiguous enough for, on the one hand, the interiority necessary to the idea of infinity to remain *real* and not apparent only, for the destiny of the interior being to be pursued in an egoist atheism refuted by nothing exterior, for it to be pursued without, in each of the movements of descent into interiority, the being descending into itself referring to exteriority by a pure play of the dialectic and in the form of an abstract correlation. But on the other hand *within the very interiority* hollowed out by enjoyment there must be produced a heteronomy that incites to another destiny than this animal complacency in oneself. If the dimension of interiority cannot belie its interiority by the apparition of a heterogeneous element in the course of this descent into itself along the path of pleasure (a descent which in fact first hollows out this dimension), still in this descent a shock must be produced which, without inverting the movement of interiorization, without breaking the thread of the interior substance, would furnish the *occasion* for a resumption of relations with exteriority. Interiority must be at the same time closed and open. The possibility of rising from the animal condition is assuredly thus described.

To this singular requirement enjoyment does indeed answer, by the insecurity troubling its fundamental security. This insecurity is not due to the heterogeneity of the world with respect to enjoyment, which would allegedly bring the sovereignty of the I to naught. The happiness of enjoyment is stronger than every disquietude, but disquietude can trouble it; here lies the gap between the animal and the human. The happiness of enjoyment is greater than all disquietude: whatever be the concerns for the morrow, the happiness of living—of breathing, of seeing, of feeling ("One minute more, Mr. Hangman!")—remains in the midst of disquietude as the term proposed to every evasion from the world troubled, to intolerability, by disquietude. *One flees life toward life.* Suicide appears as a possibility to a being already in relation with the Other, already elevated to life *for the Other*. It is the possibility of an existence already metaphysical; only a being already capable of sacrifice is capable of suicide. Before defining man as the animal that can commit suicide it is necessary to define him as capable of living for the Other and of *being* on the basis of the Other who is exterior to him. But the tragic character of suicide and of sacrifice evinces the radicality of the love of life. The primordial relation of man with the material world is not negativity, but enjoyment and agreeableness [agrément]* of life. It is uniquely with reference to this agreeableness—unsurpassable within

---

* In this term Levinas understands the form of acceptance involved in pleasure. Pleasure, the agreeable, is also what we agree to, and this very "agreeing to" is itself pleasurable.—Trans.

interiority, for it constitutes it—that the world can appear hostile, to be negated and to be conquered. If the insecurity of the world that is fully agreed to in enjoyment troubles enjoyment, the insecurity can not suppress the fundamental agreeableness of life. But this insecurity brings into the interiority of enjoyment a frontier that comes neither from the revelation of the Other nor from any heterogeneous content, but somehow from nothingness. It is due to the way the element, in which the separated being contents itself and suffices to itself, comes to this being—due to the mythological depth which prolongs the element and into which the element loses itself. This insecurity, which thus delineates a margin of nothingness about the interior life, confirming its insularity, is lived in the instant of enjoyment as the concern for the morrow.

But thus in interiority a dimension opens through which it will be able to await and welcome the revelation of transcendence. In the concern for the morrow there dawns the primordial phenomenon of the essentially uncertain future of sensibility. In order that this future arise in its signification as a postponement and a *delay* in which *labor,* by mastering the uncertainty of the future and its insecurity and by establishing *possession,* delineates separation in the form of economic independence, the separated being must be able to recollect itself [se recueillir] and have representations. *Recollection* and *representation* are produced concretely as *habitation in a dwelling* or a Home. But the interiority of the home is made of extraterritoriality in the midst of the elements of enjoyment with which life is nourished. This extraterritoriality has a positive side. It is produced in the gentleness [douceur] or the warmth of intimacy, which is not a subjective state of mind, but an event in the oecumenia of being—a delightful "lapse" of the ontological order. By virtue of its intentional structure gentleness comes to the separated being from the Other. The Other precisely *reveals* himself in his alterity not in a shock negating the I, but as the primordial phenomenon of gentleness.

The whole of this work aims to show a relation with the other not only cutting across the logic of contradiction, where the other of A is the non-A, the negation of A, but also across dialectical logic, where the same dialectically participates in and is reconciled with the other in the Unity of the system. The welcoming of the face is peaceable from the first, for it answers to the unquenchable Desire for Infinity. War itself is but a possibility and nowise a condition for it. This peaceable welcome is produced primordially in the gentleness of the feminine face, in which the separated being can recollect itself, because of which it *inhabits,* and in its dwelling accomplishes separation. Inhabitation and the intimacy of the dwelling which make the separation of the human being possible thus imply a first revelation of the Other.

Thus the idea of infinity, revealed in the face, does not only *require* a separated being; the light of the face is necessary for separation. But in founding the intimacy of the home the idea of infinity provokes separation not by some force of opposition and dialectical evocation, but by the feminine grace of its radiance. The force of opposition and of dialectical evocation would, in integrating it into a synthesis, destroy transcendence.

D. THE DWELLING

1. Habitation

Habitation can be interpreted as the utilization of an "implement" among "implements." The home would serve for habitation as the hammer for the driving in of a nail or the pen for writing. For it does indeed belong to the gear consisting of things necessary for the life of man. It serves to shelter him from the inclemencies of the weather, to hide him from enemies or the importunate. And yet, within the system of finalities in which human life maintains itself the home occupies a privileged place. Not that of an ultimate end; if one can seek it as a goal, if one can "enjoy" one's home, the home does not manifest its originality in the possibility for its enjoyment. For all "implements," besides their utility as means in view of an end, admit of an immediate interest. Thus I can *take pleasure* in handling a tool, in working, in accomplishing, using gestures which, to be sure, fit into a system of finality, but whose end is situated beyond the pleasure or pain procured by these isolated gestures themselves, which fill or *nourish* a life. The privileged role of the home does not consist in being the end of human activity but in being its condition, and in this sense its commencement. The recollection necessary for nature to be able to be represented and worked over, for it to first take form as a world, is accomplished as the home. Man abides in the world as having come to it from a private domain, from being at home with himself, to which at each moment he can retire. He does not come to it from an intersideral space where he would already be in possession of himself and from which at each moment he would have to recommence a perilous landing. But he does not find himself brutally cast forth and forsaken in the world. Simultaneously without and within, he goes forth outside from an inwardness [intimité]. Yet this inwardness opens up in a home which is situated in that outside—for the home, as a building, belongs to a world of objects. But this belongingness does not nullify the bearing

152

of the fact that every consideration of objects, and of buildings too, is produced out of a dwelling. Concretely speaking the dwelling is not situated in the objective world, but the objective world is situated by relation to my dwelling. The idealist subject which constitutes a priori its object and even the site at which it is found does not strictly speaking constitute them a priori but precisely *after the event,* after having dwelt in them as a concrete being. The event of dwelling exceeds the knowing, the thought, and the idea in which, after the event, the subject will want to contain what is incommensurable with a knowing.

The analysis of enjoyment and *living from* . . . has shown that being is not resolved into empirical events and thoughts that reflect those events or aim at them "intentionally." To present inhabitation as a becoming conscious of a certain conjuncture of human bodies and buildings is to leave aside, is to forget the outpouring of consciousness in things, which does not consist in a representation of things by consciousness, but in a specific intentionality of concretization. We can formulate it in this way: the consciousness of a world is already consciousness *through* that world. Something of that world seen is an organ or an essential means of vision: the head, the eye, the eyeglasses, the light, the lamps, the books, the school. The whole of the civilization of labor and possession arises as a concretization of the separated being effectuating its separation. But this civilization refers to the incarnation of consciousness and to inhabitation—to existence proceeding from the intimacy of a home, the first concretization. The very notion of an idealist subject has come from a failure to recognize this overflowing of concretization. The *for itself* of the subject was posited in a sort of ether, and its position added nothing to this representation of itself by itself—which included that position. Contemplation, with its pretension to constitute, after the event, the dwelling itself, assuredly evinces separation, or, better yet, is an indispensable moment of its production. But the dwelling cannot be forgotten among the conditions for representation, even if representation is a privileged conditioned, absorbing its condition. For it absorbs it only after the event, a posteriori. Hence the subject contemplating a world presupposes the event of dwelling, the withdrawal from the elements (that is, from immediate enjoyment, already uneasy about the morrow), recollection in the intimacy of the home.

The isolation of the home does not arouse magically, does not "chemically" provoke recollection, human subjectivity. The terms must be reversed: recollection, a work of separation, is concretized as existence in a dwelling, economic existence. Because the I exists recollected it takes refuge empirically in the home. Only from this recollection does the building take on the signification of being a dwelling. But "concretization" does not only reflect the possibility it concretizes, rendering explicit the articulations enveloped in it. Interiority concretely *accomplished* by the home, the passage to act—the *energy*—of recollection in the dwelling, opens up new possibilities which the possibility of recollection did not contain analytically, but which, being essential to its *energy,* are manifested only when it unfolds. How does habitation, actualizing this recollection, this intimacy and this warmth or gentleness of intimacy, make labor and representation, which complete the structure of separation, possible? We shall see shortly, but first it is important to describe the "intentional implications" of recollection itself and of the gentleness in which it is lived.

2. *Habitation and the Feminine*

Recollection, in the current sense of the term, designates a suspension of the immediate reactions the world solicits in view of a greater attention to oneself, one's possibilities, and the situation. It is already a movement of attention freed from immediate enjoyment, for no longer deriving its freedom from the agreeableness of the elements. From what then? How would a total reflection be allowed a being that never becomes the *bare fact* of existing, and whose existence is life, that is, life from something? How, in the midst of a life which is life from . . . , which enjoys elements, and which is preoccupied with overcoming the insecurity of enjoyment, is a distance to be produced? Does recollection amount to maintaining oneself in an indifferent region, in a void, in one of those interstices of being in which the Epicurean gods reside? The I would thereby lose the confirmation which as life from . . . and enjoyment of . . . it receives in the element which nourishes it, without receiving this confirmation from elsewhere. Or would the distance with regard to enjoyment, rather than signifying the cold void of the interstices of being, be lived positively as a dimension of interiority beginning with the intimate familiarity into which life is immersed?

The familiarity of the world does not only result from habits acquired in this world, which take from it its roughnesses and measure the adaptation of the living being to a world it enjoys and from which it nourishes itself; familiarity and intimacy are produced as a gentleness that spreads over the face of things. This gentleness is not only a conformity of nature with the needs of the separated being, which from the first enjoys them and constitutes itself as separate, as I, in that enjoyment, but is a gentleness coming from an affection [amitié] for that I. The intimacy which familiarity already presupposes is an *intimacy with someone*. The interiority of recollection is a solitude in a world already human. Recollection refers to a welcome.

But how can the separation of solitude, how can intimacy be produced in face of the Other? Is not the presence of the Other already language and transcendence?

For the intimacy of recollection to be able to be produced in the oecumenia of being the presence of the Other must not only be revealed in the face which breaks through its own plastic image, but must be revealed, simultaneously with this presence, in its withdrawal and in its absence. This simultaneity is not an abstract construction of dialectics, but the very essence of discretion. And the other whose presence is discreetly an absence, with which is accomplished the primary hospitable welcome which describes the field of intimacy, is the Woman. The woman is the condition for recollection, the interiority of the Home, and inhabitation.

The simple living from . . . the spontaneous agreeableness of the elements is not yet habitation. But habitation is not yet the transcendence of language. The Other who welcomes in intimacy is not the *you* [*vous*] of the face that reveals itself in a dimension of height, but precisely the *thou* [*tu*] of familiarity: a language without teaching, a silent language, an understanding without words, an expression in secret. The I-Thou in which Buber sees the category of interhuman relationship is the relation not with the interlocutor but with feminine alterity. This alterity is situated on another plane than language and nowise represents a truncated, stammering, still elementary language. On the contrary, the discretion of this presence includes all the possibilities of the transcendent relationship with the Other. It is comprehensible and exercises its function of interiorization only on the ground of the full human personality, which, however, in the woman, can be reserved so as to open up the dimension of interiority. And this is a new and irreducible possibility, a delightful lapse in being, and the source of gentleness in itself.

Familiarity is an accomplishment, an *en-ergy* of separation. With it separation is constituted as dwelling and inhabitation. To exist henceforth means to dwell. To dwell is not the simple fact of the anonymous reality of a being cast into existence as a stone one casts behind oneself; it is a recollection, a coming to oneself, a retreat home with oneself as in a land of refuge, which answers to a hospitality, an expectancy, a human welcome. In human welcome the language that keeps silence remains an essential possibility. Those silent comings and goings of the feminine being whose footsteps reverberate the secret depths of being are not the turbid mystery of the animal and feline presence whose strange ambiguity Baudelaire likes to evoke.

The separation that is concretized through the intimacy of the dwelling outlines new relations with the elements.

3. The Home and Possession

The home does not implant the separated being in a ground to leave it in vegetable communication with the elements. It is set back from the anonymity of the earth, the air, the light, the forest, the road, the sea, the river. It has a "street front," but also its secrecy. With the dwelling the separated being breaks with natural existence, steeped in a medium where its enjoyment, without security, on edge, was being inverted into care. Circulating between visibility and invisibility, one is always bound for the interior of which one's home, one's corner, one's tent, or one's cave is the vestibule. The primordial function of the home does not consist in orienting being by the architecture of the building and in discovering a site, but in breaking the plenum of the element, in opening in it the utopia in which the "I" recollects itself in dwelling at home with itself. But separation does not isolate me, as though I were simply extracted from these elements. It makes labor and property possible.

The ecstatic and immediate enjoyment to which, aspired as it were by the uncertain abyss of the element, the I was able to give itself over, is adjourned and delayed in the home. But this suspension does not reduce to nothing the relationship of the I with the elements. The dwelling remains in its own way open upon the element from which it separates. The ambiguity of distance, both removal and connection, is lifted by the window that makes possible a look that dominates, a look of him who escapes looks, the look that contemplates. The elements remain at the disposal of the I—to take or to leave. Labor will henceforth draw things from the elements and thus *discover* the world. This primordial grasp, this emprise of labor, which *arouses* things and transforms nature into a world, presupposes, just as does the contemplation of the gaze, the recollection of the I in its dwelling. The movement by which a being builds its home, opens and ensures interiority to itself, is constituted in a movement by which the separated being recollects itself. With the dwelling the latent birth of the world is produced.

The postponement of enjoyment makes accessible a world—being lying escheat, but at the disposal of whoever will take possession of it. There is here no causality: the world does not *result* from this postponement *decided* in an abstract thought. The postponement of enjoyment has no other concrete signification than this putting at one's disposal which accomplishes it, which is its en-ergy. A new conjuncture in being—accomplished by the sojourn in a dwelling and not by an abstract thought—is necessary for the deployment of this *en-ergy*. This sojourn in a dwelling, inhabitation, before imposing itself as an empirical fact, conditions every empiricism and the very structure of the fact imposed on contemplation. And conversely presence "at home with oneself" exceeds the apparent simplicity the abstract analysis of the "for itself" finds in it.

We shall describe in the pages that follow the relation that the home establishes with a world to be possessed, to be acquired, to be rendered *interior*. The first movement of economy is in fact egoist—it is not transcendence; it is not expression. The labor that draws the things from the elements in which I am steeped discovers durable substances, but forthwith suspends the independence of their durable being by acquiring them as movable goods,* transportable, put in reserve, deposited in the home.

The home that founds possession is not a possession in the same sense as the movable goods** it can collect and keep. It is possessed because it already and henceforth is hospitable for its proprietor. This refers us to its essential interiority, and to the inhabitant that inhabits it before every inhabitant, the welcoming one par excellence, welcome in itself—the feminine being. Need one add that there is no question here of defying ridicule by maintaining the empirical truth or countertruth that every

---

* "Bien-meubles."

** "Les choses meubles"—The thing (*chose*) will be defined as a "*meuble*"—being related to the home by the possessive grasp it is a "movable," a "furnishing." Cf. p. 166-161.—Trans.

home *in fact* presupposes a woman? The feminine has been encountered in this analysis as one of the cardinal points of the horizon in which the inner life takes place—and the empirical absence of the human being of "feminine sex" in a dwelling nowise affects the dimension of femininity which remains open there, as the very welcome of the dwelling.

4. Possession and Labor

The access to the world is produced in a movement that starts from the utopia of the dwelling and traverses a space to effect a primordial grasp, to seize and to take away. The uncertain future of the element is suspended. The element is fixed between the four walls of the home, is calmed in possession. It appears there as a thing, which can, perhaps, be defined by tranquillity—as in a "still life." This grasp operated on the elemental is labor.

The possession of things proceeding from the home, produced by labor, is to be distinguished from the immediate relation with the non-I in enjoyment, the possession without acquisition enjoyed by the sensibility steeped in the element, which "possesses" without taking. In enjoyment the I assumes nothing; from the first it lives from. . . . Possession by enjoyment is one with enjoyment; no activity precedes sensibility. But to possess by enjoying is also to be possessed and to be delivered to the fathomless depth, the disquieting future of the element.

Possession proceeding from the dwelling is to be distinguished from the content possessed and the enjoyment of that content. In the element, which exalts but also transports the enjoying I, labor in its possessive grasp suspends the independence of the element: its being. The thing evinces this hold or this comprehension—this ontology. Possession neutralizes this being: as property the thing is an existent that has lost its being. But in this suspension possession com-prehends the being of the existent, and only thus does the thing arise. Ontology is a relation with things which manifests things; the ontology that grasps the being of the existent is a spontaneous and pretheoretical work of every inhabitant of the earth. Possession masters, suspends, postpones the unforeseeable future of the element—its independence, its being. "Unforeseeable future," not because it exceeds the reach of vision, but because, faceless and losing itself in nothingness, it is inscribed in the fathomless depth of the element, coming from an opaque density without origin, the bad infinite or the indefinite, the *apeiron*. It has no origin because it has no substance, does not cling to a "something," quality that qualifies nothing, without zero-point through which any axis of coordinates would pass, prime matter absolutely undetermined. To suspend this independence of being, this materiality of the elemental non-I, by possession does not amount to *thinking* this suspension or obtaining it by the effect of a formula. The way of access to the fathomless obscurity of matter is not an idea of infinity, but labor. Possession is accomplished in taking-possession or labor, the destiny of the hand. The hand is the organ of grasping and taking, the first and blind grasping in the teeming mass: it relates* to me, to my egoist ends, things drawn from the element, which, beginningless and endless, bathes and inundates the separated being. But the hand *relating* the elemental to the finality of needs constitutes things only by separating its take from immediate enjoyment, depositing it in the dwelling, conferring on it the status of a possession. Labor is the very *en-ergy* of acquisition. It would be impossible in a being that had no dwelling.

The hand accomplishes its proper function prior to every execution of a plan, every projection of a project, every finality that would lead out of being at home with oneself. The hand's rigorously economic movement of seizure and acquisition is dissimulated by the traces, "wastes," and "works" this movement of acquisition, returning to the interiority of the home, leaves in its wake. These works, as city, field, garden, landscape, recommence their elemental existence. Labor in its primary intention is this acquisition, this movement toward oneself; it is not a transcendence.

Labor conforms with the elements from which it draws the things. It grasps matter as raw material. In this primordial grasp matter at the same time announces its anonymity and renounces it. It announces it, for labor, the hold on matter, is not a vision or thought in which matter already determined would be defined by relation to infinity; within the grasp matter precisely remains fundamentally indefinite and, in the intellectual sense of the term, incomprehensible. But it renounces its anonymity, since the primordial hold of labor introduces it into a world of the identifiable, masters it, and puts it at the disposal of a being recollecting and identifying itself prior to every civil status, every quality, proceeding only from itself.

Labor's hold on the indefinite does not resemble the idea of infinity.

---

* "Rapporte": to "bring back."—Trans.

Labor "defines" matter without recourse to the idea of infinity. The primordial technique does not put into practice an antecedent "knowledge," but has immediately a hold on matter. The power of the hand that grasps or tears up or crushes or kneads relates the element, not to an infinity by relation to which the thing would be defined, but to an end in the sense of a goal, to the goal of need. A fathomless depth divined by enjoyment in the element yields to labor, which masters the future and stills the anonymous rustling of the *there is,* the uncontrollable stirring of the elemental, disquieting even within enjoyment itself. This fathomless obscurity of matter is presented to labor as resistance and not as the face to face. Not as an idea of resistance, not as a resistance announced in an idea, or, as a face, announcing itself to be absolute—but already in contact with the hand that breaks it, and virtually overcome. The laborer will subjugate it; it does not oppose frontally, but as already abdicating to the hand which seeks its vulnerable point, which, already ruse and industry, reaches for it obliquely. Labor grapples with the fallacious resistance of nameless matter, the infinity of its nothingness. Thus in the last analysis labor cannot be called violence: it is applied to what is faceless, to the resistance of nothingness. It acts in the phenomenon. It attacks only the facelessness of the pagan gods whose nothingness is henceforth exposed. Prometheus stealing the fire of the heavens symbolizes industrious labor in its impiety.

Labor masters or suspends *sine die* the indeterminate future of the element. By taking hold of things, by treating being as a furnishing, transportable into a home, it disposes of the unforeseeable future in which being's ascendancy over us was portended; it reserves this future for itself. Possession removes being from change. In essence durable, it does not only endure as a state of mind; it affirms its power over time, over what belongs to nobody—over the future. Possession posits the product of labor as what remains permanent in time, a substance.

Things present themselves as solids with contours clearly delimited. Along with tables, chairs, envelopes, notebooks, pens—fabricated things —stones, grains of salt, clumps of earth, icecles, apples are things. The form which separates the object, which delineates sides for it, seems to constitute it. One thing is distinct from another because an interval separates them. But a part of a thing is in its turn a thing: the back, the leg of the chair, for example. But also any fragment of the leg is a thing, even if it does not constitute one of its articulations—everything one can detach and remove from it. The contour of the thing marks the possibility of detaching it, moving it without the others, taking it away. A thing is a movable—a *furnishing* [*meuble*]. It keeps a certain proportion relative to the human body. This proportion subjects it to the hand, and not only to enjoyment. The hand both brings the elemental qualities to enjoyment, and takes and keeps them for future enjoyment. The hand delineates a world by drawing what it grasps from the element, delineating definite beings having forms, that is, solids; the informing of the formless is solidification, emergence of the graspable, the *existent, support* of qualities. Substantiality thus does not reside in the sensible nature of things, since sensibility coincides with enjoyment enjoying an "adjective" without substantive, a pure quality, a quality without support. Abstraction, which would promote the sensible to a concept, would not confer upon it the substantiality the sensible content lacks—unless we stress, not the content of the concept, but the latent birth of the concept in the primordial hold effected by labor. The intelligibility of the concept would then designate its reference to the seizure by labor by which possession is produced. The substantiality of a thing lies in its solidity, offering itself to the hand which takes and takes away.

The hand is thus not only the point at which we communicate a certain quantity of force to matter. It traverses the indetermination of the element, suspends its unforeseeable surprises, postpones the enjoyment in which they already threaten. The hand takes and comprehends*; it recognizes the being of the existent, seizing upon the substance and not the shadow; and at the same time it suspends that being, since being is its possession. And yet this suspended, tamed being is maintained, is not worn away in the enjoyment that consumes and uses up. For a time, it is posited as durable, as *substance*. To some extent things are the non-edible, the tool, the object of everyday use, the instrument of labor, a good. The hand *comprehends* the thing not because it touches it on all sides at the same time (it does not touch it throughout), but because it is no longer a sense-organ, pure enjoyment, pure sensibility, but is mastery, domination, disposition—which do not belong to the order of sensibility. An organ for taking, for acquisition, it gathers the fruit but holds it far from the lips, keeps it, puts it in reserve, possesses it in a home. The dwelling conditions labor. The hand that acquires is burdened by what it takes; it does not found possession

---

* "... prend et comprend ..."

by itself. Moreover the very project of acquisition presupposes the recollection of the dwelling. Boutroux says somewhere that possession prolongs our body. But the body as naked body is not the first possession; it is still outside of having and not having. We dispose of our body inasmuch as we have already suspended the being of the element that bathes us, by *inhabiting*. The body is my possession according as my being maintains itself in a home at the limit of interiority and exteriority. The extraterritoriality of a home conditions the very possession of my body.

Substance refers to the dwelling, that is, in the etymological sense of the term, to economy. Possession grasps being in the object, but it grasps it, that is, forthwith contests it. In placing it in my home as a possession it confers upon it a being of pure appearance, a phenomenal being; the thing that is mine or another's is not in itself. Possession alone touches substance; the other relations with the thing only affect attributes. The function of being implement, as the value the things bear, imposes itself to spontaneous consciousness not as substance, but as one of the attributes of these beings. The access to values, usage, manipulation and manufacture rest on possession, on the hand that takes, that acquires, that brings back home. The substantiality of a thing, correlative of possession, does not consist in the thing presenting itself absolutely. In their presentation things are acquired, are given.

Because it is not in itself a thing can be exchanged and accordingly be compared, be quantified, and consequently already lose its very identity, be reflected in money. The identity of a thing is thus not its primordial structure. It disappears as soon as the thing is approached as matter. Property alone institutes permanence in the pure quality of enjoyment, but this permanence disappears forthwith in the phenomenality reflected in money. As property, merchandise, bought and sold, a thing is revealed in the market as susceptible of belonging, being exchanged, and accordingly as convertible into money, susceptible of dispersing in the anonymity of money.

But possession itself refers to more profound metaphysical relations. A thing does not resist acquisition; the other possessors—those whom one cannot possess—contest and therefore can sanction possession itself. Thus the possession of things issues in a discourse. The action that is beyond labor, presupposing the absolute resistance of the face of another being, is command and word—or the violence of murder.

5. *Labor, the Body, Consciousness*

The doctrine that interprets the *world* as a horizon from which things are presented as implements, the equipment of an existence concerned for its being, fails to recognize the being established at the threshold of an interiority the dwelling makes possible. Every manipulation of a system of tools and implements, every labor, presupposes a primordial *hold* on the things, possession, whose latent birth is marked by the home, at the frontier of interiority. The world is a possible possession, and every transformation of the world by industry is a variation of the regime of property. Proceeding from the dwelling, possession, accomplished by the quasi-miraculous grasp of a thing in the night, in the *apeiron* of prime matter, discovers a world. The grasp of a thing illuminates the very night of the *apeiron;* it is not the world that makes things possible. On the other hand, the intellectualist conception of a world as a spectacle given to impassive contemplation likewise fails to recognize the recollection of the dwelling, without which the incessant buzzing of the element cannot present itself to the hand that grasps, for without the recollection of the dwelling the hand qua hand cannot arise in the body immersed in the element. Contemplation is not the suspension of the activity of man; it comes after the suspension of the chaotic and thus independent being of the element, and after the encounter of the Other who calls in question possession itself. Contemplation in any case presupposes the very mobilization of the thing, grasped by the hand.

In the preceding considerations the body appeared not as an object among other objects, but as the very regime in which separation holds sway, as the "how" of this separation and so to speak as an adverb rather than as a substantive. It is as though in the vibration of separated existing there would by essence be produced a node where a movement of interiorization meets a movement of labor and acquisition directed toward the fathomless depth of the elements whereby the separated being is placed between two voids, in the "somewhere" in which it posits itself precisely as separate. This situation must be deduced and described more closely.

In the paradisal enjoyment, timeless and carefree, the distinction between activity and passivity is undone in agreeableness [agrément]. Enjoyment is wholly nourished by the outside it inhabits, but its agreeableness manifests its sovereignty, a sovereignty as foreign to the freedom of a *causa sui,* which nothing outside could affect, as to the Heideggerian *Geworfenheit,* which, caught up in the *other* that limits it and negates it, *suffers* from this alterity as much as would an idealist freedom. The separated being is separated or content in its joy of breathing, seeing, and feeling. The *other* in which it jubilates—the elements—is initially neither for nor against it. No assumption marks the primary relation of enjoyment, which is neither suppression of nor reconciliation with the "other". But what is distinctive about the sovereignty of the I that vibrates in enjoyment is that it is steeped in a medium and consequently undergoes *influences.* The originality of influence lies in that the autonomous being of enjoyment can be discovered, in this very enjoyment to which it cleaves, to be determined by what it is not, but without enjoyment being broken up, without violence being produced. It appears as the product of the medium in which, however, it bathes, self-sufficient. Autochthony is at the same time an attribute of sovereignty and of submission; they are simultaneous. What has influence over life seeps into it like a sweet poison. It is alienated, but even in suffering the alienation comes to it from within. This ever possible inversion of life cannot be stated in terms of limited or finite freedom. Freedom is presented here as one of the possibilities of the primordial equivocation that plays in the autochthonous life. The existence of this equivocation is the body. The sovereignty of enjoyment nourishes its independence with a dependence on the other. The sovereignty of enjoyment runs the risk of a betrayal: the alterity from which it lives already expels it from paradise. Life is a body, not only lived body [corps propre], where its self-sufficiency emerges, but a cross-roads of physical forces, body-effect. In its deep-seated fear life attests this ever possible inversion of the body-master into body-slave, of health into sickness. *To be a body* is on the one hand *to stand* [*se tenir*], to be master of oneself, and, on the other hand, to stand on the earth, to be in the *other,* and thus to be encumbered by one's body. But—we repeat—this encumberment is not produced as a pure dependence; it forms the happiness of him who enjoys it. What is necessary to my existence in order to subsist interests my existence. I pass from this dependence to this joyous independence, and in my very suffering I derive my existence from within. To be at home with oneself in something other than oneself, to be oneself while living from something other than oneself, to live from . . . , is concretized in corporeal existence. "Incarnate thought" is not initially produced as a thought that acts on the world, but as a separated existence which affirms its independence in the happy dependence of need. It is not that this equivocation amounts to two successive points of view on separation; their simultaneity constitutes the body. To neither of the aspects which reveal themselves in turn does the last word belong.

The dwelling suspends or postpones this betrayal by making acquisition and labor possible. The dwelling, overcoming the insecurity of life, is a perpetual postponement of the expiration in which life risks foundering. The consciousness of death is the consciousness of the perpetual postponement of death, in the essential ignorance of its date. Enjoyment as the body that labors maintains itself in this primary postponement, that which opens the very dimension of time.

The suffering of the recollected being, which is patience in the primary sense, pure passivity, is at the same time openness upon duration, postponement, within this suffering. In patience the imminence of defeat, but also a distance in its regard, coincide. The ambiguity of the body is *consciousness*.

There therefore exists no *duality*—lived body and physical body—which would have to be reconciled. The dwelling which lodges and prolongs life, the world life acquires and utilizes by labor, is also the physical world where labor is interpreted as a play of anonymous forces. For the forces of the exterior world the dwelling is only a postponement. The domiciled being stands out from the things only because it accords itself a delay, because it "delays the effect," because it labors.

We have not contested the spontaneity of life. We have, on the contrary, reduced the problem of the interaction of the body and the world to inhabitation, to "living from . . . ," where the schema of a freedom *causa sui* incomprehensibly limited is no longer to be found. Freedom as a relation of life with an *other* that lodges it, and by which life is *at home with itself,* is not a finite freedom; it is virtually a null freedom. Freedom is as it were the by-product of life. Its adhesion to the world in which it risks being lost is precisely, and at the same time, that by which it defends itself and is at home with itself. This body, a sector of an elemental reality, is also what permits taking hold of the world, laboring. To be free is to build a world in which one could be free. Labor comes from a being that is a thing among things and in contact with things, but, within this contact, coming from its being at home with itself. Consciousness does not fall into a body—is not incarnated; it is a disincarnation—or, more exactly, a postponing of the corporeity of the body. This is not produced in the ether of abstraction but as all the concreteness of dwelling and labor. To be conscious is to be in relation with *what is,* but as though the present of *what is* were not yet entirely accomplished and only constituted the *future* of a recollected being. To be conscious is precisely to have time—not to exceed the present time in the project that anticipates the future, but to have a distance with regard to the present itself, to be related to the element in which one is settled as to what is not yet there. All the freedom of inhabitation depends on the time that, for the inhabitant, still always remains. The incommensurable, that is, the incomprehensible format of the surrounding medium leaves time. The distance with regard to the element to which the I is given over menaces it in its dwelling only in the future. *For the moment* the present is only consciousness of danger, fear, which is feeling par excellence. The indetermination of the element, its future, becomes consciousness, the possibility of making use of time. Labor characterizes not a freedom that has detached itself from being, but a will: a being that is threatened, but has time at its disposal to ward off the threat.

The will marks, in the general economy of being, the point where the definitiveness of an event is produced as non-definitive. The strength of the will does not proceed as a force more powerful than the obstacle. It does not approach the obstacle head on, but consists in always giving oneself a distance with regard to it, catching sight of an interval between oneself and the imminence of the obstacle. To will is to forestall danger. To conceive the future is to fore-stall.* To labor is to delay its expiration. But labor is possible only in a being that has the structure of the body, a being grasping beings, that is, recollected at home with itself and only *in relation* with the non-I.

But time, which manifests itself in the recollection of dwelling, presupposes (as we will explain further) the relation with an other that is not given to labor—the relationship with the Other, with infinity, metaphysics.

This ambiguity of the body, by which the I is engaged in the other but comes always from the hither side, is *produced* in labor. Labor does not consist in being first cause in a *continuous* chain of causes such as an already illuminated thought apperceives it, being the cause that would be operative the moment thought, proceeding backward from the end,

---

* "Concevoir l'avenir, c'est pré-venir."

would stop upon the cause closest to us because coinciding with us. The different causes closely linked form a mechanism whose essence is expressed in the machine. The wheels of machinery are perfectly adjusted to one another and form an unbroken continuity. In the case of a machine one can just as well say that the result is the final cause, or the effect, of the first movement. But the movement of the body that releases the machine's action, the hand that bears itself toward the hammer or the nail that is to be driven in, is not simply the *efficient cause* of this end, while the end would be the final cause of the movement. For in the movement of the hand it is always to some measure a matter of seeking and *catching hold* of the goal, with all the contingencies this involves. This distance hollowed out and traversed by the body toward the machine or the mechanism it sets into motion may be greater or less; its margin can be much restricted in habitual gestures. But even when the gesture is habitual, skill and practice are needed to guide the habit.

In other words, the action of the body, which after the event will be statable in terms of causality, unfolds at the time under the dominion of a cause which is, in the true sense of the term, final. The intermediaries that will enable this distance to be filled in, so as to release one another automatically, are not yet found. The hand ventures forth and catches hold of its goal with an inevitable share of *chance* or of mischance, since it can miss its try. The hand is by essence groping and emprise. Groping is not a technically imperfect action, but the condition for all technique. The end is not caught sight of as an end in a disincarnate aspiration, whose destiny it would fix as the cause fixes the destiny of the effect. If the determinism of an end cannot be converted into a determinism of a cause, this is because the conception of an end is inseparable from its realization; an end does not attract, is not in some measure inevitable, but is caught hold of, and thus presupposes the body qua hand. Only a being endowed with organs can conceive a technical finality, a relation between the end and the tool. The end is a term the hand searches for in the risk of missing it. The body as possibility of a hand—and its whole corporeity can be substituted for the hand—exists in the virtuality of this movement betaking itself toward the tool.

Groping, the work of the hand par excellence, and the work adequate to the *apeiron* of the element, makes possible the whole originality of the final cause. It is said that if the attraction that an end exercises is not entirely reducible to a continuous series of shocks, a continuous propulsion, this is because the idea of the end governs the release of these shocks. But this idea of the end would be an epiphenomenon were it not manifested in the way the first shock is given: a thrust in the void, at random. In reality the "representation" of the end and the movement of the hand that plunges toward it through an unexplored distance, preceded by no searchlight, constitute but one and the same event, and define a being that, while being in the midst of a world in which it is implanted, yet comes to this world from the hither side of this world, from a dimension of *interiority*—a being that *inhabits* the world, that is, that is at home with itself in it. Groping reveals the position of the body which at the same time is integrated into being and remains in its interstices, always invited to traverse a distance at random, and maintains itself in this position all by itself. Such is the position of a separated being.

6. The Freedom of Representation and Gift

To be separated is to dwell somewhere; separation is produced positively in localization. The body does not happen as an accident to the soul. Shall we say that it is the insertion of a soul in extension? This metaphor solves nothing; there would remain the problem of understanding the insertion of the soul in the extension of the body. Appearing to representation as a thing among things, the body is in fact the *mode* in which a being, neither spatial nor foreign to geometrical or physical extension, exists separately. It is the regime of separation. The *somewhere* of dwelling is produced as a primordial event relative to which the event of the unfolding of physico-geometrical extension must be understood—and not the reverse.

And yet representational thought which nourishes itself and lives from the very being it represents to itself refers to an exceptional possibility of this separated existence. It is not that to an intention called theoretical, basis of the I, would be added volitions, desires, and sentiments, so as to transform thought into life. The strictly intellectualist thesis subordinates life to representation. It maintains that in order to will it is first necessary to represent to oneself what one wills; in order to desire, represent one's goal to oneself; in order to feel, represent to oneself the object of the sentiment; and in order to act, represent to oneself what one will do. But how would the tension and care of a life arise from impassive representation? The converse thesis presents no fewer difficulties. Does representation, as the limit case of an engagement in reality, the residue of an act suspended and hesitant, representation as the misfire of action, exhaust the essence of theory?

If it is not possible to draw from an impassive contemplation of an object the finality necessary for action, is it easier to derive from commitment, from action, from care, the freedom of contemplation representation evinces?

Moreover the philosophical meaning of representation does not become evident from the simple opposition of representation to action. Does impassiveness opposed to commitment sufficiently characterize representation? Is the freedom with which it is linked an absence of relation, an outcome of history in which nothing remains *other,* and consequently a sovereignty in the void?

Representation is conditioned. Its transcendental pretension is constantly belied by the life that is already implanted in the being representation claims to constitute. But representation claims to substitute itself *after the event* for this life in reality, so as to constitute this very reality. Separation has to be able to account for this constitutive conditioning accomplished by representation—though representation be produced *after the event.* The theoretical, being after the event, being essentially memory, is to be sure not creative; but its critical essence—its retrogressive movement—is no wise a possibility of enjoyment and labor. It evinces a new energy, oriented upstream, counter-current, which the impassiveness of contemplation expresses only superficially.

That representation is conditioned by life, but that this conditioning could be reversed after the event—that idealism is an eternal temptation —results from the very event of separation, which must not at any moment be interpreted as an abstract cleavage in space. The fact of the after-the-event does show that the possibility of constitutive representation does not restore to abstract eternity or to the instant the privilege of measuring all things; it shows, on the contrary, that the production of separation is bound to time, and even that the articulation of separation in time is produced thus in itself and not only secondarily, for us.

The possibility of a representation that is constitutive but already rests on the enjoyment of a real completely constituted indicates the radical character of the uprootedness of him who is recollected in a home, where the I, while steeped in the elements, takes up its position before a Nature. The elements in and from which I live are also that to which I am opposed. The feat of having limited a part of this world and having closed it off, having access to the elements I enjoy by way of the door and the window, realizes extraterritoriality and the sovereignty of thought, anterior to the world to which it is posterior. *Anterior posteriorly:* separation is not thus "known"; it is thus produced. Memory is precisely the accomplishment of this ontological structure. A marsh wave that returns to wash the strand beneath the line it left, a spasm of time conditions remembrance. Thus only do I see without being seen, like Gyges, am no longer invaded by nature, no longer immersed in a tone or an atmosphere. Thus only does the equivocal essence of the home hollow out interstices in the continuity of the earth. The Heideggerian analyses of the world have accustomed us to think that the "in view of oneself" that characterizes *Dasein,* care in situation, in the last analysis conditions every human product. In *Being and Time* the home does not appear apart from the system of implements. But can the "in view of oneself" characteristic of care be brought about without a disengagement from the situation, without a recollection and without extraterritoriality—without *being at home with oneself?* Instinct remains inserted in its situation; the hand that gropes traverses a void at random.

Whence does this transcendental energy come to me, this postponement which is time itself, this future in which memory will lay hold of a past that was before the past, the "deep past, never past enough"—an energy already presupposed by recollection in a home?

We have defined representation as a determination of the other by the same, without the same being determined by the other. This definition excluded representation from reciprocal relations, whose terms meet and limit one another. To represent to oneself that from which I live would be equivalent to remaining exterior to the elements in which I am steeped. But if I cannot quit the space in which I am steeped, with a dwelling I can but *approach* these elements, possess things. I can indeed recollect myself in the midst of my life, which is life from. . . . However, the negative moment of this *dwelling* which determines possession, the recollection which draws me out of submergence, is not a simple echo of possession. We may not see in it the counterpart of presence to things, as though the possession of things, as a presence to them, dialectically contained the withdrawal from them. This withdrawal implies a new event; I must have been in relation with something I do not live from. This event is the relation with the Other who welcomes me in the Home, the discreet presence of the Feminine. But in order that I be able to free myself from the very possession that the welcome of the

Home establishes, in order that I be able to see things in themselves, that is, represent them to myself, refuse both enjoyment and possession, I must know how *to give* what I possess. Only thus could I situate myself absolutely above my engagement in the non-I. But for this I must encounter the indiscreet face of the Other that calls me into question. The Other—the absolutely other—paralyzes possession, which he contests by his epiphany in the face. He can contest my possession only because he approaches me not from the outside but from above. The same can not lay hold of this other without suppressing him. But the untraversable infinity of the negation of murder is announced by this dimension of height, where the Other comes to me concretely in the ethical impossibility of commiting this murder. I welcome the Other who presents himself in my home by opening my home to him.

The calling in question of the I, coextensive with the manifestation of the Other in the face, we call language. The height from which language comes we designate with the term teaching. Socratic maieutics prevailed over a pedagogy that introduced ideas into a mind by violating or seducing (which amounts to the same thing) that mind. It does not preclude the openness of the very dimension of infinity, which is height, in the face of the Master. This voice coming from another shore teaches transcendence itself. Teaching signifies the whole infinity of exteriority. And the whole infinity of exteriority is not first produced, to then teach: teaching is its very production. The first teaching teaches this very height, tantamount to its exteriority, the ethical. In this commerce with the infinity of exteriority or of height the naïveté of the direct impulse, the naïveté of the being exercising itself as a force on the move, is ashamed of its naïveté. It discovers itself as a violence, but thereby enters into a new dimension. Commerce with the alterity of infinity does not offend like an opinion; it does not limit a mind in a way inadmissible to a philosopher. Limitation is produced only within a totality, whereas the relation with the Other breaks the ceiling of the totality. It is fundamentally pacific. The other is not opposed to me as a freedom other than, but similar to my own, and consequently hostile to my own. The Other is not another freedom as arbitrary as my own, in which case it would traverse the infinity that separates me from him and enter under the same concept. His alterity is manifested in a mastery that does not conquer, but teaches. Teaching is not a species of a genus called domination, a hegemony at work within a totality, but is the presence of infinity breaking the closed circle of totality.

Representation derives its freedom with regard to the world that nourishes it from the relation essentially moral, that with the Other. Morality is not added to the preoccupations of the I, so as to order them or have them judged; it calls in question, and puts at a distance from itself, the I itself. Representation began not in the presence of a thing exposed to my violence but empirically escaping my powers, but in my possibility of calling this violence into question, in a possibility produced by the commerce with infinity, by society.

The positive deployment of this pacific relation with the other, without frontier or any negativity, is produced in language. Language does not belong among the relations that could appear through the structures of formal logic; it is contact across a distance, relation with the non-touchable, across a void. It takes place in the dimension of absolute desire by which the same is in relation with an other that was not simply lost by the same. We are not required to take contact or vision to be the archetypal gestures of straightforwardness. The Other is neither initially nor ultimately what we grasp or what we thematize. For truth is neither in seeing nor in grasping, which are modes of enjoyment, sensibility, and possession; it is in transcendence, in which absolute exteriority presents itself in expressing itself, in a movement at each instant recovering and deciphering the very signs it emits.

But the transcendence of the face is not enacted outside of the world, as though the economy by which separation is produced remained beneath a sort of beatific contemplation of the Other (which would thereby turn into the idolatry that brews in all contemplation). The "vision" of the face as face is a certain mode of sojourning in a home, or—to speak in a less singular fashion—a certain form of economic life. No human or interhuman relationship can be enacted outside of economy; no face can be approached with empty hands and closed home. Recollection in a home open to the Other—hospitality—is the concrete and initial fact of human recollection and separation; it coincides with the Desire for the Other absolutely transcendent. The chosen home is the very opposite of a root. It indicates a disengagement, a wandering [errance] which has made it possible, which is not a *less* with respect to installation, but the surplus of the relationship with the Other, metaphysics.

But the separated being can close itself up in its egoism, that is, in the very accomplishment of its isolation. And this possibility of forgetting the transcendence of the Other—of banishing with impunity all hospitality (that is, all language) from one's home, banishing the transcendental relation that alone permits the I to shut itself up in itself—evinces the absolute truth, the radicalism, of separation. Separation is not only dialectically correlative with transcendence, as its reverse; it is accomplished as a positive event. The relation with infinity remains as another possibility of the being recollected in its dwelling. The possibility for the home to open to the Other is as essential to the essence of the home as closed doors and windows. Separation would not be radical if the possibility of shutting oneself up at home with oneself could not be produced without internal contradiction as an event in itself, as atheism itself is produced—if it should only be an empirical, psychological fact, an illusion. Gyges's ring symbolizes separation. Gyges plays a double game, a presence to the others and an absence, speaking to "others" and evading speech; Gyges is the very condition of man, the possibility of injustice and radical egoism, the possibility of accepting the rules of the game, but cheating.

Our work in all its developments strives to free itself from the conception that seeks to unite events of existence affected with opposite signs in an ambivalent condition which alone would have ontological dignity, while the events themselves proceeding in one direction or in another would remain empirical, articulating nothing ontologically new. The method practiced here does indeed consist in seeking the condition of empirical situations, but it leaves to the developments called empirical, in which the conditioning possibility is accomplished—it leaves to the *concretization*—an ontological role that specifies the meaning of the fundamental possibility, a meaning invisible in that condition.

The relationship with the Other is not produced outside of the world, but puts in question the world possessed. The relationship with the Other, transcendence, consists in speaking the world to the Other. But language accomplishes the primordial putting in common—which refers to possession and presupposes economy. The universality a thing receives from the word that extracts it from the *hic et nunc* loses its mystery in the ethical perspective in which language is situated. The *hic et nunc* itself issues from possession, in which the thing is grasped, and language, which designates it to the other, is a primordial dispossession, a first donation. The generality of the word institutes a common world. The ethical event at the basis of generalization is the underlying intention of language. The relation with the Other does not only stimulate, provoke generalization, does not only supply it with the pretext and the occasion (this no one has ever contested), but is this generalization itself. Generalization is a universalization—but universalization is not the entry of a sensible thing into a no man's land* of the ideal, is not purely negative like a sterile renunciation, but is the offering of the world to the Other. Transcendence is not a vision of the Other, but a primordial donation.

Language does not exteriorize a representation preexisting in me: it puts in common a world hitherto mine. Language *effectuates* the entry of things into a new ether in which they receive a name and become concepts. It is a first action over and above labor, an action without action, even though speech involves the effort of labor, even though, as incarnate thought, it inserts us into the world, with the risks and hazards of all action. At each instant it exceeds this labor by the generosity of the offer it forthwith makes of this very labor. The analyses of language that tend to present it as one meaningful action among others fail to recognize this *offering* of the world, this offering of contents which answers to the face of the Other or which questions him, and first opens the perspective of the meaningful.

The "vision" of the face is inseparable from this offering language is. To see the face is to speak of the world. Transcendence is not an optics, but the first ethical gesture.

---

* In English in the original.—Trans.

E. THE WORLD OF PHENOMENA
AND EXPRESSION

1. Separation Is an Economy

In affirming separation we are not transposing into an abstract formula the empirical image of a spatial interval which joins its extremities by the very space that separates them. Separation must take form outside of this formalism, as an event that is not equivalent to its contrary as soon as it is produced. To separate oneself, to not remain bound up with a totality, is positively to be *somewhere,* in the home, to be economically. The "somewhere" and the home render egoism, the primordial mode of being in which separation is produced, explicit. Egoism is an ontological event, an effective rending, and not a dream running along the surface of being, negligible as a shadow. The rending of a totality can be produced only by the throbbing of an egoism that is neither illusory nor subordinated in any way whatever to the totality it rends. Egoism is life: life from . . . , or enjoyment. Enjoyment, given over to the elements which content it but lead it off into the "nowhere" and menace it, withdraws into a dwelling. So many opposed movements —the submergence in the elements which begins to open up interiority, the sojourn, happy and needy, on the earth, time, and the consciousness which loosens the vice of being and ensures the mastery of a world—are united in the corporeal being of man—nakedness and indigence, exposed to the anonymous exteriority of heat and cold but recollecting in the interiority of being at home with oneself, and hence labor and possession. In laboring possession reduces to the same what at first presented itself as other. Despite the infinite extension of needs it makes possible economic existence remains within the same (just as animal existence). Its movement is centripetal.

But is not this interiority manifested on the outside by works? Do not works succeed in breaking through the crust of separation? Do not actions, gestures, manners, objects utilized and fabricated recount their

175

author? To be sure—but only if they have been clothed with the signification of language, which is instituted above and beyond works. Through works alone the I does not come outside; it withdraws from them or congeals in them as though it did not appeal to the Other and did not respond to him, but in its activity sought comfort, privacy, and sleep. The lines of meaning traced in matter by activity are immediately charged with equivocations, as though action, in pursuing its design, were *without regard* for exteriority, without attention. In undertaking what I willed I realized so many things I did not will: the work rises in the midst of the wastes of labor. The worker does not hold in his hands all the threads of his own action. He is exteriorized by acts that are already in a sense abortive. If his works deliver signs, they have to be deciphered without his assistance. If he participates in this deciphering, he speaks. Thus the product of labor is not an inalienable possession, and it can be usurped by the Other. Works have a destiny independent of the I, are integrated in an ensemble of works: they can be exchanged, that is, be maintained in the anonymity of money. Integration in an economic world does not commit the interiority from which works proceed. This inner life does not die away like a straw fire, but it does not recognize itself in the existence attributed to it within economy. This is attested in the consciousness the person has of the tyranny of the State. The State awakens the person to a freedom it immediately violates. The State which realizes its essence in works slips toward tyranny and thus attests *my absence* from those works, which across the economic necessities return to me as alien. From the work I am only deduced and am already ill-understood, betrayed rather than expressed.

But neither do I break through the crust of separation by approaching the Other in his works, which, like my own, are delivered over to the anonymous field of the economic life, in which I maintain myself egoist and separated, identifying in the diverse my own identity as the same, through labor and possession. The Other signals himself but does not present himself. The works symbolize him. The symbolism of life and labor symbolizes in that very particular sense Freud discovered in all our conscious manifestations and in our dreams, and which is the essence of every sign, its primordial definition: it reveals only in concealing. In this sense the signs constitute and protect my privacy. To be expressed by one's life, by one's works, is precisely to decline expression. Labor remains economic; it comes from the home and returns to it, a movement of Odyssey where the adventure pursued in the world is but the accident of a return. Absolutely speaking, the interpretation of the symbol can assuredly lead to an intention divined; but we penetrate into this interior world as by burglary and without conjuring the absence. The word alone—but disengaged from its density as a linguistic product —can put an end to this absence.

2. Works and Expression

Things manifest themselves as answering to a question relative to which they have a meaning—the question *quid*? This question calls for a substantive and an adjective—inseparably. To this quest corresponds a content, sensible or intellectual, a "comprehension" by concept. The author of the work, approached from the work, will be present only as a content. This content can not be detached from the context, from the system in which the works themselves are integrated, and it answers to the question by its place in the system. To ask *what* is to ask *as what:* it is not to take the manifestation for itself.

But the question that asks about the quiddity is put to someone. He who is to respond has long already *presented* himself, responding thus to a question prior to every question in search of quiddities. In fact the "who is it?" is not a question and is not satisfied by a knowing. He to whom the question is put *has already presented himself,* without being a content. He has presented himself as a face. The face is not a modality of quiddity, an answer to a question, but the correlative of what is prior to every question. What is prior to every question is not in its turn a question nor a knowledge possessed a priori, but is Desire. The *who* correlative of Desire, the *who* to whom the question is put, is, in metaphysics, a "notion" as fundamental and as universal as quiddity and being and the existent and the categories.

To be sure, most of the time the *who* is a *what*. We ask "Who is Mr. X?" and we answer: "He is the President of the State Council," or "He is Mr. So-and-so." The answer presents itself as a quiddity; it refers to a system of relations. To the question *who?* answers the non-qualifiable presence of an existent who *presents himself* without reference to anything, and yet distinguishes himself from every other existent. The question *who?* envisages a face. The notion of the face differs from every represented content. If the question *who?* does not question in the same sense as the question *what?* it is that here what one asks and he whom one questions coincide. To aim at a face is to put the question *who?* to the very face that is the answer to this question; the answerer and the answered coincide. The face, preeminently expression, formulates the first word: the signifier arising at the thrust of his sign, as eyes that look at you.

The *who* involved in activity is not *expressed* in the activity, is not *present,* does not attend his own manifestation, but is simply signified in it by a sign in a system of signs, that is, as a being who is manifested precisely as absent from his manifestation: a manifestation in the absence of being—a phenomenon. When we understand man on the basis of his works he is more surprised than understood.* His life and his labor mask him. As symbols they call for interpretation. Here phenomenality does not simply designate a relativity of knowledge, but a *mode of being* where nothing is ultimate, where everything is a sign, a present absenting itself from its presence and in this sense a dream. With the exteriority that is not that of things symbolism disappears and the order of being begins, and a day dawns from whose depths no new day is to dawn. What inward existence lacks is not a being in the superlative, prolonging and amplifying the equivocations of interiority and of its symbolism, but an order where all the symbolisms are deciphered by beings that present themselves absolutely—that express themselves. The same is not the Absolute; its reality expressed in its work is absent from its work. In its economic existence its reality is not total.

It is only in approaching the Other that I attend to myself. This does not mean that my existence is constituted in the thought of the others. An existence called objective, such as is reflected in the thought of the others, and by which I count in universality, in the State, in history, in the totality, does not express me, but precisely dissimulates me. The face I welcome makes me pass from phenomenon to being in another sense: in discourse I expose myself to the questioning of the Other, and this urgency of the response—acuteness of the present—engenders me for responsibility; as responsible I am brought to my final reality. This extreme attention does not actualize what was in potency, for it is not conceivable without the other. Being attentive signifies a surplus of consciousness, and presupposes the call of the other. To be attentive is to recognize the mastery of the other, to receive his command, or, more exactly, to receive from him the command to command. When I seek my final reality, I find that my existence as a "thing in itself" begins

---

* ". . . il est plus surpris que compris."

with the presence in me of the idea of Infinity. But this relation already consists in serving the Other.

Death is not this master. Always future and unknown it gives rise to fear or flight from responsibilities. Courage exists in spite of it. It has its ideal elsewhere; it commits me to life. Death, source of all myths, is *present* only in the Other, and only in him does it summon me urgently to my final essence, to my responsibility.

For the totality of contentment to reveal its phenomenality and its inadequateness to the absolute it does not suffice that a discontent be substituted for contentment. Discontent still remains within the horizons of a totality, as an indigence which, in need, anticipates its satisfaction. Such is a lower proletariat that would covet but the comfort of the bourgeois interior and its fleshpot horizons. The totality of contentment betrays its own phenomenality when an exteriority that does not slip into the void of needs gratified or frustrated supervenes. The totality of contentment reveals its phenomenality when this exteriority, incommensurable with needs, breaks interiority by this very incommensurability. Interiority then discovers itself to be insufficient, but this insufficiency does not designate any limitation imposed by this exteriority. The insufficiency of interiority is not immediately convertible into needs presaging their satisfaction or suffering from their penury; the broken interiority is not mended in the horizons outlined by needs. Such an exteriority reveals an insufficiency of the separated being that is without possible satisfaction—not only unsatisfied *in fact,* but outside of every perspective of satisfaction or unsatisfaction. The exteriority foreign to needs would then reveal an insufficiency full of this very insufficiency and not of hopes, a distance more precious than contact, a non-possession more precious than possession, a hunger that nourishes itself not with bread but with hunger itself. This is not some romantic dream, but what from the beginning of this research imposed itself as Desire. Desire does not coincide with an unsatisfied need; it is situated beyond satisfaction and nonsatisfaction. The relationship with the Other, or the idea of Infinity, accomplishes it. Each can live it in the strange desire of the Other that no voluptuosity comes to fulfill, nor close, nor put to sleep. By virtue of this relationship man, withdrawn from the element, recollected in a home, represents a world to himself. Because of it, because of presence before the face of the Other, man does not permit himself to be deceived by his glorious triumph as a living being, and unlike the animal can know the difference between being and

phenomenon, can recognize his phenomenality, the penury of his plenitude, a penury inconvertible into needs which, being beyond plenitude
and void, cannot be gratified.

3. Phenomenon and Being

The epiphany of exteriority, which exposes the deficiency of the sovereign interiority of the separated being, does not situate interiority, as one
part limited by another, in a totality. We here enter the order of Desire
and the order of relations irreducible to those governing totality. The
contradiction between the free interiority and the exteriority that should
limit it is reconciled in the man open to teaching.

Teaching is a discourse in which the master can bring to the student
what the student does not yet know. It does not operate as maieutics,
but continues the placing in me of the idea of infinity. The idea of
infinity implies a soul capable of containing more than it can draw from
itself. It designates an interior being that is capable of a relation with
the exterior, and does not take its own interiority for the totality of
being. This whole work seeks only to present the spiritual according to
this Cartesian order, prior to the Socratic order. For the Socratic
dialogue already presupposes beings who have decided for discourse, who
consequently have accepted its rules, whereas teaching leads to the logical
discourse without rhetoric, without flattery or seduction and hence without violence, and maintaining the interiority of him who welcomes.

The man of enjoyment who remains in interiority, who ensures
his separation, can be unaware of his phenomenality. This possibility of
ignorance does not denote an inferior degree of consciousness, but is the
very price of separation. Separation as a break with participation
was deduced from the Idea of Infinity. It is therefore also a relation
extending over the irremediable abyss of this separation. If separation
had to be described in terms of enjoyment and economy, this is because
the sovereignty of man was nowise a simple reverse of the relation with
the Other. Separation not being reducible to a simple counterpart of
relation, the relationship with the Other does not have the same status as
the relations given to objectifying thought, where the distinction of terms
also reflects their union. The relationship between me and the Other
does not have the structure formal logic finds in all relations. The terms
remain absolute despite the relation in which they find themselves. The
relation with the Other is the only relation where such an overturning of

formal logic can occur. But we then understand that the idea of infinity, which requires separation, requires it unto atheism, so profoundly that the idea of infinity could be forgotten. The forgetting of transcendence is not produced as an accident in a separated being; the possibility of this forgetting is necessary for separation. The distance and interiority remain intact in the resumption of the relationship; and when the soul opens, in the marvel of teaching, the transitivity of teaching is neither less nor more authentic than the freedom of the master and the student, though the separated being thereby leaves the plane of economy and labor.

We have said that this moment when the separated being is discovered without expressing itself, when it appears but absents itself from its apparition, corresponds rather exactly to the meaning of phenomenon. The phenomenon is the being that appears, but remains absent. It is not an appearance, but a reality that lacks reality, still infinitely removed from its being. In the work someone's intention has been divined, but he has been judged in absentia. Being has not come to the assistance of itself (as Plato says about written discourse); the interlocutor has not *attended* his own revelation. One has penetrated into his interior, but in his absence. He has been understood like a prehistoric man who has left hatchets and drawings but no words. Everything comes to pass as though the word, that word that lies and dissimulates, were absolutely indispensable for the trial, to clarify the items of a dossier and the objects constituting evidence, as though the word alone could assist the judges and render the accused present, as though by the word alone the multiple concurrent possibilities of the symbol, which symbolizes in silence and in twilight, could be sorted out and give birth to the truth. Being is a world in which one speaks and of which one speaks. Society is the presence of being.

Being, the thing in itself, is not, with respect to the phenomenon, the hidden. Its presence presents itself in its word. To posit the thing in itself as hidden would be to suppose that it is with respect to the phenomenon what the phenomenon is to the appearance. The truth of disclosure is at most the truth of the phenomenon hidden under the appearances; the truth of the thing in itself is not disclosed. The thing in itself expresses itself. Expression manifests the presence of being, but not by simply drawing aside the veil of the phenomenon. It is of itself presence of a face, and hence appeal and teaching, *entry into relation* with me—the ethical relation. And expression does not manifest the presence of being by referring from the sign to the signified; it presents the signifier. The signifier, he who gives a sign, is not signified. It is necessary to have already been in the society of signifiers for the sign to be able to appear as a sign. Hence the signifier must present himself before every sign, by himself—present a face.

Speech is an incomparable manifestation: it does not accomplish the movement from the sign to the signifier and the signified; it unlocks what every sign closes up at the very moment it opens the passage that leads to the signified, by making the signifier *attend* this manifestation of the signified. This attendance measures the surplus of spoken language over written language, which has again become signs. Signs are a mute language, a language impeded. Language does not group symbols into systems, but deciphers the symbols. But when this primordial manifestation of the Other has already taken place, when an existent has *presented* himself and come to the assistance of himself, not only verbal signs but all signs can serve as language. But speech itself does not always find the welcome that ought to be reserved to speech. For it involves non-speech, and can express in the sense that implements, clothing, and gestures express. In its mode of articulation, in its style, speech signifies as an activity and as a product. It is to pure speech what writing for graphologists is to the written expression for the reader. Speech taken as an activity signifies as do furnishings or implements. It does not have the total transparence of the gaze directed upon the gaze, the absolute *frankness* of the face to face proffered at the bottom of all speech. From my speech-activity I absent myself, as I am missing from all my products. But I am the unfailing source of ever renewed deciphering. And this renewal is precisely presence, or my attendance to myself.

As long as the existence of man remains interiority it remains phenomenal. The language by which a being exists for another is his unique possibility to exist with an existence that is more than his interior existence. The surplus that language involves with respect to all the works and labors that manifest a man measures the distance between the living man and the dead—who, however, is alone recognized by history, which approaches him objectively in his work or his heritage. Between the subjectivity shut up in its interiority and the subjectivity poorly heard in history there is the attendance of the subjectivity that speaks.

The return to univocal being from the world of signs and symbols proper to phenomenal existence does not consist in being integrated into a whole such as understanding conceives and politics establishes it.

There the independence of the separated being is lost, unrecognized, and oppressed. To return to exterior being, to being in the univocal sense, the sense that hides no other sense, is to enter into the straightforwardness of the face to face. This is not a play of mirrors but my responsibility, that is, an existence already obligated. It places the center of gravitation of a being outside of that being. The surpassing of phenomenal or inward existence does not consist in receiving the recognition of the Other, but in offering him one's being. To be in oneself is to express oneself, that is, already to serve the Other. The ground of expression is goodness. To be καθ'αὐτό is to be good.

SECTION III

EXTERIORITY AND THE FACE

A. SENSIBILITY AND THE FACE

Is not the face given to vision? How does the epiphany as a face determine a relationship different from that which characterizes all our sensible experience?

The idea of intentionality has compromised the idea of sensation by removing the character of being a concrete datum from this allegedly purely qualitative and subjective state, foreign to all objectification. Already the classical analysis had shown, from a psychological point of view, its constructed character—the sensation graspable by introspection is already a perception. It was said that we always find ourselves among things: color is always extended and objective, the color of a dress, a lawn, a wall; sound is a noise of a passing car, or a voice of someone speaking. In fact nothing psychological would correspond to the simplicity of the physiological definition of sensation. Sensation as a simple quality floating in the air or in our soul represents an abstraction because, without the object to which it refers, quality can have the signification of being a quality only in a relative sense: by turning over a painting we can see the colors of the objects painted as colors in themselves—but in fact already as colors of the canvas that bears them. —Unless their purely aesthetic effect would consist in this detachment from the object . . . . But then sensation would result from a long thought process.

This critique of sensation failed to recognize the plane on which the sensible life is lived as enjoyment. This mode of life is not to be interpreted in function of objectification. Sensibility is not a fumbling objectification. Enjoyment, by essence satisfied, characterizes all sensations whose representational content dissolves into their affective content. The very distinction between representational and affective content is tantamount to a recognition that enjoyment is endowed with a dynamism other than that of perception. But we can speak of enjoyment or of sensation even in the domain of vision and audition, when one has seen or heard much, and the object revealed by the experiences is steeped in the enjoyment—or suffering—of pure sensation, in which one has bathed and

187

lived as in qualities without support. The notion of sensation is thus somewhat rehabilitated. In other words, sensation recovers a "reality" when we see in it not the subjective counterpart of objective qualities, but an enjoyment "anterior" to the crystallization of consciousness, I and non-I, into subject and object. This crystallization occurs not as the ultimate finality of enjoyment but as a moment of its becoming, to be interpreted in terms of enjoyment. Rather than taking sensations to be contents destined to fill a priori forms of objectivity, a transcendental function *sui generis* must be recognized in them (and for each qualitative specificity in its own mode) ; a priori formal structures of the non-I are not necessarily structures of objectivity. The specificity of each sensation reduced precisely to that "quality without support or extension" the sensualists sought in it designates a structure not necessarily reducible to the schema of an object endowed with qualities. The senses have a meaning that is not predetermined as objectification. It is for having neglected in the sensibility this function of pure sensibility in the Kantian sense of the term and a whole "transcendental aesthetics" of "contents" of experience that we are led to posit the non-I in a univocal sense, as the objectivity of the object. In fact we reserve a transcendental function for visual and tactile qualities, and leave to qualities coming from other senses only the role of adjectives clinging to the visible and touched object—which is inseparable from labor and the home. The object disclosed, discovered, appearing, a phenomenon, is the visible or touched object. Its objectivity is interpreted without the other sensations taking part in it. The ever self-identical objectivity would be found in the perspectives of vision or the movements of the hand that palpates. As Heidegger, after St. Augustine, pointed out, we use the term vision indifferently for every experience, even when it involves other senses than sight. And we also use the grasp in this privileged sense. Idea and concept cover with the whole of experience. This interpretation of experience on the basis of vision and touch is not due to chance and can accordingly expand into a civilization. It is incontestable that objectification operates in the gaze in a privileged way; it is not certain that its tendency to inform every experience is inscribed, and unequivocably so, in being. A phenomenology of sensation as enjoyment, a study of what we could call its transcendental function, which does not necessarily issue in the object nor in the qualitative specification of an object (as such simply seen), would be required. The *Critique of Pure Reason,* in discovering the transcendental activity of the mind, has made familiar the idea of a spiritual activity that does not issue in an object, even though this revolutionary idea was in Kantian philosophy attenuated in that the activity in question constituted the *condition* for the object. A transcendental phenomenology of sensation would justify the return to the term sensation to characterize the transcendental function of the quality corresponding to it. For the ancient conception of sensation, in which the affecting of a subject by an object did enter, would evoke this function better than the naïvely realist language of the moderns. We have maintained that enjoyment—which does not fit in the schema of objectification and vision—does not exhaust its meaning in qualifying the visible object. All our analyses of the preceding section were guided by this conviction. They were also guided by the idea that representation is not a work of the look by itself, but of language. But in order to distinguish look and language, that is, the look and the welcome of the face which language presupposes, we must analyse more closely the privilege of vision.

As Plato noted, besides the eye and the thing, vision presupposes the light. The eye does not see the light, but the object in the light. Vision is therefore a relation with a "something" established within a relation with what is not a "something." We are in the light inasmuch as we encounter the thing in nothingness. The light makes the thing appear by driving out the shadows; it empties space. It makes space arise specifically as a void. Inasmuch as the movement of the hand that touches traverses the "nothing" of space, touch resembles vision. Nevertheless vision has over the touch the privilege of maintaining the object in this void and receiving it always from this nothingness as from an origin, whereas in touch nothingness is manifested to the free movement of palpation. Thus for vision and for touch a being comes as though from nothingness, and in this precisely resides their traditional philosophical prestige. This coming forth from void is thus their coming from their origin; this "openness" of experience or this experience of openness explains the privilege of objectivity and its claim to coincide with the very being of *existents*. We find this schema of vision from Aristotle to Heidegger. In the light of generality which does not exist is established the relation with the individual. For Heidegger, an openness upon Being, which is not *a being,* which is not a "something," is necessary in order that, in general, a "something" manifest itself. In the rather formal fact that an existent is, in its work or its exercise of Being—in its very independence—resides its intelligibility. Thus appear the structures of vision, where the relation of the subject with the object is subordinated to the relation of the object with the void of openness, which is not an object. The comprehension of an existent consists in precisely going beyond the existent, into the open. To comprehend the particular being is to apprehend it out of an illuminated site it does not fill.

But is not this spatial void a "something"—the form of all experience, the object of geometry, something *seen* in its turn? In fact, it is necessary to make a stroke in order to see a line. Whatever be the significance of the passage to the limit, the notions of intuitive geometry will impose themselves upon us from the things seen: the line is the limit of a thing; the plane the surface of an object. It is on the basis of a something that geometrical notions impose themselves. They are experimental "notions" not because they would be contrary to reason, but because they become objects of view only on the basis of things: they are limits of things. But illuminated space involves the attenuation of these limits unto nothingness, their vanishing. Considered in itself, illuminated space, emptied by light of the obscurity that filled it, is nothing. To be sure, this void is not equivalent to absolute nothingness; to traverse it is not equivalent to transcending. But if empty space differs from nothingness, and if the distance it opens does not justify a claim to transcendence in the movement that traverses it, yet its "plenitude" nowise returns it to the status of an object. This "plenitude" is of another order. If the void that light produces in the space from which it drives out darkness is not equivalent to nothingness, even in the absence of any particular object, *there is* this void itself. It does not exist by virtue of a play on words. The negation of every qualifiable thing allows the impersonal *there is* to arise again, returning intact behind every negation, whatever be the degree of negation. The silence of infinite spaces is terrifying. The invasion of this *there is* does not correspond to any representation. We have described elsewhere its vertigo.* And the elemental essence of the element, with the mythical facelessness from which it comes, participates in the same vertigo.

In driving out darkness the light does not arrest the incessant play of the *there is*. The void the light produces remains an indeterminate density which has no meaning of itself prior to discourse, and does not yet triumph over the return of mythical gods. But vision in the light is precisely the possibility of forgetting the horror of this interminable

---

***Existence and Existents*, trans. A. F. Lingis, The Hague, Nijhoff, 1978, pp. 57-64.—Trans.

return, this *aperion,* maintaining oneself before this semblance of
nothingness which is the void, and approaching objects as though at their
origin, out of nothingness. This deliverance from the horror of the *there
is* is evinced in the contentment of enjoyment. The void of space is not
the absolute interval from which the absolutely exterior being can arise.
It is a modality of enjoyment and separation.

Illuminated space is not the absolute interval. The connection between vision and touch, between representation and labor, remains essential. Vision moves into grasp. Vision opens upon a perspective, upon a
horizon, and describes a traversable distance, invites the hand to movement and to contact, and ensures them. Socrates made fun of Glaucon
who wished to take the vision of the starlit sky for an experience of
height. The forms of objects call for the hand and the grasp. By the
hand the object is in the end comprehended, touched, taken, borne and
referred to other objects, clothed with a signification, *by reference to*
other objects.* Empty space is the condition for this relationship; it is
not a breach of the horizon. Vision is not a transcendence. It ascribes a
signification by the *relation* it makes possible. It opens nothing that,
beyond the same, would be absolutely other, that is, in itself. Light
conditions the relations between data; it makes possible the signification
of objects that border one another. It does not enable one to approach
them face to face. Intuition, taken in this very general sense, is not
opposed to the thought of relations. It is already relationship, since it is
vision; it catches sight of the space across which things are transported
toward one another. Space, instead of transporting beyond, simply
ensures the condition for the *lateral* signification of things within the
same.

To see is hence always to see on the horizon. The vision that
apprehends on the horizon does not encounter a being out of what is
beyond all being. Vision is a forgetting of the *there is* because of the
essential satisfaction, the agreeableness [agrément] of sensibility, enjoyment, contentment with the finite without concern for the infinite. In
fleeing itself in vision consciousness returns to itself.

But is not light in another sense origin of itself—as the source of light,
in which its being and its appearing coincide, as fire and as sun? Here,
to be sure, is the figure of every relation with the absolute. But it is only

---

* "Par la main, l'objet est en fin de compte compris, touché, pris, porté et
rapporté à d'autres objets, revêt une signification, par *rapport* à d'autres objets."

a figure. The light as sun is an object. If in the diurnal vision light makes seen and is not seen, the nocturnal light is seen as source of light. In the vision of brilliancy the juncture of light with object takes place. The sensible light qua visual datum does not differ from other data, and itself remains relative to an elemental and obscure ground. A relation with what in another sense comes absolutely from itself is needed to make possible the consciousness of radical exteriority. A light is needed to see the light.

Does not science make possible the transcending of the subjective condition of sensibility? Even if we distinguish from qualitative science that which the work of Léon Brunschvicg extolled, we can still ask whether mathematical thought itself breaks with sensation? The phenomenological message essentially answers in the negative. The realities physico-mathematical science reach derive their meaning from procedures that proceed from the sensible.

Total alterity, in which a being does not refer to enjoyment and presents itself out of itself, does not shine forth in the *form* by which things are given to us, for beneath form things conceal themselves. The surface can be transformed into an interior: one can melt the metal of things to make new objects of them, utilize the wood of a box to make a table out of it by chopping, sawing, planing: the hidden becomes open and the open becomes hidden. This consideration may seem naïve—as though the interiority or the essence of the thing which the form hides would have to be taken in the spatial sense. But in fact the depth of the thing can have no other meaning than that of its matter, and the revelation of matter is essentially superficial.

It would seem that between the different surfaces there exists a more profound difference: that of the obverse and the reverse. One surface is offered to the gaze, and one can turn over the garment, as one remints a coin. But does not the distinction between the obverse and the reverse bring us beyond these superficial considerations? Does it not indicate to us another plane than that with which our last remarks were intentionally concerned? The obverse would be the essence of the thing whose servitudes are supported by the reverse, where the threads are invisible. Yet Proust admired the reverse of the sleeves of a lady's gown, like those dark corners of cathedrals, nonetheless worked with the same art as the façade. It is art that endows things with something like a *façade*—that by which objects are not only seen, but are as objects on exhibition. The darkness of matter would denote the state of a being that precisely has no façade. The notion of façade borrowed from building suggests to us that architecture is perhaps the first of the fine arts. But in it is constituted the beautiful, whose essence is indifference, cold splendor, and silence. By the façade the thing which keeps its secret is exposed enclosed in its monumental essence and in its myth, in which it gleams like a splendor but does not deliver itself. It captivates by its grace as by magic, but does not reveal itself. If the transcendent cuts across sensibility, if it is openness preeminently, if its vision is the vision of the very openness of being, it cuts across the vision of forms and can be stated neither in terms of contemplation nor in terms of practice. It is the face; its revelation is speech. The relation with the Other alone introduces a dimension of transcendence, and leads us to a relation totally different from experience in the sensible sense of the term, relative and egoist.

B. ETHICS AND THE FACE

1. Infinity and the Face

Inasmuch as the access to beings concerns vision, it dominates those beings, exercises a power over them. A thing is *given,* offers itself to me. In gaining access to it I maintain myself within the same.

The face is present in its refusal to be contained. In this sense it cannot be comprehended, that is, encompassed. It is neither seen nor touched—for in visual or tactile sensation the identity of the I envelops the alterity of the object, which becomes precisely a content.

The Other is not other with a relative alterity as are, in a comparison, even ultimate species, which mutually exclude one another but still have their place within the community of a genus—excluding one another by their definition, but calling for one another by this exclusion, across the community of their genus. The alterity of the Other does not depend on any quality that would distinguish him from me, for a distinction of this nature would precisely imply between us that community of genus which already nullifies alterity.

And yet the Other does not purely and simply negate the I; total negation, of which murder is the temptation and the attempt, refers to an antecedent relation. The relation between the Other and me, which dawns forth in his expression, issues neither in number nor in concept. The Other remains infinitely transcendent, infinitely foreign; his face in which his epiphany is produced and which appeals to me breaks with the world that can be common to us, whose virtualities are inscribed in our *nature* and developed by our existence. Speech proceeds from absolute difference. Or, more exactly, an absolute difference is not produced in a process of specification descending from genus to species, in which the order of logical relations runs up against the given, which is not reducible to relations. The difference thus encountered remains bound up with the logical hierarchy it contrasts with, and appears against the ground of the common genus.

194

Absolute difference, inconceivable in terms of formal logic, is established only by language. Language accomplishes a relation between terms that breaks up the unity of a genus. The terms, the interlocutors, absolve themselves from the relation, or remain absolute within relationship. Language is perhaps to be defined as the very power to break the continuity of being or of history.

The incomprehensible nature of the presence of the Other, which we spoke of above, is not to be described negatively. Better than comprehension, *discourse* relates with what remains essentially transcendent. For the moment we must attend to the formal work of language, which consists in presenting the transcendent; a more profound signification will emerge shortly. Language is a relation between separated terms. To the one the other can indeed present himself as a theme, but his presence is not reabsorbed in his status as a theme. The word that bears on the Other as a theme seems to contain the Other. But already it is said to the Other who, as interlocutor, has quit the theme that encompassed him, and upsurges inevitably behind the said. Words are said, be it only by the silence kept, whose weight acknowledges this evasion of the Other. The knowledge that absorbs the Other is forthwith situated within the discourse I address to him. Speaking, rather than "letting be," solicits the Other. Speech cuts across vision. In knowledge or vision the object seen can indeed determine an act, but it is an act that in some way appropriates the "seen" to itself, integrates it into a world by endowing it with a signification, and, in the last analysis, constitutes it. In discourse the divergence that inevitably opens between the Other as my theme and the Other as my interlocutor, emancipated from the theme that seemed a moment to hold him, forthwith contests the meaning I ascribe to my interlocutor. The formal structure of language thereby announces the ethical inviolability of the Other and, without any odor of the "numinous," his "holiness."

The fact that the face maintains a relation with me by discourse does not range him in the same; he remains absolute within the relation. The solipsist dialectic of consciousness always suspicious of being in captivity in the same breaks off. For the ethical relationship which subtends discourse is not a species of consciousness whose ray emanates from the I; it puts the I in question. This putting in question emanates from the other.

The presence of a being not entering into, but overflowing, the sphere of the same determines its "status" as infinite. This overflowing is to be distinguished from the image of liquid overflowing a vessel, because this overflowing presence is effectuated as a position *in face of* the same. The facing position, opposition par excellence, can be only as a moral summons. This movement proceeds from the other. The idea of infinity, the infinitely more contained in the less, is concretely produced in the form of a relation with the face. And the idea of infinity alone maintains the exteriority of the other with respect to the same, despite this relation. Thus a structure analogous to the ontological argument is here produced: the exteriority of a being is inscribed in its essence. But what is produced here is not a reasoning, but the epiphany that occurs as a face. The metaphysical desire for the absolutely other which animates intellectualism (or the radical empiricism that confides in the teaching of exteriority) deploys its *en-ergy* in the vision of the face [vision du visage], or in the idea of infinity. The idea of infinity exceeds my powers (not quantitatively, but, we will see later, by calling them into question); it does not come from our a priori depths—it is consequently experience par excellence.

The Kantian notion of infinity figures as an ideal of reason, the projection of its exigencies in a beyond, the ideal completion of what is given incomplete—but without the incomplete being confronted with a privileged *experience* of infinity, without it drawing the limits of its finitude from such a confrontation. The finite is here no longer conceived by relation to the infinite; quite the contrary, the infinite presupposes the finite, which it amplifies infinitely (although this passage to the limit or this projection implicates in an unacknowledged form the idea of infinity, with all the consequences Descartes drew from it, and which are presupposed in this idea of projection). The Kantian finitude is described positively by sensibility, as the Heideggerian finitude by the being for death. This infinity referring to the finite marks the most anti-Cartesian point of Kantian philosophy as, later, of Heideggerian philosophy.

Hegel returns to Descartes in maintaining the positivity of the infinite, but excluding all multiplicity from it; he posits the infinite as the exclusion of every "other" that might maintain a relation with the infinite and thereby limit it. The infinite can only encompass all relations. Like the god of Aristotle it refers only to itself, though now at the term of a history. The relation of a particular with infinity would be equivalent to the entry of this particular into the sovereignty of a State. It becomes infinite in negating its own finitude. But this outcome does not succeed in smothering the protestation of the private individual, the apology of the separated being (though it be called empirical and animal), of the individual who experiences as a tyranny the State willed by his reason, but in whose impersonal destiny he no longer recognizes his reason. We recognize in the finitude to which the Hegelian infinite is opposed, and which it encompasses, the finitude of man before the elements, the finitude of man invaded by the *there is,* at each instant traversed by faceless gods against whom labor is pursued in order to realize the security in which the "other" of the elements would be revealed as the same. But the other absolutely other —the Other—does not limit the freedom of the same; calling it to responsibility, it founds it and justifies it. The relation with the other as face heals allergy. It is desire, teaching received, and the pacific opposition of discourse. In returning to the Cartesian notion of infinity, the "idea of infinity" put in the separated being by the infinite, we retain its positivity, its anteriority to every finite thought and every thought of the finite, its exteriority with regard to the finite; here there was the possibility of separated being. The idea of infinity, the overflowing of finite thought by its content, effectuates the relation of thought with what exceeds its capacity, with what at each moment it learns without suffering shock. This is the situation we call welcome of the face. The idea of infinity is produced in the *opposition* of conversation, in sociality. The relation with the face, with the other absolutely other which I can not contain, the other in this sense infinite, is nonetheless my Idea, a commerce. But the relation is maintained without violence, in peace with this absolute alterity. The "resistance" of the other does not do violence to me, does not act negatively; it has a positive structure: ethical. The first revelation of the other, presupposed in all the other relations with him, does not consist in grasping him in his negative resistance and in circumventing him by ruse. I do not struggle with a faceless god, but I respond to his expression, to his revelation.

2. Ethics and the Face

The face resists possession, resists my powers. In its epiphany, in expression, the sensible, still graspable, turns into total resistance to the grasp. This mutation can occur only by the opening of a new dimension. For the resistance to the grasp is not produced as an insurmountable resistance, like the hardness of the rock against which the effort of the hand comes to naught, like the remoteness of a star in the immensity of space. The expression the face introduces into the world does not defy the feebleness of my powers, but my ability for power.* The face, still a thing among things, breaks through the form that nevertheless delimits it. This means concretely: the face speaks to me and thereby invites me to a relation incommensurate with a power exercised, be it enjoyment or knowledge.

And yet this new dimension opens in the sensible appearance of the face. The permanent openness of the contours of its form in expression imprisons this openness which breaks up form in a caricature. The face at the limit of holiness and caricature is thus still in a sense exposed to powers. In a sense only: the depth that opens in this sensibility modifies the very nature of power, which henceforth can no longer take, but can kill. Murder still aims at a sensible datum, and yet it finds itself before a datum whose being can not be *suspended* by an appropriation. It finds itself before a datum absolutely non-neutralizable. The "negation" effected by appropriation and usage remained always partial. The grasp that contests the independence of the thing preserves it "for me." Neither the destruction of things, nor the hunt, nor the extermination of living beings aims at the face, which is not of the world. They still belong to labor, have a finality, and answer to a need. Murder alone lays claim to total negation. Negation by labor and usage, like negation by representation, effect a grasp or a comprehension, rest on or aim at affirmation; they can. To kill is not to dominate but to annihilate; it is to renounce comprehension absolutely. Murder exercises a power over what escapes power. It is still a power, for the face expresses itself in the sensible, but already impotency, because the face rends the sensible. The alterity that is expressed in the face provides the unique "matter" possible for total negation. I can wish to kill only an existent absolutely independent, which exceeds my powers infinitely, and therefore does not oppose them but paralyzes the very power of power. The Other is the sole being I can wish to kill.

But how does this disproportion between infinity and my powers differ from that which separates a very great obstacle from a force applied to it? It would be pointless to insist on the banality of murder, which reveals the quasi-null resistance of the obstacle. This most banal incident of human history corresponds to an exceptional possibility—since it

---

* "Mon pouvoir de pouvoir."

claims the total negation of a being. It does not concern the force that this being may possess as a part of the world. The Other who can sovereignly say *no* to me is exposed to the point of the sword or the revolver's bullet, and the whole unshakeable firmness of his "for itself" with that intransigent *no* he opposes is obliterated because the sword or the bullet has touched the ventricles or auricles of his heart. In the contexture of the world he is a quasi-nothing. But he can oppose to me a struggle, that is, oppose to the force that strikes him not a force of resistance, but the very *unforeseeableness* of his reaction. He thus opposes to me not a greater force, an energy assessable and consequently presenting itself as though it were part of a whole, but the very transcendence of his being by relation to that whole; not some superlative of power, but precisely the infinity of his transcendence. This infinity, stronger than murder, already resists us in his face, is his face, is the primordial *expression*, is the first word: "you shall not commit murder." The infinite paralyses power by its infinite resistance to murder, which, firm and insurmountable, gleams in the face of the Other, in the total nudity of his defenceless eyes, in the nudity of the absolute openness of the Transcendent. There is here a relation not with a very great resistance, but with something absolutely *other:* the resistance of what has no resistance—the ethical resistance. The epiphany of the face brings forth the possibility of gauging the infinity of the temptation to murder, not only as a temptation to total destruction, but also as the purely ethical impossibility of this temptation and attempt. If the resistance to murder were not ethical but real, we would have a *perception* of it, with all that reverts to the subjective in perception. We would remain within the idealism of a *consciousness* of struggle, and not in relationship with the Other, a relationship that can turn into struggle, but already overflows the consciousness of struggle. The epiphany of the face is ethical. The struggle this face can threaten *presupposes* the transcendence of expression. The face threatens the eventuality of a struggle, but this threat does not exhaust the epiphany of infinity, does not formulate its first word. War presupposes peace, the antecedent and non-allergic presence of the Other; it does not represent the first event of the encounter.

The impossibility of killing does not have a simply negative and formal signification; the relation with infinity, the idea of infinity in us, conditions it positively. Infinity presents itself as a face in the ethical resistance that paralyses my powers and from the depths of defenceless eyes rises firm and absolute in its nudity and destitution. The comprehension of this destitution and this hunger establishes the very proximity of the other. But thus the epiphany of infinity is expression and discourse. The primordial essence of expression and discourse does not reside in the information they would supply concerning an interior and hidden world. In expression a being presents itself; the being that manifests itself attends its manifestation and consequently appeals to me. This attendance is not the **neutrality** [*le neutre*] of an image, but a solicitation that concerns me by its destitution and its Height. To speak to me is at each moment to surmount what is necessarily plastic in manifestation. To manifest oneself as a face is to *impose onself* above and beyond the manifested and purely phenomenal form, to present oneself in a mode irreducible to manifestation, the very straightforwardness of the face to face, without the intermediary of any image, in one's nudity, that is, in one's destitution and hunger. In *Desire* are conjoined the movements unto the Height and unto the Humility of the Other.

Expression does not radiate as a splendor that spreads unbeknown to the radiating being—which is perhaps the definition of beauty. To manifest oneself in attending one's own manifestation is to invoke the interlocutor and expose oneself to his response and his questioning. Expression does not impose itself as a true representation or as an action. The being offered in true representation remains a possibility of appearance. The world which invades me when I engage myself in it is powerless against the "free thought" that suspends that engagement, or even refuses it interiorly, being capable of living hidden. The being that expresses itself imposes itself, but does so precisely by appealing to me with its destitution and nudity—its hunger—without my being able to be deaf to that appeal. Thus in expression the being that imposes itself does not limit but promotes my freedom, by arousing my goodness. The order of responsibility, where the gravity of ineluctable being freezes all laughter, is also the order where freedom is ineluctably invoked. It is thus the irremissible weight of being that gives rise to my freedom. The ineluctable has no longer the inhumanity of the fateful, but the severe seriousness of goodness.

This bond between expression and responsibility, this ethical condition or essence of language, this function of language prior to all disclosure of being and its cold splendor, permits us to extract language from subjection to a preexistent thought, where it would have but the servile function of translating that preexistent thought on the outside, or of universalizing its interior movements. The presentation of the face is not true, for the true refers to the non-true, its eternal contemporary, and ineluctably meets with the smile and silence of the skeptic. The presentation of being in the face does not leave any logical place for its contradictory. Thus I cannot evade by silence the discourse which the epiphany that occurs as a face opens, as Thrasymachus, irritated, tries to do, in the first book of the *Republic* (moreover without succeeding). "To leave men without food is a fault that no circumstance attenuates; the distinction between the voluntary and the involuntary does not apply here," says Rabbi Yochanan.[1] Before the hunger of men responsibility is measured only "objectively"; it is irrecusable. The face opens the primordial discourse whose first word is obligation, which no "interiority" permits avoiding. It is that discourse that obliges the entering into discourse, the commencement of discourse rationalism prays for, a "force" that convinces even "the people who do not wish to listen"[2] and thus founds the true universality of reason.

Preexisting the disclosure of being in general taken as basis of knowledge and as meaning of being is the relation with the existent that expresses himself; preexisting the plane of ontology is the ethical plane.

3. Reason and the Face

Expression is not produced as the manifestation of an intelligible form that would connect terms to one another so as to establish, across distance, the assemblage of parts in a totality, in which the terms joined up already derive their meaning from the situation created by their community, which, in its turn, owes its meaning to the terms combined. This "circle of understanding" is not the primordial event of the logic of being. Expression precedes these coordinating effects visible to a third party.

The event proper to expression consists in bearing witness to oneself, and guaranteeing this witness. This attestation of oneself is possible only as a face, that is, as speech. It produces the commencement of intelligibility, initiality itself, principality, royal sovereignty, which commands unconditionally. The principle is possible only as command. A search for the influence that expression would have undergone or an unconscious source from which it would emanate would presuppose

---

[1] Treatise *Synhedrin*, 104 b.
[2] Plato, *Republic*, 327 b.

an inquiry that would refer to new testimonies, and consequently to an original sincerity of an expression.

Language as an exchange of ideas about the world, with the mental reservations it involves, across the vicissitudes of sincerity and deceit it delineates, presupposes the originality of the face without which, reduced to an action among actions whose meaning would require an infinite psychoanalysis or sociology, it could not commence. If at the bottom of speech there did not subsist this originality of expression, this break with every influence, this dominant position of the speaker foreign to all compromise and all contamination, this straightforwardness of the face to face, speech would not surpass the plane of activity, of which it is evidently not a species—even though language can be integrated into a system of acts and serve as an instrument. But language is possible only when speaking precisely renounces this function of being action and returns to its essence of being expression.

Expression does not consist in *giving* us the Other's interiority. The Other who expresses himself precisely does not *give* himself, and accordingly retains the freedom to lie. But deceit and veracity already presuppose the absolute authenticity of the face—the privileged case of a presentation of being foreign to the alternative of truth and non-truth, circumventing the ambiguity of the true and the false which every truth risks—an ambiguity, moreover, in which all values move. The presentation of being in the face does not have the status of a value. What we call the face is precisely this exceptional presentation of self by self, incommensurable with the presentation of realities simply given, always suspect of some swindle, always possibly dreamt up. To seek truth I have already established a relationship with a face which can guarantee itself, whose epiphany itself is somehow a word of honor. Every language as an exchange of verbal signs refers already to this primordial word of honor. The verbal sign is placed where someone signifies something to someone else. It therefore already presupposes an authentification of the signifier.

The ethical relation, the face to face, also cuts across every relation one could call mystical, where events other than that of the presentation of the original being come to overwhelm or sublimate the pure sincerity of this presentation, where intoxicating equivocations come to enrich the primordial univocity of expression, where discourse becomes incantation as prayer becomes rite and liturgy, where the interlocutors find themselves playing a role in a drama that has begun outside of them. Here resides the rational character of the ethical relation and of language. No fear, no trembling could alter the straightforwardness of this relationship, which preserves the discontinuity of relationship, resists fusion, and where the response does not evade the question. To poetic activity—where influences arise unbeknown to us out of this nonetheless conscious activity, to envelop it and beguile it as a rhythm, and where action is borne along by the very work it has given rise to, where in a dionysiac mode the artist (according to Nietzsche's expression) becomes a work of art—is opposed the language that at each instant dispels the charm of rhythm and prevents the initiative from becoming a role. Discourse is rupture and commencement, breaking of rhythm which enraptures and transports the interlocutors—prose.

The face in which the other—the absolutely other—presents himself does not negate the same, does not do violence to it as do opinion or authority or the thaumaturgic supernatural. It remains commensurate with him who welcomes; it remains terrestrial. This presentation is preeminently nonviolence, for instead of offending my freedom it calls it to responsibility and founds it. As nonviolence it nonetheless maintains the plurality of the same and the other. It is peace. The relation with the other—the absolutely other—who has no frontier with the same is not exposed to the allergy that afflicts the same in a totality, upon which the Hegelian dialectic rests. The other is not for reason a scandal which launches it into dialectical movement, but the first rational teaching, the condition for all teaching. The alleged scandal of alterity presupposes the tranquil identity of the same, a freedom sure of itself which is exercised without scruples, and to whom the foreigner brings only constraint and limitation. This flawless identity freed from all participation, independent in the I, can nonetheless lose its tranquillity if the other, rather than countering it by upsurging on the same plane as it, speaks to it, that is, shows himself in expression, in the face, and comes from on high. Freedom then is inhibited, not as countered by a resistance, but as arbitrary, guilty, and timid; but in its guilt it rises to responsibility. Contingency, that is, the irrational, appears to it not outside of itself in the other, but within itself. It is not limitation by the other that constitutes contingency, but egoism, as unjustified of itself. The relation with the Other as a relation with his transcendence—the relation with the Other who puts into question the brutal spontaneity of one's immanent destiny—introduces into me what was not in me. But this "action" upon my freedom precisely puts an end to violence and contingency, and, in this sense also, founds Reason. To affirm that the passage of a content from one mind to the other is produced without violence only if the truth taught by the master is from all eternity in the student is to extrapolate maieutics beyond its legitimate usage. The idea of infinity in me, implying a content overflowing the container, breaks with the prejudice of maieutics without breaking with rationalism, since the idea of infinity, far from violating the mind, conditions nonviolence itself, that is, establishes ethics. The other is not for reason a scandal that puts it in dialectical movement, but the first teaching. A being *receiving* the idea of Infinity, *receiving* since it cannot derive it from itself, is a being taught in a non-maieutic fashion, a being whose very existing consists in this incessant reception of teaching, in this incessant overflowing of self (which is time). To think is to have the idea of infinity, or to be taught. Rational thought refers to this teaching. Even if we confine ourselves to the formal structure of logical thought, which starts from a definition, infinity, relative to which concepts are delimited, can not be defined in its turn. It accordingly refers to a "knowledge" of a new structure. We seek to fix it as a relation with the face and to show the ethical essence of this relation. The face is the evidence that makes evidence possible—like the divine veracity that sustains Cartesian rationalism.

4. Discourse Founds Signification

Language thus conditions the functioning of rational thought: it gives it a commencement in being, a primary identity of signification in the face of him who speaks, that is, who presents himself by ceaselessly undoing the equivocation of his own image, his verbal signs. Language conditions thought—not language in its physical materiality, but language as an attitude of the same with regard to the Other irreducible to the representation of the Other, irreducible to an intention of thought, irreducible to a consciousness of . . . , since relating to what no consciousness can contain, relating to the infinity of the Other. Language is not enacted within a consciousness; it comes to me from the Other and reverberates in consciousness by putting it in question. This event is irreducible to consciousness, where everything comes about from within—even the strangeness of suffering. To regard language as an attitude of the mind does not amount to disincarnating it, but is precisely to account for its incarnate essence, its difference from the constitutive, egological nature of the transcendental thought of idealism. The originality of discourse with respect to constitutive intentionality, to pure consciousness, destroys the concept of immanence: the idea of infinity in consciousness is an overflowing of a consciousness whose incarnation offers new powers to a soul no long paralytic—powers of welcome, of gift, of full hands, of hospitality. But to take incarnation as a primary fact of language, without indicating the ontological structure it accomplishes, would be to assimilate language to activity, to that prolongation of thought in corporeity, the *I think* in the *I can,* which has indeed served as a prototype for the category of the lived body [corps propre] or incarnate thought, which dominates one part of contemporary philosophy. The thesis we present here separates radically language and activity, expression and labor, in spite of all the practical side of language, whose importance we may not underestimate.

Until very recently the fundamental function of discourse in the upsurge of reason was not recognized. The function of words was understood in their dependence on reason: words reflected thought. Nominalism was the first to seek in words another function: that of an *instrument* of reason. A symbolic function of the word symbolizing the non-thinkable rather than signifying thought contents, this symbolism amounted to association with a certain number of conscious, intuitive data, an association that would be self-sufficient and would not require thought. The theory had no other purpose than to explain a divergence between thought, incapable of aiming at a general object, and language, which does seem to refer to general objects. Husserl's critique, completely subordinating words to reason, showed this divergency to be only apparent. The word is a window; if it forms a screen it must be rejected. With Heidegger Husserl's esperantist words take on the color and weight of a historical reality. But they remain bound to the process of comprehension.

The mistrust of verbalism leads to the incontestable primacy of rational thought over all the *operations* of expression that insert a thought into a particular language as into a system of signs, or bind it to a system of language presiding over the choice of these signs. Modern investigations in the philosophy of language have made familiar the idea of an underlying solidarity of thought with speech. Merleau-Ponty, among others, and better than others, showed that disincarnate thought thinking speech before speaking it, thought constituting the world of speech, adding a world of speech to the world antecedently constituted out of significations in an always transcendental operation, was a myth. Already thought consists in foraging in the system of signs, in the particular tongue of a people or civilization, and receiving signification from this very operation. It ventures forth at random, inasmuch as it does not start with an antecedent representation, or with those significations, or with phrases to be articulated. Hence one might say thought operates in the "I can" of the body. It operates in it before representing this body to itself or constituting it. Signification surprises the very thought that thought it.

But why is language, the recourse to the system of signs, necessary for thought? Why does the object, and even the perceived object, need a name in order to become a signification? What is it to have a meaning? Signification, though received from this incarnate language, nonetheless remains, thoughout this conception, an "intentional object." The structure of constitutive consciousness recovers all its rights after the mediation of the body that speaks or writes. Does not the surplus of signification over representation consist in a new mode of being presented (new with respect to constitutive intentionality), whose secret the analysis of "body intentionality" does not exhaust? Does the mediation of the sign constitute the signification because it would introduce into an objective and static representation the "movement" of symbolic relation? But then language would again be suspected of taking us away from "the thing themselves.". . .

It is the contrary that must be affirmed; it is not the mediation of the sign that forms signification, but signification (whose primordial event is the face to face) that makes the sign function possible. The primordial essence of language is to be sought not in the corporeal operation that discloses it to me and to others and, in the recourse to language, builds up a thought, but in the presentation of meaning. This does not bring us back to a transcendental consciousness constituting objects, against which the theory of language we have just evoked protests with such just rigor. For significations do not present themselves to theory, that is, to the constitutive freedom of a transcendental consciousness; *the being of signification consists in putting into question in an ethical relation constitutive freedom itself.* Meaning is the face of the Other, and all recourse to words takes place already within the primordial face to face of language. Every recourse to words presupposes the comprehension of the primary signification, but this comprehension, before being interpreted as a "consciousness of," is society and obligation. Signification is the Infinite, but infinity does not present itself to a transcendental thought, nor even to meaningful activity, but presents itself in the Other; the Other faces me and puts me in question and *obliges* me by his essence qua infinity. That "something" we call signification arises in being with language because the essence of language is the relation with the Other. This relation is not added to the interior monologue—be it Merleau-Ponty's "corporeal intentionality"—like an address added to the fabricated object one puts in the mailbox; the welcoming of the being that appears in the face, the ethical event of sociality, already commands inward discourse. And the epiphany that is produced as a face is not constituted as are all other beings, precisely because it "reveals" infinity. Signification is infinity, that is, the Other. The intelligible is not a concept, but an intelligence. Signification precedes *Sinngebung,* and rather than justifying idealism, marks its limit.

In a sense signification is to perception what the symbol is to the object symbolized. The symbol marks the inadequateness of what is given in consciousness with regard to the being it symbolizes, a consciousness needy and hungry for the being it lacks, for the being announced in the very precision with which its absence is lived, a potency that evinces the act. Signification resembles it, as an overflowing of the intention that envisages by the being envisaged. But here the inexhaustible surplus of infinity overflows the actuality of consciousness. The shimmer of infinity, the face, can no longer be stated in terms of consciousness, in metaphors referring to light and the sensible. It is the ethical exigency of the face, which puts into question the consciousness that welcomes it. The consciousness of obligation is no longer a consciousness, since it tears consciousness up from its center, submitting it to the Other.

If the face to face founds language, if the face brings the first signification, establishes signification itself in being, then language does not only serve reason, but is reason. Reason in the sense of an impersonal legality does not permit us to account for discourse, for it absorbs the plurality of the interlocutors. Reason, being unique, cannot speak to another reason. A reason immanent in an individual consciousness is, to be sure, conceivable, in the way of naturalism, as a system of laws that regulate the nature of this consciousness, individuated like all natural beings but in addition individuated also as oneself. The concordance between consciousnesses would then be explained by the resemblance of beings constituted in the same fashion. Language would be reduced to a system of signs awakening, from one consciousness to the other, like thoughts. In that case one must disregard the intentionality of rational thought, which opens upon a universal order, and run all the risks of naturalist psychologism, against which the arguments of the first volume of the *Logische Untersuchungen* are ever valid.

Retreating from these consequences, and in order to conform oneself more to the "phenomenon," one can call reason the internal coherence of an ideal order realized in being in the measure that the individual consciousness, in which it is learnt or set up, would renounce its particularity as an individual and an ipseity, and either withdraw unto a noumenal sphere, from which it would exercise intemporally its role as absolute subject in the I think, or be reabsorbed in the universal order of the State, which at first it seemed to foresee or constitute. In both cases the role of language would be to dissolve the ipseity of individual consciousness, fundamentally antagonistic to reason, either to transform it into an "I think" which no longer speaks, or to make it disappear into its own discourse, whereupon, having entered into the State, it could only undergo the judgment of history, rather than remain me, that is, judge that history.

In such a rationalism there is no longer any society, that is, no longer any relation whose terms absolve themselves from the relation.

The Hegelians may attribute to human animality the consciousness of tyranny the individual feels before impersonal law, but they have yet to make understandable how a rational animal is possible, how the particularity of oneself can be affected by the simple universality of an idea, how an egoism can abdicate?

If, on the contrary, reason lives in language, if the first rationality gleams forth in the opposition of the face to face, if the first intelligible, the first signification, is the infinity of the intelligence that presents itself (that is, speaks to me) in the face, if reason is defined by signification rather than signification being defined by the impersonal structures of reason, if society precedes the apparition of these impersonal structures, if universality reigns as the presence of humanity in the eyes that look at me, if, finally, we recall that this look appeals to my responsibility and consecrates my freedom as responsibility and gift of self—then the pluralism of society could not disappear in the elevation to reason, but would be its condition. It is not the impersonal in me that Reason would establish, but an I myself capable of society, an I that has arisen in enjoyment as separated, but whose separation would itself be necessary for infinity *to be*—for its infinitude is accomplished as the "facing."

5. *Language and Objectivity*

A meaningful world is a world in which there is the Other through whom the world of my enjoyment becomes a theme having a significa-tion. Things acquire a rational signification, and not only one of simple usage, because an other is associated with my relations with them. In designating a thing I designate it to the Other. The act of designating modifies my relation of enjoyment and possession with things, places the things in the perspective of the Other. Utilizing a sign is therefore not limited to substituting an indirect relation for the direct relation with a thing, but permits me to render the things offerable, detach them from my own usage, alienate them, render them exterior. The word that designates things attests their apportionment between me and the others. The objectivity of the object does not follow from a suspension of usage and enjoyment, in which I possess things without assuming them. Objectivity results from language, which permits the putting into question of possession. This disengagement has a positive meaning: the entry of the thing into the sphere of the other. The thing becomes a theme. To thematize is to offer the world to the Other in speech. "Distance" with regard to the object thus exceeds its spatial signification.

This objectivity is correlative not of some trait in an isolated subject, but of his relation with the Other. Objectification is produced in the very work of language, where the subject is detached from the things possessed as though it hovered over its own existence, as though it were detached from it, as though the existnece it exists had not yet completely reached it. This distance is more radical than every distance in the world. The subject must find itself "at a distance" from its own being, even with regard to that taking distance that is inherent in the home, by which it is still in being. For negation remains within the totality, even when it bears upon the totality of the world. In order that objective distance be hollowed out, it is necessary that while in being the subject be not yet in being, that in a certain sense it be not yet born—that it not be in nature. If the subject capable of objectivity *is* not yet completely, this "not yet," this state of potency relative to act, does not denote a less than being, but denotes time. Consciousness of the object—thematization—rests on distance with regard to oneself, which can only be time; or, if one prefers, it rests on self-consciousness, if we recognize the "distance from self to self" in self-consciousness to be "time." However, time can designate a "not yet" that nevertheless would not be a "lesser being"—it can remain distant both from being and from death—only as the inexhaustible future of infinity, that is, as what is produced in the very relationship of language. In designating what it possesses to the other, in speaking, the subject hovers over its own existence. But it is from the welcoming of the infinity of the other that it receives the freedom with regard to itself that this dispossession requires. It detains it finally from the Desire which does not arise from a lack or a limitation but from a surplus, from the idea of Infinity.

Language makes possible the objectivity of objects and their thematization. Already Husserl affirmed that the objectivity of thought consists in being valid for everyone. To know objectively would therefore be to constitute my thought in such a way that it already contained a reference to the thought of the others. What I communicate therefore is already constituted in function of others. In speaking I do not transmit to the Other what is objective for me: the objective becomes objective only through communication. But in Husserl the Other who makes this communication possible is first constituted for a monadic thought. The basis of objectivity is constituted in a purely subjective process. In positing the relation with the Other as ethical, one surmounts a difficulty that would be inevitable if, contrary to Descartes, philosophy started from a *cogito* that would posit itself absolutely independently of the Other.

For the Cartesian *cogito* is discovered, at the end of the Third Meditation, to be supported on the certitude of the divine existence qua infinite, by relation to which the finitude of the *cogito,* or the doubt, is posited and conceivable. This finitude could not be determined without recourse to the infinite, as is the case in the moderns, for whom finitude is, for example, determined on the basis of the mortality of the subject. The Cartesian subject is given a point of view exterior to itself from which it can apprehend itself. If, in a first movement, Descartes takes a consciousness to be indubitable of itself by itself, in a second movement—the reflection on reflection—he recognizes conditions for this certitude. This certitude is due to the clarity and distinctness of the *cogito,* but certitude itself is sought because of the presence of infinity in this finite thought, which without this presence would be ignorant of its own finitude: ". . . *manifeste intelligo plus realitatis esse in substantia*

infinita quam in finita, ac proinde priorem quodammodo in me esse per-
ceptionem infiniti quam finiti, hoc est Dei quam mei ipsius. Qua enim
ratione intelligerem me dubitare me cupere, hoc est aliquid mihi deesse, et
me non esse omnino perfectum si nulla idea entis perfectionis in me esset,
ex cujus comparatione defectus meos cognoscerem?"[3]

Is the position of thought in the midst of the infinite that created it
and has given it the idea of infinity discovered by a reasoning or an
intuition that can posit only themes? The infinite can not be thematized, and the distinction between reasoning and intuition does not apply
to the access to infinity. Is not the relation with infinity, in the twofold
structure of infinity present to the finite, but present outside of the finite,
foreign to theory? We have seen in it the ethical relation. If Husserl
sees in the *cogito* a subjectivity without any support outside of itself, this
cogito constitutes the idea of infinity itself and gives it to itself as an
object. The non-constitution of infinity in Descartes leaves a door open;
the reference of the finite *cogito* to the infinity of God does not consist in
a simple thematization of God. I of myself account for every object; I
contain them. The idea of infinity is not for me an object. The
ontological argument lies in the mutation of this "object" into being, into
independence with regard to me; God is the other. If to think consists
in referring to an object, we must suppose that the thought of infinity is
not a thought. What is it positively? Descartes does not raise the
question. It is in any case evident that the intuition of infinity retains a
rationalist meaning, and will not become any sort of invasion of God
across an inward emotion. Decartes, better than an idealist or a realist,
discovers a relation with a total alterity irreducible to interiority, which
nevertheless does not do violence to interiority—a receptivity without
passivity, a relation between freedoms.

The last paragraph of the Third Meditation brings us to a relation
with infinity in thought which overflows thought and becomes a personal
relation. Contemplation turns into admiration, adoration, and joy. It

---

[3] Ed. Tannery, T. VII, pp. 45-6. ["... there is manifestly more reality in
the infinite substance than in the finite substance, and my awareness of the
infinite must therefore be in some way prior to my awareness of the finite,
that is to say, my awareness of God must be prior to that of myself. For
how could I know that I doubt and desire, i.e., know that something is lacking to me and that I am not wholly perfect, save by having in me the idea
of a being more perfect than myself, by comparison with which I may recognize my deficiencies." Eng. trans. by Norman Kemp Smith, Descartes, *Philosophical Writings* (New York, 1958), p. 205.]

is a question no longer of an "infinite object" still known and thematized, but of a majesty: *". . . placet hic aliquamdiu in ipsius Dei contemplatione immorari, eius attributa apud me expendere et immensi huius luminis pulchritudinem quantum caligantis ingenii mei acies ferre poterit, intueri, admirari, adorare. Ut enim in hac sola divinae majestatis contemplatione summan alterius vitae felicitatem consistere fide credimus, ita etiam jam ex eadem licet multo minus perfecta, maximum cujus in hac vita capaces simus voluptatem percipi posse experimur . . ."**

To us this paragraph appears to be not a stylistic ornament or a prudent hommage to religion, but the expression of this transformation of the idea of infinity conveyed by knowledge into Majesty approached as a face.

6. The Other and the Others

The presentation of the face, expression, does not disclose an inward world previously closed, adding thus a new region to comprehend or to take over.** On the contrary, it calls to me above and beyond the given that speech already puts in common among us. What one gives, what one takes reduces itself to the phenomenon, discovered and open to the grasp, carrying on an existence which is suspended in possession—whereas the presentation of the face puts me into relation with being. *The existing of this being,* irreducible to phenomenality understood as a reality without reality, is effectuated in the non-postponable urgency with which he requires a response. This response differs from the "reaction" that the given gives rise to in that it cannot remain "between us," as is the case with the steps I take with regard to a thing. Everything that takes place here "between us" concerns everyone, the face that looks at it places itself in the full light of the public order, even if I draw back from it to seek with the interlocutor the complicity of a private relation and a clandestinity.

---

* ". . . it seems to me right to linger for a while on the contemplation of this all-perfect God, to ponder at leisure His marvelous attributes, to intuit, to admire, to adore, the incomparable beauty of this inexhaustible light, so far at least as the powers of my mind may permit, dazzled as they are by what they are endeavoring to see. For just as by faith we believe that the supreme felicity of the life to come consists in the contemplation of the Divine majesty, so do we now experience that a similar meditation, though one so much less perfect, can enable us to enjoy the highest contentment of which we are capable in this present life." *Ibid.,* p. 211.

** ". . . à comprendre ou à prendre."

Language as the presence of the face does not invite complicity with the preferred being, the self-sufficient "I-Thou" forgetful of the universe; in its frankness it refuses the clandestinity of love, where it loses its frankness and meaning and turns into laughter or cooing. The third party looks at me in the eyes of the Other—language is justice. It is not that there first would be the face, and then the being it manifests or expresses would concern himself with justice; the epiphany of the face qua face opens humanity. The face in its nakedness as a face presents to me the destitution of the poor one and the stranger; but this poverty and exile which appeal to my powers, address me, do not deliver themselves over to these powers as givens, remain the expression of the face. The poor one, the stranger, presents himself as an equal. His equality within this essential poverty consists in referring to the *third party,* thus present at the encounter, whom in the midst of his destitution the Other already serves. He comes to *join* me. But he joins me to himself for service; he commands me as a Master. This command can concern me only inasmuch as I am master myself; consequently this command commands me to command. The *thou* is posited in front of a *we.* To be *we* is not to "jostle" one another or get together around a common task. The presence of the face, the infinity of the other, is a destituteness, a presence of the third party (that is, of the whole of humanity which looks at us), and a command that commands commanding. This is why the relation with the Other, discourse, is not only the putting in question of my freedom, the appeal coming from the other to call me to responsibility, is not only the speech by which I divest myself of the possession that encircles me by setting forth an objective and common world, but is also sermon, exhortation, the prophetic word. By essence the prophetic word responds to the epiphany of the face, doubles all discourse not as a discourse about moral themes, but as an irreducible movement of a discourse which by essence is aroused by the epiphany of the face inasmuch as it attests the presence of the third party, the whole of humanity, in the eyes that look at me. Like a shunt every social relation leads back to the presentation of the other to the same without the intermediary of any image or sign, solely by the expression of the face. When taken to be like a genus that unites like individuals the essence of society is lost sight of. There does indeed exist a human race as a biological genus, and the common function men may exercise in the world as a totality permits the applying to them of a common concept. But the human community instituted by language, where the interlocutors remain absolutely separated, does not constitute the unity of genus. It is stated as a kinship of men. That all men are brothers is not explained by their resemblance, nor by a common cause of which they would be the effect, like medals which refer to the same die that struck them. Paternity is not reducible to a causality in which individuals would mysteriously participate, and which would determine, by no less mysterious an effect, a phenomenon of solidarity.

It is my responsibility before a face looking at me as absolutely foreign (and the epiphany of the face coincides with these two moments) that constitutes the original fact of fraternity. Paternity is not a causality, but the establishment of a unicity with which the unicity of the father does and does not coincide.[4] The non-coincidence consists, concretely, in my position as brother; it implies other unicities at my side. Thus my unicity qua I contains both self-sufficiency of being and my partialness, my position before the other as a face. In this welcoming of the face (which is already my responsibility in his regard, and where accordingly he approaches me from a dimension of height and dominates me), equality is founded. Equality is produced where the other commands the same and reveals himself to the same in responsibility; otherwise it is but an abstract idea and a word. It cannot be detached from the welcoming of the face, of which it is a moment.

The very status of the human implies fraternity and the idea of the human race. Fraternity is radically opposed to the conception of a humanity united by resemblance, a multiplicity of diverse families arisen from the stones cast behind by Deucalion, and which, across the struggle of egoisms, results in a human city. Human fraternity has then two aspects: it involves individualities whose logical status is not reducible to the status of ultimate differences in a genus, for their singularity consists in each referring to itself. (An individual having a common genus with another individual would not be removed enough from it.) On the other hand, it involves the commonness of a father, as though the commonness of race would not bring together enough. Society must be a fraternal community to be commensurate with the straightforwardness, the primary proximity, in which the face presents itself to my welcome. Monotheism signifies this human kinship, this idea of a human race that refers back to the approach of the Other in the face, in a dimension of height, in responsibility for oneself and for the Other.

---

[4] See below, p. 278.

7. *The Asymmetry of the Interpersonal*

The presence of the face coming from beyond the world, but committing me to human fraternity, does not overwhelm me as a numinous essence arousing fear and trembling. To be in relationship while absolving oneself from this relation is to speak. The Other does not only *appear* in his face, as a phenomenon subject to the action and domination of a freedom; infinitely distant from the very relation he enters, he presents himself there from the first as an absolute. The I disengages itself from the relationship, but does so within relationship with a being absolutely separated. The face with which the Other turns to me is not reabsorbed in a representation of the face. To hear his destitution which cries out for justice is not to represent an image to oneself, but is to posit oneself as responsible, both as more and as less than the being that presents itself in the face. Less, for the face summons me to my obligations and judges me. The being that presents himself in the face comes from a dimension of height, a dimension of transcendence whereby he can present himself as a stranger without opposing me as obstacle or enemy. More, for my position as *I* consists in being able to respond to this essential destitution of the Other, finding resources for myself. The Other who dominates me in his transcendence is thus the stranger, the widow, and the orphan, to whom I am obligated.

These differences between the Other and me do not depend on different "properties" that would be inherent in the "I," on the one hand, and, on the other hand, in the Other, nor on different psychological dispositions which their minds would take on from the encounter. They are due to the I-Other conjuncture, to the inevitable *orientation* of being "starting from oneself" toward "the Other." The priority of this orientation over the terms that are placed in it (and which cannot arise without this orientation) summarizes the theses of the present work.

Being *is* not *first,* to afterwards, by breaking up, give place to a diversity all of whose terms would maintain reciprocal relations among themselves, exhibiting thus the totality from which they proceed, and in which there would on occasion be produced a being existing for itself, an I, facing another I (incidents that could be accounted for by an impersonal discourse exterior to those incidents). Not even the language that narrates it can depart from the orientation of the I to the Other. Language does not take place *in front of* a correlation from which the I would derive its identity and the Other his alterity. The separation involved in language does not denote the presence of two beings in an ethereal space where union simply echos separation. Separation is first the fact of a being that lives *somewhere,* from *something,* that is, that enjoys. The identity of the I comes to it from its egoism whose insular sufficiency is accomplished by enjoyment, and to which the face teaches the infinity from which this insular sufficiency is separated. This egoism is indeed founded on the infinitude of the other, which can be accomplished only by being produced as the idea of Infinity in a separated being. The other does indeed invoke this separated being, but this invocation is not reducible to calling for a correlative. It leaves room for a process of being that is deduced from itself, that is, remains separated and capable of shutting itself up against the very appeal that has aroused it, but also capable of welcoming this face of infinity with all the resources of its egoism: economically. Speech is not instituted in a homogeneous or abstract medium, but in a world where it is necessary to aid and to give. It presupposes an I, an existence separated in its enjoyment, which does not welcome empty-handed the face and its voice coming from another shore. Multiplicity in being, which refuses totalization but takes form as fraternity and discourse, is situated in a "space" essentially asymmetrical.

8. Will and Reason

Discourse conditions thought, for the first intelligible is not a concept, but an intelligence whose inviolable exteriority the face states in uttering the "you shall not commit murder." The essence of discourse is ethical. In stating this thesis, idealism is refused.

The idealist intelligible constitutes a system of coherent ideal relations whose presentation before the subject is equivalent to the entry of the subject into this order and its absorption into those ideal relations. The subject has no resource in itself that does not dry up under the intelligible sun. Its will is reason and its separation illusory (even though the possibility of illusion attests the existence of an at least subterranean subjective source which the intelligible cannot dry up).

Idealism completely carried out reduces all ethics to politics. The Other and the I function as elements of an ideal calculus, receive from this calculus their real being, and approach one another under the dominion of ideal necessities which traverse them from all sides. They play the role of moments in a system, and not that of origin. Political society appears as a plurality that expresses the multiplicity of the articulations of a system. In the kingdom of ends, where persons are indeed defined as wills, but where the will is defined as what permits itself to be affected by the universal—where the will wishes to be reason, be it practical reason —multiplicity rests in fact only on the hope of happiness. The so-called animal principle of happiness, ineluctable in the description of the will, even taken as practical reason, maintains pluralism in the society of minds.

In this world without multiplicity language loses all social significa- tion; interlocutors renounce their unicity not in desiring one another but in desiring the universal. Language would be equivalent to the constitution of rational institutions in which an impersonal reason which is already at work in the persons who speak and already sustains their effective reality would become objective and effective: each being is posited apart from all the others, but the will of each, or ipseity, from the start consists in willing the universal or the rational, that is, in negating its very particularity. In accomplishing its essence as discourse, in becoming a discourse universally coherent, language would at the same time realize the universal State, in which multiplicity is reabsorbed and discourse comes to an end, for lack of interlocutors.

To distinguish formally will and understanding, will and reason, nowise serves to maintain plurality in being or the unicity of the person if one forthwith decides to consider only the will that adheres to clear ideas or decides only through respect for the universal to be a good will. If the will can aspire to reason in one way or another, it is reason, reason seeking or forming itself; its true essence is revealed in Spinoza or in Hegel. This identification of will and reason, which is the ultimate intention of idealism, is opposed by the entire pathetic experience of humanity, which the Hegelian or Spinozist idealism relegates to the subjective or the imaginary. The interest of this opposition does not lie in the very protestation of the individual who refuses the system and reason, that is, in his arbitrariness, which the coherent discourse could hence not silence by persuasion—but in the affirmation that makes this opposition live. For the opposition does not consist in shutting one's eyes to being and thus striking one's head madly against the wall so as to surmount in oneself the consciousness of one's deficiencies of being, one's destitution, and one's exile, and so as to transform a humiliation into desperate pride. This opposition is inspired by the certainty of the sur- plus which an existence separated from and thus desiring the full or immutable being or being in act involves by relation to that being, *that is, the surplus that is produced by the society of infinity,* an incessant surplus that accomplishes the infinitude of infinity. The protestation against the identification of the will with reason does not indulge in arbitrariness, which, by its absurdity and immorality, would immediately justify this identification. It proceeds from the certitude that the ideal of a being accomplished from all eternity, thinking only itself, can not serve as the ontological touchstone for a life, a becoming, capable of renewal, of Desire, of society. Life is not comprehensible simply as a diminution, a fall, or an embryo or virtuality of being. The individual and the personal count and act independently of the universal, which would mould them. Moreover, the existence of the individual on the basis of the universal, or the fall from which it arises, remains unexplained. *The individual and the personal are necessary for Infinity to be able to be produced as infinite.*[5] The impossibility of treating life in function of being is manifested compellingly in Bergson, where duration no longer imitates, in its fallenness, an immobile eternity, or in Heidegger, where possibility no longer is referred to ἔργον as a δύναμις. Heidegger dissociates life from the finality of potency tending toward act. That there could be a more than being or an above being is expressed in the idea of creation which, in God, exceeds a being eternally satisfied with itself. But this notion of the being above being does not come from theology. If it has played no role in the Western philosophy issued from Aristotle, the Platonic idea of the Good ensures it the dignity of a philosophical thought—and it therefore should not be traced back to any oriental wisdom.

If the subjectivity were but a deficient mode of being, the distinguishing between will and reason would indeed result in conceiving the will as arbitrary, as a pure and simple negation of an embryonic or virtual reason dormant in an I, and consequently as a negation of that I and a violence in regard to oneself. If, on the contrary, the subjectivity is fixed as a separated being in relation with an other absolutely other, the Other, if the face brings the first signification, that is, the very upsurge of the rational, then the will is distinguished fundamentally from the intelligible, which it must not comprehend and into which it must not disappear, for the intelligibility of this intelligible resides precisely in ethical behavior, that is, in the responsibility to which it invites the will. The will is free to assume this responsibility in whatever sense it likes; it

---

[5] See below, "The Truth of the Will," pp. 240 ff.

is not free to refuse this responsibility itself; it is not free to ignore the meaningful world into which the face of the Other has introduced it. *In the welcoming of the face the will opens to reason.* Language is not limited to the maieutic awakening of thoughts common to beings. It does not accelerate the inward maturation of a reason common to all; it teaches and introduces the new into a thought. The introduction of the new into a thought, the idea of infinity, is the very work of reason. The absolutely new is the Other. The rational is not opposed to the experienced; absolute experience, the experience of what is in no way a priori, is reason itself. In discovering, as correlative of experience, the Other, him who, being in himself essentially, can speak, and nowise sets himself up as an object, the *novelty* contributed by experience is reconciled with the ancient Socratic exigency of a mind nothing can force, an exigency Leibniz again answers to in refusing the monads windows. The ethical presence is both other and imposes itself without violence. As the activity of reason commences with speech, the subject does not abdicate his unicity, but confirms his separation. He does not enter into his own discourse to disappear in it; it remains an apology. The passage to the rational is not a dis-individuation precisely because it is language, that is, a response to the being who in a face speaks to the subject and tolerates only a personal response, that is, an ethical act.

C. THE ETHICAL RELATION
AND TIME

1. Subjectivity and Pluralism

Separation, effected in the concrete as habitation and economy, makes possible the relation with the detached, absolute exteriority. This relation, metaphysics, is brought about primordially by the epiphany of the Other in the face. Separation opens up between terms that are absolute and yet in relation, that absolve themselves from the relation they maintain, that do not abdicate in it in favor of a totality this relation would sketch out. Thus the metaphysical relation realizes a multiple existing [un exister multiple]—a pluralism. But this relation would not realize pluralism if the formal structure of relationship exhausted the essence of relationship. We must explicate the power that beings placed in relation have of absolving themselves from the relation. This power entails a different sense of absolution for each of the separated terms; the Metaphysician is not absolute in the same sense as the Metaphysical. The dimension of height from which the Metaphysical comes to the Metaphysician indicates a sort of non-homogeneity of space, such that a radical multiplicity, distinct from numerical multiplicity, can here be produced. Numerical multiplicity remains defenseless against totalization. For a multiplicity to be able to be produced in the order of being, *disclosure* (where being does not only manifest itself, but effectuates itself, or exerts itself, or holds sway, or reigns) is not enough; it is not enough that its *production* radiate in the cold splendor of truth. In this splendor the diverse is united—under the panoramic look it calls for. Contemplation is itself absorbed into this totality, and precisely in this way founds that objective and eternal being or that "impassive nature resplendent in its eternal beauty" (according to Pushkin's expression), in which common sense recognizes the prototype of being, and which, for the philosopher, confers its prestige on totality. The subjectivity of knowledge cannot break with this totality, which is reflected in the subject or reflects the subject. The objective totality *remains exclusionary* of every *other,* despite its being laid bare, that is, despite its apparition to an other. Contemplation is to be defined, perhaps, as a process by which being is revealed without ceasing to be one. The philosophy it commands is a suppression of pluralism.

For a multiplicity to be maintained, there must be produced in it the subjectivity that could not seek congruence with the being in which it is produced. Being must hold sway as revealing itself, that is, in its very being flowing toward an I that approaches it, but flowing toward it infinitely without running dry, burning without being consumed. But this approach can not be conceived as a cognition in which the knowing subject is reflected and absorbed. That would be to forthwith destroy this exteriority of being by a total reflection—which cognition aims at. The impossibility of total reflection must not be posited negatively—as the finitude of a knowing subject who, being mortal and already engaged in the world, does not reach truth—but rather as the *surplus* of the social relation, where the subjectivity remains in face of . . . , in the straight-forwardness of this welcome, and is not measured by truth. The social relation itself is not just another relation, one among so many others that can be produced in being, but is its ultimate event. The very utterance by which I state it and whose claim to truth, postulating a total reflection, refutes the unsurpassable character of the face to face relation, nonetheless confirms it by the very fact of stating this truth—of telling it to the Other. Multiplicity therefore implies an objectivity posited in the impossibility of total reflection, in the impossibility of conjoining the I and the non-I in a whole. This impossibility is not negative—which would be to still posit it by reference to the idea of truth contemplated. It results from the surplus of the epiphany of the other, who dominates me from his height.

This foundation of pluralism does not congeal in isolation the terms that constitute the plurality. While maintaining them against the total-ity that would absorb them, it leaves them in commerce or in war. At no moment are they posited as causes of themselves—which would be to remove from them all receptivity and all activity, shut them up each in its own interiority, and isolate them like the Epicurean gods living in the interstices of being, or like the gods immobilized in the between-time[1] of

---

[1] Cf. our article "La réalité et son ombre," *Les Temps modernes,* Nov., 1948.

art, left for all eternity on the edge of the interval, at the threshold of a future that is never produced, statues looking at one another with empty eyes, idols which, contrary to Gyges, are exposed and do not see. Our analyses of separation have opened another perspective. The primordial form of this multiplicity is not, however, produced as war, nor as commerce. War and commerce presuppose the face and the transcendence of the being appearing in the face. War can not be derived from the empirical fact of the multiplicity of beings that limit one another, under the pretext that where the presence of the one inevitably limits the other, violence is identical with this limitation. Limitation is not of itself violence. Limitation is conceivable only within a totality where the parts mutually define one another. Definition, far from doing violence to the identity of the terms united into a totality, ensures this identity. The limit separates and unites in a whole. The reality fragmented into concepts that mutually limit one another forms a totality by virtue of that very fragmentation. As a play of antagonistic forces the world forms a whole, and is deducible or should be deducible, in a completed scientific thought, from one unique formula. What one is tempted to call antagonism of forces or of concepts presupposes a subjective perspective, and a pluralism of wills. The point at which this perspective converges does not form a part of the totality. Violence in nature thus refers to an existence precisely not limited by an other, an existence that maintains itself outside of the totality. But the exclusion of violence by beings susceptible of being integrated into a totality is not equivalent to peace. Totality absorbs the multiplicity of beings, which peace implies. Only beings capable of war can rise to peace. War like peace presupposes beings structured otherwise than as parts of a totality.

War therefore is to be distinguished from the logical opposition of the *one* and the *other* by which both are defined within a totality open to a panoramic view, to which they would owe their very opposition. In war beings refuse to belong to a totality, refuse community, refuse law; no frontier stops one being by another, nor defines them. They affirm themselves as transcending the totality, each identifying itself not by its place in the whole, but by its *self*.

War presupposes the transcendence of the antagonist; it is waged against man. It is surrounded with honors and pays the last honors; it aims at a presence that comes always from elsewhere, a being that appears in a face. It is neither the hunt nor struggle with an element. The possibility, retained by the adversary, of thwarting the best laid calculations expresses the separation, the breach of totality, across which the adversaries approach one another. The warrior runs a risk; no logistics guarantees victory. The calculations that make possible the determination of the outcome of a play of forces within a totality do not decide war. It lies at the limit of a supreme confidence in oneself and a supreme risk. It is a relation between beings exterior to totality, which hence are not in touch with one another.

But would the violence that is impossible among beings ready to constitute a totality—that is, to reconstitute it—then be possible among separated beings? How could separated beings maintain any relation, even violence? It is that the refusal of totality in war does not refuse relationship—since in war the adversaries seek out one another.

Relationship between separated being would indeed be absurd were the terms posited as substances, each *causa sui,* since, as pure activities, capable of receiving no action, the terms could undergo no violence. But the relation of violence does not remain at the level of the wholly formal conjuncture of relationship. It implies a specific structure of the terms in relation. Violence bears upon only a being both graspable and escaping every hold. Without this living contradiction in the being that undergoes violence the deployment of violent force would reduce itself to a labor.

Thus for relationship between separated beings to be possible, the multiple terms would have to be partially independent and partially in relation. The notion of finite freedom then imposes itself to reflection. But how is such a notion to be formed? To say that a being is partially free immediately raises the problem of the relation existing in it between the free part, *causa sui,* and the non-free part. To say that the free part is impeded in the non-free part would bring us back indefinitely to the same difficulty: how can the free part, *causa sui,* undergo anything whatever from the non-free part? The finitude of freedom must therefore not signify some limit within the substance of the free being, divided into one part endowed with a causality of its own and one part subject to exterior causes. The notion of independence must be grasped elsewhere than in causality. Independence would not be equivalent to the idea of *causa sui,* which, moreover, is belied by birth, non-chosen and impossible to choose (the great drama of contemporary thought), which situates the will in an anarchic world, that is, a world without origin.

Thus freedom, an abstraction that reveals itself to be self-contradictory when one supposes it to have a limitation, can not describe beings in the relation that does not constitute totality, beings in war.

A being independent of and yet at the same time exposed to the other is a temporal being: to the inevitable violence of death it opposes its time, which is postponement itself. It is not finite freedom that makes the notion of time intelligible; it is time that gives a meaning to the notion of **finite freedom.** Time is precisely the fact that the whole existence of the mortal being—exposed to violence—is not being for death, but the "not yet" which is a way of being against death, a retreat before death in the very midst of its inexorable approach. In war death is brought to what is moving back, to what *for the moment* exists completely. Thus in war the reality of the time that separates a being from its death, the reality of a being taking up a position with regard to death, that is, the reality of a conscious being and its interiority, is recognized. As *causa sui* or freedom beings would be immortal, and could not, in a kind of dumb and absurd hatred,* grapple on to one another. Were beings only given over to violence, only mortal, they would be dead in a world where nothing opposes anything, a world whose time would break up into eternity. The notion of a mortal but temporal being, apprehended in the will (a notion we shall develop) differs fundamentally from every causality leading to the idea of the *causa sui.* Such a being is exposed, but also opposed to violence. Violence does not befall it as an accident that befalls a sovereign freedom. The hold that violence has over this being—the mortality of this being—is the primordial fact. Freedom itself is but its adjournment by time. What is at issue is not finite freedom in which a singular compound of activity and passivity would be produced, but rather a freedom originally null, offered in death to the other, but in which time arises as a détente: the free will is necessity relaxed and postponed rather than finite freedom. It is détente or distension—postponement by virtue of which nothing is definitive yet, nothing consummated, skill which finds for itself a dimension of retreat there where the inexorable is imminent.

The contact of the soul with the body it has at its disposal is inverted into the non-contact of a blow struck in the void. The adversary's skill, which cannot be summed up in forces, has to be taken into account—but how take it into account? My skill postpones the inevitable. To hit, the blow must be struck there where the adversary has absented himself; to be parried, I have to pull back from the point at which he

---

* ". . . haine sourde et absurde . . ."

touches me. Ruse and ambush—Ulysses' craft—constitute the essence of war. This skill is inscribed in the very existence of the body; it is suppleness—a simultaneity of absence and presence. Corporeity is the mode of existence of a being whose presence is postponed at the very moment of his presence. Such a distension in the tension of the instant can only come from an infinite dimension which separates me from the other, both present and still to come, a dimension opened by the face of the Other. War can be produced only when a being postponing its death is exposed to violence. It can be produced only where discourse was possible: discourse subtends war itself. Moreover violence does not aim simply at disposing of the other as one disposes of a thing, but, already at the limit of murder, it proceeds from unlimited negation. It can aim at only a presence itself infinite despite its insertion in the field of my powers. Violence can aim only at a face.

It is therefore not freedom that accounts for the transcendence of the Other, but the transcendence of the Other that accounts for freedom—a transcendence of the Other with regard to me which, being infinite, does not have the same signification as my transcendence with regard to him. The risk that war involves measures the distance that separates bodies within their hand-to-hand struggle. The Other, in the hands of forces that break him, exposed to powers, remains unforeseeable, that is, transcendent. This transcendence is not to be described negatively, but is manifested positively in the moral resistance of the face to the violence of murder. The force of the Other is already and henceforth moral. Freedom, be it that of war, can be manifested only outside totality, but this "outside totality" opens with the transcendence of the face. To think of freedom as *within* totality is to reduce freedom to the status of an indetermination in being, and forthwith to integrate it into a totality by closing the totality over the "holes" of indetermination—and seeking with psychology the laws of a free being!

But the relation that subtends war, an asymmetrical relation with the other who, as infinity, opens time, transcends and dominates the subjectivity (the I not being transcendent with regard to the other in the same sense that the other is transcendent with regard to me), can take on the aspect of a symmetrical relation. The face, whose ethical epiphany consists in soliciting a response (which the violence of war and its murderous negation alone can seek to reduce to silence), is not satisfied with a "good intention" and a benevolence wholly Platonic. The "good intention" and the "benevolence wholly Platonic" are only the residue of an attitude assumed where one enjoys things, where one can divest one-self of them and offer them.   Henceforth the independence of the I and its position before the absolutely other can figure in a history and a politics.   Separation is embedded in an order in which the asymmetry of the interpersonal relation is effaced, where I and the other become interchangeable in commerce, and where the particular man, an individuation of the genus man, appearing in history, is substituted for the I and for the other.

Separation is not effaced in this ambiguity.   We must now show in what concrete form the freedom of separation is lost, and in what sense it is maintained even in its very loss, and can resurrect.

2. *Commerce, the Historical Relation, and the Face*

The will at work ensures the separated being's *being at home with itself*.   But in its work, which has a signification but remains mute, the will remains unexpressed.   Labor, in which it is exerted, is visibly inserted in the things, but the will forthwith absents itself from them, since works take on the anonymity of merchandise, an anonymity into which, as a wage-earner, the worker himself may disappear.

The separated being can, to be sure, shut itself up in its interiority.   Things can not counter it absolutely, and Epicurean wisdom lives from this truth.   But the will, whereby a being wields itself by somehow holding in its own hands all the strings that operate its being, is by its work exposed to the Other.   Its exertion is seen as a thing, if only by virtue of the insertion of its body in the world of things.   Corporeity thus describes the ontological regime of a primary self-alienation, con-temporaneous with the very event by which the self ensures, against the unknown factor of the elements, its own independence, that is, its self-possession or its security.   The will equivalent to atheism—which refuses the Other as an influence being exerted on an I or holding it in its invisible meshes, which refuses the Other as a God inhabiting the I—the will which tears itself from this possession, from this enthusiasm, as the very power of rupture, delivers itself over to the Other in its work, the very work which permits it to ensure its interiority.   Interiority thus does not exhaust the existence of the separated being.

The idea of *fatum* accounted for the reversal every heroism in a role suffers.   The hero finds himself playing a role in a drama exceeding his heroic intentions, which, by their very opposition to that drama, hasten the accomplishment of designs foreign to them. The absurdity of the *fatum* foils the sovereign will. In fact inscription in a foreign will is produced through the mediation of the work, which separates itself from its author, his intentions, and his possession, and which another will lays hold of. The labor which brings being into our possession ipso facto relinquishes it, is in the very sovereignty of its powers unceremoniously delivered over to the Other.

Every will separates itself from its work. The movement proper to action consists in issuing in the unknown—in not being able to measure all its consequences. The unknown does not result from a factual ignorance; the unknown upon which action issues resists all knowledge, does not stand out in the light, since it represents the meaning the work receives from the other. The other can dispossess me of my work, take it or buy it, and thus direct my very behavior; I am exposed to instigation. The work is destined to this alien *Sinngebung* from the moment of its origin in me. It is to be emphasized that this destination of the work to a history that I cannot foresee—for I cannot see it—is inscribed in the very essence of my power, and does not result from the contingent presence of other persons alongside of me.

Power is not entirely one with its own impetus, does not accompany its work up to the end. A separation opens between the producer and the product. At a given moment the producer no longer *follows up*, remains behind. His transcendence stops mid-way. In contrast with the transcendence of expression, in which the being that expresses himself personally attends the work of expression, production attests the author of the work in his absence, as a plastic form. This inexpressive character of the product is reflected positively in its market value, in its suitability for others, in its capability to assume the meaning others will give it, to enter into an entirely different context from that which engendered it. The work does not defend itself against the Other's *Sinngebung*, and exposes the will that produced it to contestation and unrecognition; it lends itself to the designs of a foreign will and allows itself to be appropriated. The willing of the living will *postpones* this subjection, and accordingly wills against the Other and his threat. But this way a will plays in history a role it has not willed marks the limits of interiority: the will finds itself caught up in events that will appear only to the historian. Historical events link up in works. Wills without works will constitute no history; there is no purely interior history. History, in which the interiority of each will manifests itself only in plastic form—in the muteness of products—is an economic history. In history the will is congealed into a personage interpreted on the basis of his work, in which the essential of the will productive of things, dependent on things, but struggling against this dependence which delivers it to the Other, is obscured. As long as the will, in a being who speaks, takes up again and defends his work against a foreign will, history lacks the distance it lives from. Its reign commences in the world of realities-results, the world of "complete works," the heritage of dead wills.

The whole being of willing is hence not enacted within oneself. The capacity of the independent I does not contain its own being; willing escapes willing. The work is always in a certain sense an abortive action. I am not entirely what I want to do. Thus there lies open an unlimited field of investigation for psychoanalysis or sociology, which apprehend the will on the basis of its apparition in the work, in its behavior, or in its products.

The order hostile to the will dispossessed of its work, from which the willing is thus turned, depends on foreign wills. The work has a meaning for other wills; it can serve another and eventually turn against its author. The "misconstruction" acquired by the result of the will that has withdrawn from its work is due to the will that has survived. The absurd has a meaning for someone. Fate does not precede history; it follows it. Fate is the history of the historiographers, accounts of the survivors, who interpret, that is, utilize the works of the dead. The historical distance which makes this historiography, this violence, this subjection possible is proportionate to the time necessary for the will to lose its work completely. Historiography recounts the way the survivors appropriate the works of dead wills to themselves; it rests on the usurpation carried out by the conquerors, that is, by the survivors; it recounts enslavement, forgetting the life that struggles against slavery.

The fact that the will escapes itself, that the will does not contain itself, amounts to the possibility the others have of laying hold of the work, alienating, acquiring, buying, stealing it. The will itself thus takes on a meaning for the other, as though it were a thing. In the historical relation one will, to be sure, does not approach another as a thing. This relation does not resemble that which characterizes labor: in commerce and war the relation with the work remains a relation with the worker. But across the gold that buys him or the steel that kills him the Other is not approached face to face; even though they traverse the interval of a transcendence commerce aims at the anonymous market, war is waged against a mass. Material things, bread and wine, clothing and the home, like the blade of steel, have a hold on the "for itself" of the will. The part of eternal truth that materialism involves lies in the fact that the human will can be laid hold of in its works. The point of the sword, a physical reality, can exclude a meaningful activity, a subject, a "for itself," from the world. This great banality is nonetheless most astonishing: the for itself of the will, unshakeable in its happiness, is exposed to violence; spontaneity *undergoes,* turns into its contrary. The steel touches not an inert being, the gold attracts not a thing but a will which qua will, qua "for itself," should have been immune from every attack. Violence recognizes, but bends the will. Threat and seduction act by slipping into the interstice that separates the work from the will. Violence is corruption—seduction and threat, where the will is betrayed. This status of the will is the body.

The body exceeds the categories of a thing, but does not coincide with the role of "lived body" ["corps propre"] which I dispose of in my voluntary action and by which *I can.* The ambiguity of corporeal resistance which turns into a means and from means turns into a resistance does not account for its ontological *hybris.* The body in its very activity, in its for itself, inverts into a thing to be treated as a thing. This is what we express concretely in saying that it abides between health and sickness. Through it one not only fails to recognize, one can mistreat the "for itself" of the person; one does not only offend him, one coerces him. "I am anything you like," says Sganarelle, under the blows. One does not adopt successively and independently the biological point of view on it and the "point of view" which from the interior maintains it as a lived body; the originality of the body consists of the coinciding of two points of view. This is the paradox and the essence of time itself proceeding unto death, where the will is affected as a thing by the things —by the point of steel or by the chemistry of the tissues (due to a murderer or to the impotency of the doctors)—but gives itself a reprieve and postpones the contact by the against-death of postponement. The will essentially violable harbors treason in its own essence. It is not only offendable in its dignity—which would confirm its inviolable character —but is susceptible of being coerced and enslaved as a will, becoming a servile soul. Gold and threats force it not only to sell its products but to sell itself. Or again, the human will is not heroic.

The corporeity of the will must be understood on the basis of this ambiguity of voluntary power, exposing itself to the others in its centripetal movement of egoism. The body is its ontological regime, and not an object. The body, where expression can dawn forth and where the egoism of the will becomes discourse and primal opposition, at the same time conveys the entry of the I into the calculations of the Other. An interaction of wills or a history then becomes possible—an interaction of wills each defined as *causa sui*, since action upon a pure activity would presuppose a passivity in that activity. The ambiguity of the ontological regime of the body is founded in mortality, which we shall treat of below.

But is not total independence of the will realized in courage? Courage, the power to face death, at first sight does seem to carry out the total independence of the will; he who has accepted his death remains exposed to the violence of the assassin, but does he not refuse his consent to a foreign will to the end? —Unless the Other wills that very death. Then, while refusing consent, the will gives satisfaction to the foreign will in spite of itself, by the result of its behavior, precisely by its *work*. In the extreme situation of the struggle unto death the refusal to acquiese to a foreign will can revert into satisfaction given to this hostile will. The acceptance of death therefore does not enable me to resist with certainty the murderous will of the Other. Absolute dissention with a foreign will does not preclude the carrying out of his designs. Refusing to serve another by one's life does not preclude serving him by one's death. The being that wills does not exhaust the destiny of his existence in his will. This destiny does not necessarily imply a tragedy, for resolute opposition to the foreign will is, perhaps, madness, since one can speak to the Other and desire him.

The Other's designs do not present themselves to me as do the laws of things. His schemes show themselves to be inconvertible into data of a problem, which the will might calculate. The will that refuses the foreign will is obliged to recognize this foreign will as absolutely exterior, as untranslatable into thoughts that would be immanent in itself. Whatever be the extension of my thoughts, limited by nothing, the Other cannot be contained by me: he is unthinkable—he is infinite and recognized as such. This recognition is not produced again as a thought, but is produced as morality. The total refusal of the other, the will preferring death to servitude, annihilating its own existence in order to cut short every relation with the exterior, cannot prevent this work, which does not express him, from which he absents himself (for it is not a word), from being entered in this alien reckoning, which it defies, but recognizes precisely in its supreme courage. By its work the sovereign and self-enclosed will confirms the foreign will it means to ignore, and finds itself "made game of" by the Other. Thus a plane is manifested in which the will, though it have broken with participation, finds itself inscribed, and in which, in spite of itself, impersonally, even its supreme initiative, the breaking with being, is transcribed. In its effort to escape the Other in dying, it recognizes the other. The suicide to which it resolves itself in order to escape servitude is inseparable from the pain of "losing," whereas this death should have shown the absurdity of every game. Macbeth wishes for the destruction of the world in his defeat and his death ("and wish th'estate o'th'world were now undone")—or more profoundly still, he wishes that the nothingness of death be a void as total as that which would have reigned had the world never been created.

And yet in its separation from the work and in the possible betrayal that threatens it in the course of its very exercise, the will becomes aware of this betrayal and thereby keeps itself at a distance from it. Thus, faithful to itself, it remains in a certain sense inviolable, escapes its own history, and renews itself. There is no inward history. The inwardness of the will posits itself subject to a jurisdiction which scrutinizes its intentions, before which the meaning of its being coincides totally with its inward will. The volitions of the will do not weigh on it, and from the jurisdiction to which it opens comes pardon, the power to efface, to absolve, to undo history. The will thus moves between its betrayal and its fidelity which, simultaneous, describe the very originality of its power. But the fidelity does not forget the betrayal—and the religious will remains a relation with the Other. Fidelity is won by repentance and prayer (a privileged word in which the will seeks its fidelity to itself); and the pardon which ensures it this fidelity comes to it from the outside. Hence the rights of the inward will, its certitude of being a misunderstood will, still reveal a relation with exteriority. The will awaits its investiture and pardon. It awaits them from an exterior will, but one from which it would experience no longer shock but judgment, an exteriority withdrawn from the antagonism of wills, withdrawn from history. This possibility of justification and pardon, as religious consciousness in which interiority tends to coincide with being, opens before the Other, to whom I can speak. I speak a word that, in the measure that it welcomes the Other as Other, offers or sacrifices to him a product of labor, and consequently does not play above economy. Thus we see expression, the other extremity of the voluntary power that is separated from its work and betrayed by it, nonetheless referring to the inexpressive work by which the will, free with regard to history, partakes of history.

The will, in which the identity of the same holds sway in its fidelity to itself and in its betrayal, does not result from the empirical accident that would have placed a being in the midst of a multiplicity of beings which contest its identity. The will contains this duality of betrayal and fidelity in its mortality, which is produced or holds sway in its corporeity. A being in which multiplicity does not designate the simple divisibility of a whole into parts nor the simple unity of number of the gods living each for itself in the interstices between beings requires mortality and corporeity. For otherwise either the imperialist will would reconstitute a whole, or, as a physical body, neither mortal nor immortal, it would form a simple block. The postponement of death in a mortal will—time—is the mode of existence and reality of a separated being that has entered into relation with the Other. This space of time has to be taken as the point of departure. In it is enacted a meaningful life which one must not measure against an ideal of eternity, taking its duration and its interests to be absurd or illusory.

3. The Will and Death

Death is interpreted in the whole philosophical and religious tradition either as a passage to nothingness or as a passage to another existence, continuing in a new setting. It is thought within the alternative of being and nothingness, which is accredited by the death of our relatives, who do indeed cease to exist in the empirical world, which, for this world, means disappearance or departure. More profoundly and as it were a priori we approach death as nothingness in the passion for murder. The spontaneous intentionality of this passion aims at annihilation. Cain, when he slew Abel, should have possessed this knowledge of death. The identifying of death with nothingness befits the death of the other in murder. But at the same time this nothingness presents itself there as a sort of impossibility. For the Other cannot present himself as Other outside of my conscience, and his face expresses my moral impossibility of annihilating. This interdiction is to be sure not equivalent to pure and simple impossibility, and even presupposes the possibility which precisely it forbids—but in fact the interdiction already dwells in this very possibility rather than presupposing it; it is not added to it after the event, but looks at me from the very depths of the eyes I want to extinguish, looks at me as the eye that in the tomb shall look at Cain. The movement of annihilation in murder is therefore a purely relative annihilation, a passage to the limit of a negation attempted within the world. In fact it leads us toward an order of which we can say nothing, not even being, antithesis of the impossible nothingness.

One might wonder that we contest here the truth of the thought that situates death either in nothingness or in being, as though the alternative of being and nothingness were not ultimate. Shall we deny that *tertium non datur?*

And yet my relation with my own death places me before a category that does not enter into either term of this alternative. The sense of my death is contained in the refusal of this ultimate alternative. My death is not deduced from the death of the others by analogy; it is inscribed in the fear I can have for my being. The "knowledge" of the threatening precedes every experience reasoned in terms of the death of the Other; in naturalist language this is termed an instinctive knowledge of death. It is not the knowledge of death that defines menace; it is in the imminence of death, in its irreducible oncoming movement, that menace originally consists, that the "knowledge of death" is (if one may put it so) uttered and articulated. Fear measures this movement. The imminence of the menace does not come from a precise point of the future. *Ultima latet.* The unforeseeable character of the ultimate instant is not due to an empirical ignorance, to the limited horizon of our understanding, which a greater understanding would have been able to overcome. The unforeseeable character of death is due to the fact that it does not lie within any horizon. It is not open to grasp. It takes me without leaving me the chance I have in a struggle, for in reciprocal struggle I grasp what takes hold of me. In death I am exposed to absolute violence, to murder in the night. But in fact already in struggle I contend with the invisible. Struggle must not be confounded with the collision of two forces whose issue one can foresee and calculate. Struggle is already, or again, *war,* where between the forces that confront one another gapes open the interval of transcendence across which death comes and strikes without being received. The Other, inseparable from the very event of transcendence, is situated in the region from which death, possibly murder, comes. The unwonted hour of its coming approaches as the hour of fate fixed by someone. Hostile and malevolant powers, more wily, more clever than I, absolutely other and only thereby hostile, retain its secret. Death, in its absurdity, maintains an interpersonal order, in which it tends to take on a signification—as in the primitive mentality where, according to Levy-Bruhl, it is never natural, but requires a magical explanation. The things that bring death to me, being graspable and subject to labor, obstacles rather than menaces, refer to a malevolence, are the residue of a bad will which surprises and stalks. Death threatens me from beyond. This unknown that frightens, the silence of the infinite spaces that terrify, comes from the other, and this alterity, precisely as absolute, strikes me in an evil design or in a judgment of justice. The solitude of death does not make the Other vanish, but remains in a consciousness of hostility, and consequently still renders possible an appeal to the Other, to his friendship and his medication. The doctor is an a priori principle of human mortality. Death approaches in the fear of someone, and hopes in someone. "The Eternal brings death and brings life." A social conjuncture is maintained in this menace. It does not sink into the anxiety that would transform it into a "nihilation of nothingness." In the being for death of fear I am not faced with nothingness, but faced with what is *against me,* as though murder, rather than being one of the occasions of dying, were inseparable from the essence of death, as though the approach of death remained one of the modalities of the relation with the Other. The violence of death threatens as a tyranny, as though proceeding from a foreign will. The order of necessity that is carried out in death is not like an implacable law of determinism governing a totality, but is rather like the alienation of my will by the Other. It is, of course, not a question of inserting death into a primitive (or developed) religious system that would explain it; but it is a question of showing, behind the threat it brings against the will, its reference to an interpersonal order whose signification it does not annihilate.

One does not know when death will come. What will come? With what does death threaten me? With nothingness or with recommencement? I do not know. In this impossibility of knowing the after my death resides the essence of the last moment. I can absolutely not apprehend the moment of death; it is "out of reach," as Montaigne would say. *Ultima latet*—contrary to all the instants of my life, which are spread out between my birth and my death, and which can be recalled or anticipated. My death comes from an instant upon which I can in no way exercise my power. I do not run up against an obstacle which at least I touch in that collision, which, in surmounting or in enduring it, I integrate into my life, suspending its alterity. Death is a menace that approaches me as a mystery; its secrecy determines it—it approaches without being able to be assumed, such that the time that separates me from my death dwindles and dwindles without end, involves a sort of last interval which my consciousness cannot traverse, and where a leap will somehow be produced from death to me. The last part of the route will be crossed without me; the time of death flows upstream; the I in its projection toward the future is overturned by a movement of imminence, pure menace, which comes to me from an absolute alterity. Thus in a tale by Edgar Allen Poe, as the walls that imprison the narrator close in inexorably, he looks upon death with a look which as a look has always an expanse before it, but perceives also the uninterrupted approach of an instant infinitely future for the I who awaits it—*ultima latet*—which, in a countercurrent movement, will efface this infinitesimal—but untraversable—distance. This interference of movements across the distance that separates me from the last moment distinguishes the temporal interval from spatial distance.

But imminence is at the same time menace and postponement. It pushes on, and it leaves time. To be temporal is both to be for death and to still have time, to be against death. In the way the menace affects me in imminence resides my being implicated by the menace, and the essence of fear. It is a relation with an instant whose exceptional character is due not to the fact that it is at the threshold of nothingness or of a rebirth, but to the fact that, in life, it is the impossibility of every possibility, the stroke of a total passivity alongside of which the passivity of the sensibility, which moves into activity, is but a distant imitation. Thus the fear for my being which is my relation with death is not the fear of nothingness, but the fear of violence—and thus it extends into fear of the Other, of the absolutely unforeseeable.

It is in mortality that the interaction of the psychic and the physical appears in its primordial form. The interaction of the physical and the psychic, when approached from the psychic, posited as for itself or as *causa sui,* and from the physical, posited as unfolding in function of the "other," gives rise to a problem due to the abstraction to which the terms in relation are reduced. Mortality is the concrete and primary phenomenon. It forbids the positing of a for itself that would not be already delivered over to the Other and consequently be a *thing.* The for itself, essentially mortal, does not only represent things to itself, but is subject to them.

But if the will is mortal and susceptible to violence from a blade of steel, from the chemistry of poison, from hunger and thirst, if it is a body maintaining itself between health and sickness, this is not only because it would be surrounded by nothingness. This nothingness is an interval beyond which lurks a hostile will. I am a passivity threatened not only by nothingness in my being, but by a will in my will. In my action, in the for itself of my will, I am exposed to a foreign will. This is why death cannot drain all meaning from life. I am exposed not merely because of a Pascalian diversion, or a fall into the anonymity of everyday life in the Heideggerian sense of the term. The enemy or the God over whom I can have no power* and who does not form a *part* of my world remains yet in relation with me and permits me to will, but with a will that is not egoist, a will that flows into the essence of desire whose center of gravitation does not coincide with the I of need, the desire that is for the Other. Murder, at the origin of death, reveals a cruel world, but one to the scale of human relations. The will, already betrayal and alienation of itself but postponing this betrayal, on the way to death but a death ever future, exposed to death but not *immediately,* has time to be for the Other, and thus to recover meaning despite death. This existence for the Other, this Desire of the other, this goodness liberated from the egoist gravitation, nonetheless retains a personal character. The being thus defined has its time at its disposal precisely because it postpones violence, that is, because a meaningful order subsists beyond death, and thus all the possibilities of discourse are not reduced to desperate blows of a head struck against the wall. The Desire into which the threatened will dissolves no longer defends the powers of a will, but, as the goodness whose meaning death cannot efface, has its center outside of itself. We shall have to show this in the course of bringing to light the other chance that the will seizes upon in the time left it by its being against death: the founding of institutions in which the will ensures a meaningful, but impersonal world beyond death.

4. Time and the Will: Patience

In affirming that the human will is not heroic we have not declared for human cowardice, but have indicated the precarity of courage, always on the verge of its own failure by reason of the essential mortality of the

---

* "Je ne peux pouvoir"—the power meant here is that primordial ability of the "I can" that holds sway in the "I know."—Trans.

will, which in its exercise betrays itself. But in this very failing we have caught sight of the marvel of time, as futurition and postponement of this expiration. The will combines a contradiction: an immunity from every exterior attack to the point of positing itself as uncreated and immortal, endowed with a force above every quantifiable force (nothing less is attested by the self-consciousness in which the inviolable being takes refuge: "Not for eternity will I waver")—and the permanent fallibility of this inviolable sovereignty, to the point that voluntary being lends itself to techniques of seduction, propaganda, and torture. The will can succumb to tyrannical pressure and corruption, as though only the quantity of energy it puts forth to resist or the quantity of energy exerted upon it distinguished cowardice from courage. When the will triumphs over its passions, it manifests itself not only as the strongest passion, but as above all passion, determining itself by itself, inviolable. But when it has succumbed, it reveals itself to be exposed to influences, to be a force of nature, absolutely tractable, resolving itself purely and simply into its components. In its self-consciousness it is violated. Its "freedom of thought" is extinguished: the pressure of forces initially adverse ends up appearing as a penchant. In a sort of inversion it loses even the consciousness of the bent of its penchants. The will remains on this moving limit between inviolability and degeneration.

This inversion is more radical than sin, for it threatens the will in its very structure as a will, in its dignity as *origin* and identity. But at the same time this inversion is infinitely less radical, for it only threatens, is indefinitely postponed, is consciousness. Consciousness is resistance to violence, because it leaves the time necessary to forestall it. Human freedom resides in the future, always still minimally future, of its non-freedom, in consciousness—the prevision of the violence imminent in the time that still remains. To be conscious is to have time—not to overflow the present by anticipating and hastening the future, but to have a distance with regard to the present: to relate oneself to being as to a being to come, to maintain a distance with regard to being even while already coming under its grip. To be free is to have time to forestall one's own abdication under the threat of violence.

By virtue of time, the being defined, that is, self-identical, by reason of its place within the whole, the natural being (for birth describes precisely the entry into the whole that preexists and outlives), has not yet reached its term, remains at a distance from itself, is still preparatory, in the vestibule of being, still this side of the fatality of the non-chosen birth, not yet accomplished. The being defined by its birth can thus take up a position with regard to its nature; it disposes of a background and, in this sense, is not completely born, remains anterior to its definition or its nature. One instant does not link up with another to form a present. The identity of the present splits up into an inexhausible multiplicity of possibles that suspend the instant. And this gives meaning to initiative, which nothing definitive paralyses, and to consolation—for how could one sole tear, though it be effaced, be forgotten, how could reparation have the least value, if it did not correct the instant itself, if it did not let it escape in its being, if the pain that glints in the tear did not exist "pending," if it did not exist with a still provisional being, if the present were consummated?

The privileged situation where the ever future evil becomes present—at the limit of consciousness—is reached in the suffering called physical. We find ourselves here backed up to being. We do not only know suffering as a disagreeable sensation, *accompanying* the fact of being at bay and struck; this fact is suffering itself, the "dead end" of the contact. The whole acuity of suffering lies in the impossibility of fleeing it, of being protected in oneself from oneself; it lies in being cut off from every living spring. And it is the impossiblity of retreat. Here the only future negation of the will in fear, the imminence of what escapes power, is inserted into the present; here the other grasps me, the world affects, touches the will. In suffering reality acts on the in itself of the will, which turns despairingly into total submission to the will of the Other. In suffering the will is defeated by sickness. In fear death is yet future, at a distance from us; whereas suffering realizes in the will the extreme proximity of the being menacing the will.

But we still witness this turning of the I into a thing; we are at the same time a thing and at a distance from our reification, an abdication minimally distant from abdication. Suffering remains ambiguous: it is already the present of the pain acting on the for itself of the will, but, as consciousness, the pain is always yet to come. In suffering the free being ceases to be free, but, while non-free, is yet free. It remains at a distance from this pain by its very consciousness, and consequently can become a heroic will. This situation where the consciousness deprived of all freedom of movement maintains a minimal distance from the present, this ultimate passivity which nonetheless desperately turns into action and into hope, is *patience*—the passivity of undergoing, and yet mastery itself. In patience a disengagement within engagement is effected—

neither the impassibility of a contemplation hovering over history nor irrevocable engagement in its visible objectivity. The two positions merge. The being that does violence to me and has a hold on me is not yet upon me; it continues to threaten from the future, is not yet upon me, is only conscious. But in this extreme consciousness, where the will reaches mastery in a new sense, where death no longer touches it, extreme passivity becomes extreme mastery. The egoism of the will stands on the verge of an existence that no longer accents itself.

The supreme ordeal of freedom is not death, but suffering. This is known very well in hatred, which seeks to grasp the ungraspable, to humiliate, from on high, through the suffering in which the Other exists as pure passivity. Hatred wills this passivity in the eminently active being that is to bear witness to it. Hatred does not always desire the death of the Other, or at least it desires the death of the Other only in inflicting this death as a supreme suffering. The one who hates seeks to be the cause of a suffering to which the despised being must be witness. To inflict suffering is not to reduce the Other to the rank of object, but on the contrary is to maintain him superbly in his subjectivity. In suffering the subject must know his reification, but in order to do so he must precisely remain a subject. Hatred wills both things. Whence the insatiable character of hatred; it is satisfied precisely when it is not satisfied, since the Other satisfies it only by becoming an object, but can never become object enough, since at the same time as his fall, his lucidity and witness are demanded. In this lies the logical absurdity of hatred.

The supreme ordeal of the will is not death, but suffering. In patience, at the limit of its abdication, the will does not sink into absurdity, for—over and beyond the nothingness that would reduce the space of time that elapses from birth to death to the purely subjective, the interior, the illusory, the meaningless—the violence the will endures comes from the other as a tyranny. But for this very reason it is produced as an absurdity breaking out on the ground of signification. Violence does not stop Discourse; all is not inexorable. Thus alone does violence remain endurable in patience. It is produced only in a world where I can die *as a result of someone* and *for someone*. This situates death in a new context and modifies its conception, empties it of the pathos that comes to it from the fact of its being my death. In other words, in patience the will breaks through the crust of its egoism and as it were displaces its center of gravity outside of itself, to will as Desire and Goodness limited by nothing.

The analysis below will bring to light the dimension of fecundity, from which, ultimately, flows the time of patience itself—and the dimension of the political, which we now encounter.

5. *The Truth of the Will*

The will is subjective—it does not keep hold on all its being, for with death there comes to it an event that escapes its power absolutely. Death marks the subjectivity of the will not as an end, but as supreme violence and alienation. But in patience, where the will is transported to a life *against someone* and *for someone,* death no longer touches the will. But is this immunity *true* or simply subjective?

In raising this question we are not implying the existence of a real sphere opposed to the inner life, which would be possibly inconsistent and illusory. We seek to present the inner ilfe not as an epiphenomenon and an appearance, but as an *event* of being, as the openness of a dimension indispensable, in the economy of being, for the production of infinity. The power for illusion is not a simple aberration of thought, but a movement in being itself. It has an ontological import. The plane of the inner life is that of apology; it is nowise to be sublated, under pain of reducing anew the inner life to an epiphenomenon. But does not apology of itself, precisely in escaping itself in death, call for a confirmation, in which it escapes death? The apology demands a judgment, not in order to pale under the light that would be projected upon it and flee as an inconsistent shade, but rather in order to obtain justice. Judgment would confirm the event of the apology in its original and fundamental movement, ineluctable in the production of Infinity. The will, whose spontaneity and mastery are belied by death, are stifled in a historical context, that is, in the works that remain of them, of itself seeks to place itself under a judgment, and to receive the truth from it upon its own witness. What is this exisence the will enters into, placing itself under a judgment that dominates the apology, but does not reduce it to silence? For does not judgment, the act of situating by reference to infinity, necessarily have its source outside the being judged; does it not come from the other, from history? But the other above all alienates a will. The verdict of history is pronounced by the survivor who no longer speaks to the being he judges, and to whom the will appears and offers itself as a result and as a work. Thus the will seeks judgment in order to be confirmed against death, whereas judgment taken as the judgment of history kills the will qua will.

This dialectical situation of the search for and the denial of justice has a concrete meaning: the freedom that animates the elementary fact of consciousness forthwith manifests its inanity as a paralytic's freedom and as premature. Hegel's great meditation on freedom permits us to understand that the good will by itself is not a true freedom as long as it does not dispose of the means to realize itself. To proclaim the universality of God in consciousness, to think that everything is consummated while the peoples that tear one another to pieces belie this universality in fact, is not only to prepare the irreligion of a Voltaire, but is to shock reason itself. Interiority cannot replace universality. Freedom is not realized outside of social and political institutions, which open to it the access to fresh air necessary for its expansion, its respiration, and even, perhaps, its spontaneous generation. Apolitical freedom is to be explained as an illusion due to the fact that its partisans or its beneficiaries belong to an advanced stage of political evolution. An existence that is free, and not a velleity for freedom, presupposes a certain organization of nature and of society; the sufferings of torture, stronger than death, can extinguish inward freedom. Even he who has accepted death is not free. The insecurity of the morrow, hunger and thirst scoff at freedom. And, to be sure, in the midst of torture understanding the reasons for the torture reestablishes the famous inward freedom, in spite of the betrayal and degradation portended. But these reasons themselves appear only to the beneficiaries of historical evolution and institutions. In order to oppose inward freedom to the absurd and its violence it is necessary to have received an education.

Hence freedom would cut into the real only by virtue of institutions. Freedom is engraved on the stone of the tables on which laws are inscribed—it exists by virtue of this incrustation of an institutional existence. Freedom depends on a written text, destructible to be sure, but durable, on which freedom is conserved for man outside of man. Human freedom, exposed to violence and to death, does not reach its goal all at once, with a Bergsonian élan; it takes refuge from its own perfidy in institutions. History is not an eschatology. The animal fabricating tools frees itself from its animal condition when its momentum seems interrupted and broken, when instead of going of itself to its goal as an inviolable will it fabricates tools and fixes the powers of its future action in transmissible and receivable things. Thus a political and technical existence ensures the will its truth, renders it objective (as we say today), without opening upon goodness, without emptying it of its egoist weight. The mortal will can escape violence by driving violence and murder from the world, that is, by profiting from time to delay always further the hours of expiration.

Objective judgment is pronounced by the very existence of rational institutions, in which the will is secured against death and against its own perfidy. It consists in the submission of the subjective will to the universal laws which reduce the will to its objective signification. In the respite that the postponement of death, or time, leaves to the will it relies on institutions. It henceforth exists reflected by the public order, in the equality which the universality of laws ensures it. Henceforth it exists as though it were dead and signified only in its own heritage, as though everything that was existence in the first person in it, subjective existence, were but the aftereffect of its animality. But the will now knows another tyranny: that of works alienated, already foreign to man, which reawaken the ancient nostalgia for cynicism. There exists a tyranny of the universal and of the impersonal, an order that is inhuman though distinct from the brutish. Against it man affirms himself as an irreducible singularity, exterior to the totality into which he enters, and aspiring to the religious order where the recognition of the individual concerns him in his singularity, an order of joy which is neither cessation nor antithesis of pain, nor flight before it (as the Heideggerian theory of *Befindlichkeit* would have us think). The judgment of history is always pronounced in absentia. The will's absence from this judgment lies in the fact that it is present there only in the third person. It figures in this discourse as in an indirect discourse where it no longer bears unicity and commencement, where it has already lost its voice. But speech in the first person, direct discourse—useless for the objective wisdom of the universal judgment, or simply a datum of its investigation—consists precisely in *incessantly* supplying a datum to be added to what, being object of universal wisdom, admits of no further adjunction. This word is therefore not of the same sort as the other words of judgment. It presents the will at its trial; it is produced as its defense. The subjectivity's presence at the judgment which ensures it truth is not a purely numerical fact of being there, but is an apology. The subjectivity cannot maintain itself altogether in its apologetic position, and lays itself open to the violence of death. To maintain itself entirely within its relation with itself it would have to be able, over and beyond apology, to will its judgment. It is not the nothingness of death that has to be surmounted, but the passivity to which the will is exposed inasmuch as it is mortal, incapable of absolute attention or absolute vigilance, and necessarily surprised, exposed to murder. But the possibility of seeing itself from the outside does not harbor truth either, if I pay for it the price of my depersonalization. In this judgment, by which the subjectivity is maintained in being absolutely, the singularity and unicity of the I who thinks must not be engulfed, as a result of having been absorbed into its own thought and entered into its discourse. Judgment must be borne upon a will that could defend itself during the adjudication and through its apology be present at its trial, and does not disappear into the totality of a coherent discourse.

The judgment of history is set forth in the visible. Historical events are the visible par excellence; their truth is produced in evidence. The visible forms, or tends to form, a totality. It excludes the apology, which undoes the totality in inserting into it, at each instant, the unsurpassable, unencompassable present of its very subjectivity. The judgment at which the subjectivity is to remain apologetically present has to be made against the evidence of history (and against philosophy, if philosophy coincides with the evidence of history). The invisible must manifest itself if history is to lose its right to the last word, necessarily unjust for the subjectivity, inevitably cruel. But the manifestation of the invisible can not mean the passage of the invisible to the status of the visible; it does not lead back to evidence. It is produced in the goodness reserved to subjectivity, which thus is subject not simply to the truth of judgment, but to the source of this truth. The truth of the invisible is ontologically produced by the subjectivity which states it. For the invisible is not the "provisionally invisible," nor what remains invisible for a superficial and rapid glance, and which a more attentive and scrupulous investigation would render visible, nor what remains unexpressed as hidden movements of the soul, nor what, gratuitously and lazily, is affirmed to be a mystery. The invisible is the offense that inevitably results from the judgment of visible history, even if history unfolds rationally. The virile judgment of history, the virile judgment of "pure reason," is cruel. The universal norms of this judgment silence the unicity in which the apology is contained and from which it draws its arguments. Inasmuch as the invisible is ordered into a totality it offends the subjectivity, since, by essence, the judgment of history consists in translating every apology into visible arguments, and in drying up the inexhaustible source of the singularity from which they proceed and against which no argument can prevail. For there can be no place for singularity in a totality. The idea of a judgment of God represents the limit idea of a judgment that, on the one hand, takes into account the invisible and essential offense to a singularity that results from judgment (even a judgment that is rational and inspired by universal principles, and consequently is visible and evident) and, on the other hand, is fundamentally discreet, and does not silence by its majesty the voice and the revolt of the apology. God sees the invisible and sees without being seen. But how is that situation which we can call judgment of God, and to which the will that wills in truth and not only subjectively submits, concretely brought about?

The invisible offense that results from the judgment of history, a judgment on the visible, will attest subjectivity to be prior to judgment or to be a refusal of judgment, if it is only produced as cry and protestation, if it is felt within me. But it is produced as judgment itself when it looks at me and accuses me in the face of the Other—whose very epiphany is brought about by this offense suffered, by this status of being stranger, widow, and orphan. The will is under the judgment of God when its fear of death is inverted into fear of committing murder.

To be judged thus does not consist in hearing a verdict set forth impersonally and implacably out of universal principles. Such a voice would interrupt the direct discourse of the being subject to judgment, would silence the apology, whereas the adjudication in which the defense makes itself heard should confirm in truth the singularity of the will it judges. But not by indulgence, which would indicate a lapse in the judgment. The exaltation of the singularity in judgment is produced precisely in the infinite responsibility of the will to which the judgment gives rise. Judgment is pronounced upon me in the measure that it summons me to respond. Truth takes form in this response to a summons. The summons exalts the singularity precisely because it is addressed to an infinite responsibility. *The infinity of responsibility denotes not its actual immensity, but a responsibility increasing in the measure that it is assumed;* duties become greater in the measure that they are accomplished. The better I accomplish my duty the fewer rights I have; the more I am just the more guilty I am. The I, which we have seen arise in enjoyment as a separated being having apart, in itself, the center around which its existence gravitates, is confirmed in its singularity by purging itself of this gravitation, purges itself interminably, and is confirmed precisely in this incessant effort to purge itself. This is termed goodness. Perhaps the possibility of a point of the universe where such an overflow of responsibility is produced ultimately defines the I.

In the justice that indicts my arbitrary and partial freedom I therefore am not simply called upon to concur, to consent and assume—to seal my pure and simple entry into the universal order, my abdication and the end of the apology, whose remanence would then be interpreted as a residue or aftereffect of animality. In reality, justice does not include me in the equilibrium of its universality; justice summons me to go beyond the straight line of justice, and henceforth nothing can mark the end of this march; behind the straight line of the law the land of goodness extends infinite and unexplored, necessitating all the resources of a singular presence. I am therefore necessary for justice, as responsible beyond every limit fixed by an objective law. The I is a privilege and an election. The sole possibility in being of going beyond the straight line of the law, that is, of finding a place lying beyond the universal, is to be I. The morality called inward and subjective exercises a function which universal and objective law cannot exercise, but which it calls for. Truth cannot *be* in tyranny, as it cannot *be* in the subjective. Truth can *be* only if a subjectivity is called upon to tell it, in the sense that the Psalmist exclaims: "The dust will give thanks to you, will tell your truth." The call to infinite responsibility confirms the subjectivity in its apologetic position. The dimension of its interiority is brought from the level of the subjective to that of being. Judgment no longer alienates the subjectivity, for it does not make it enter into and dissolve in the order of an objective morality, but leaves it a dimension whereby it deepens in itself. To utter "I," to affirm the irreducible singularity in which the apology is pursued, means to possess a privileged place with regard to responsibilities for which no one can replace me and from which no one can release me. To be unable to shirk: this is the I. The personal character of apology is maintained in this election by which the I is accomplished qua I. The accomplishing of the I qua I and morality constitute one sole and same process in being: morality comes to birth not in equality, but in the fact that infinite exigencies, that of serving the poor, the stranger, the widow, and the orphan, converge at one point of the universe. Thus through morality alone are I and the others produced in the universe. The alienable subjectivity of need and will, which claims to be already and henceforth in possession of itself, but which death makes mockery of, is transfigured by the election which invests it, turning it toward the resources of its own interiority. These resources are infinite—in the incessant overflowing of duty accomplished, by ever broader responsibilities. The person is thus confirmed in objective judgment and no longer reduced to his place within a totality. But this confirmation does not consist in flattering his subjective tendencies and consoling him for his death, but in existing for the Other, that is, in being called in question and in dreading murder more than death—a *salto mortale* whose perilous space is opened forth and measured already by patience (and this is the meaning of suffering), but which the singular being par excellence—an I—can alone accomplish. The truth of the will lies in its coming under judgment; but its coming under judgment lies in a new orientation of the inner life, called to infinite responsibilities.

Justice would not be possible without the singularity, the unicity of subjectivity. In this justice subjectivity does not figure as a formal reason, but as individuality; formal reason is incarnate in a being only in the measure that it loses its election and is equivalent to all the others. Formal reason is incarnate only in a being who does not have the strength to suppose that, under the visible that is history, there is the invisible that is judgment.

The deepening of the inner life can no longer be guided by the evidences of history. It is given over to risk and to the moral creation of the I—to horizons more vast than history, in which history itself is judged. Objective events and the evidence of philosophers can only conceal these horizons. If subjectivity cannot be judged in Truth without its apology, if judgment, instead of reducing it to silence, exalts it, then there must be a discord between events and the good, or, more exactly, events must have an invisible meaning which only a subjectivity, a singular being, can determine. To place oneself beyond the judgment of history, under the judgment of truth, is not to suppose behind the apparent history another history called judgment of God—but equally failing to recognize the subjectivity. To place oneself under the judgment of God is to exalt the subjectivity, called to moral overstepping beyond laws, which is henceforth in truth because it surpasses the limits of its being. The judgment of God that judges me at the same time confirms me. But it confirms me precisely in my interiority, whose justice is more severe than the judgment of history. Concretely to be an I presenting itself at a trial—which requires all the resources of subjectivity—means for it to be able to see, beyond the universal judgements of history, that offense of the offended which is inevitably produced in the very judgment issued from universal principles. What is above all invisible is the offense universal history inflicts on particulars. To be I and not only an incarnation of a reason is precisely to be capable of seeing the offense of the offended, or the face. The deepening of my responsibility in the judgment that is borne upon me is not of the order of universalization: beyond the justice of universal laws, the I enters under judgment by the fact of being good. Goodness consists in taking up a position in being such that the Other counts more than myself. Goodness thus involves the possibility for the I that is exposed to the alienation of its powers by death to not be for death.

The inner life is exalted by the truth of being—by the existence of being in the truth of judgment. It is indispensable for truth, being the dimension in which something can be opposed clandestinely to the visible judgment of history which seduces the philosopher. Yet this inner life cannot forgo all visibility. The judgment of consciousness must refer to a reality beyond the sentence pronounced by history, which is also a cessation and an end. Hence truth requires as its ultimate condition an infinite time, the condition for both goodness and the transcendence of the face. The fecundity of subjectivity, by which the I survives itself, is a condition required for the truth of subjectivity, the clandestine dimension of the judgment of God. But for this condition to be realized, it is not enough that an infinite time be given.

It is necessary to go back to the primary phenomenon of time in which the phenomenon of the "not yet" is rooted. It is necessary to go back to paternity, without which time is but the image of eternity. Without it the time necessary for the manifestation of truth behind visible history (but which remains time—that is, is temporalized relative to a present situated in itself and identifiable) would be impossible. Biological fecundity is but one of the forms of paternity. Paternity, as a primordial effectuation of time, can, among men, be borne by the biological life, but be lived beyond that life.

SECTION IV

BEYOND THE FACE

The relation with the Other does not nullify separation. It does not arise within a totality nor does it establish a totality, integrating me and the other. Nor does the face to face conjuncture presuppose the existence of universal truths into which subjectivity could be absorbed, and which it would be enough to contemplate for me and the other to enter into a relation of communion. Rather, here the converse thesis must be maintained: the relation between me and the other commences in the *inequality* of terms, transcendent to one another, where alterity does not determine the other in a formal sense, as where the alterity of B with respect to A results simply from the identity of B, distinct from the identity of A. Here the alterity of the other does not result from its identity, but constitutes it: the other is the Other. The Other qua Other is situated in a dimension of height and of abasement—glorious abasement; he has the face of the poor, the stranger, the widow, and the orphan, and, at the same time, of the master called to invest and justify my freedom. This inequality does not appear to the third party who would count us. It precisely signifies the absence of a third party capable of taking in me and the other, such that the primordial multiplicity is observed within the very face to face that constitutes it. It is produced in multiple singularities and not in a being exterior to this number who would count the multiples. The inequality *is* in this impossibility of the exterior point of view, which alone could abolish it. The relationship that is established—the relationship of teaching, of mastery, of transitivity—is language, and is produced only in the speaker who, consequently, himself *faces*. Language is not added to the impersonal thought dominating the same and the other; impersonal thought is produced in the movement that proceeds from the same to the other, and consequently in

251

the interpersonal and not only impersonal language. An order common
to the interlocutors is established by the positive act of the one *giving* the
world, his possession, to the other, or by the positive act of the one
justifying himself in his freedom before the other, that is, by apology.
Apology does not blindly affirm the self, but already appeals to the
Other. It is the primordial phenomenon of reason, in its insurmountable
bipolarity. The interlocutors as singularities, irreducible to the concepts
they constitute in communicating their world or in appealing to the
justification of the Other, preside over communication. Reason presupposes these singularities or particularities, not as individuals open to
conceptualization, or divesting themselves of their particularity so as to
find themselves to be identical, but precisely as interlocutors, irreplaceable beings, unique in their genus, faces. The difference between the
two theses: "reason creates the relations between me and the other"
and "the Other's teaching me creates reason" is not purely theoretical.
The consciousness of the tyranny of the State—though it be rational—
makes this difference actual. Does the impersonal reason, to which man
rises in the third stage of knowledge, leave him outside of the State?
Does it spare him all violence? Does it make him confess that this constraint obstructs nothing but the animal in him? The freedom of the I
is neither the arbitrariness of an isolated being nor the conformity
of an isolated being with a rational and universal law incumbent upon all.

My arbitrary freedom reads its shame in the eyes that look at me. It is
apologetic, that is, refers already from itself to the judgment of the Other
which it solicits, and which thus does not offend it as a limit. It thus
reveals itself to be contrary to the conception for which every alterity
is an offense. It is not a *causa sui* simply diminished or, as it is put,
finite. For if this freedom were partially negated, it would be negated
totally. By reason of my apologetic position, my being is not called
upon to appear to itself in its reality: my being does not equal its apparition in consciousness.

But neither will my being be what I have been for the others in terms
of an impersonal reason. If I am reduced to my role in history I remain
as unrecognized as I was deceptive when I appeared in my own consciousness. Existence in history consists in placing my consciousness
outside of me and in destroying my responsibility.

The inhumanity of a humanity where the self has its consciousness
outside of itself resides in the consciousness of the violence that is within
oneself. The renunciation of one's partiality as an individual is imposed

as though by a tyranny. Moreover, if the partiality of the individual, understood as the very principle of his individuation, is a principle of incoherence, by what magic would the simple addition of incoherencies produce a coherent impersonal discourse, and not the disordered din of the crowd? My individuality is hence quite different from this animal partiality, to which would be added a reason that issues from the contradiction in which the hostile impulses of animal particularities oppose one another. Its singularity is at the very level of its reason; it is apology, that is, personal discourse, from me to the others. My being is produced in producing itself before the others in discourse; it is what it reveals of itself to the others, but while participating in, attending, its revelation. I am *in truth* by being produced in history under the judgment it bears upon me, but under the judgment that it bears upon me in my presence—that is, while letting me speak. We have shown above the issuance of this apologetic disclosure in goodness. The difference between "to appear in history" (without a right to speak) and to appear to the Other while attending one's own apparition distinguishes again my political being from my religious being.

In my religious being I am *in truth*. Will the violence death introduces into this being make truth impossible? Does not the violence of death reduce to silence the subjectivity without which truth could neither be said nor be—or (to put it in a word, the word so often used in this exposition, and which includes appearing and being) without which truth could not be *produced?* —Unless, revolted by the violence of reason that reduces the apology to silence, the subjectivity could not only accept to be silent, but could renounce itself by itself, renounce itself without violence, cease the apology for itself. This would not be a suicide nor a resignation, but would be love. The submission to tyranny, the resignation to a universal law, though it be rational, which stops the apology, compromises the truth of my being.

Hence we must indicate a plane both presupposing and transcending the epiphany of the Other in the face, a plane where the I bears itself beyond death and recovers also from its return to itself. This plane is that of love and fecundity, where subjectivity is posited in function of these movements.

A. THE AMBIGUITY OF LOVE

The metaphysical event of transcendence—the welcome of the Other, hospitality—Desire and language—is not accomplished as love. But the transcendence of discourse is bound to love. We shall show how in love transcendence goes both further and less far than language.

Has love no other term than a person? The person here enjoys a privilege—the loving intention goes unto the Other, unto the friend, the child, the brother, the beloved, the parents. But a thing, an abstraction, a book can likewise be objects of love. It is that by an essential aspect love, which as transcendence goes unto the Other, throws us back this side of immanence itself: it designates a movement by which a being seeks that to which it was bound before even having taken the initiative of the search and despite the exteriority in which it finds it. The supreme adventure is also a predestination, a choice of what had not been chosen. Love as a relation with the Other can be reduced to this fundamental immanence, be divested of all transcendence, seek but a connatural being, a sister soul, present itself as incest. The myth Aristophanes tells in Plato's *Symposium,* in which love reunites the two halves of one sole being, interprets the adventure as a return to self. The enjoyment justifies this interpretation. It brings into relief the ambiguity of an event situated at the limit of immanence and transcendence. This desire —a movement ceaselessly cast forth, an interminable movement toward a future never future enough—is broken and satisfied as the most egoist and cruelist of needs. It is as though the too great audacity of the loving transcendence were paid for by a throw-back this side of need. But this *this side* itself, by the depths of the unavowable to which it leads, by the occult influence it exercises over all the powers of being, bears witness to an exceptional audacity. Love remains a relation with the Other that turns into need, and this need still presupposes the total, transcendent exteriority of the other, of the beloved. But love also goes beyond the beloved. This is why through the face filters the obscure light coming from beyond the face, from what *is not yet,* from a future never future

254

enough, more remote than the possible. An enjoyment of the transcendent almost contradictory in its terms, love is stated with truth neither in erotic talk where it is interpreted as sensation nor in the spiritual language which elevates it to being a desire of the transcendent. The possibility of the Other appearing as an object of a need while retaining his alterity, or again, the possibility of enjoying the Other, of placing oneself at the same time beneath and beyond discourse—this position with regard to the interlocutor which at the same time reaches him and goes beyond him, this simultaneity of need and desire, of concupiscence and transcendence, tangency of the avowable and the unavowable, constitutes the originality of the erotic which, in this sense, is *the equivocal* par excellence.

B. PHENOMENOLOGY OF EROS

Love aims at the Other; it aims at him in his frailty [faiblesse]. Frailty does not here figure the inferior degree of any attribute, the relative deficiency of a determination common to me and the other. Prior to the manifestation of attributes, it qualifies alterity itself. To love is to fear for another, to come to the assistance of his frailty. In this frailty as in the dawn rises the Loved, who is the Beloved.* An epiphany of the Loved, the feminine is not added to an object and a Thou antecedently given or encountered in the neuter (the sole gender formal logic knows). The epiphany of the Beloved is but one with her *regime* of tenderness. The *way* of the tender consists in an extreme fragility, a vulnerability. It manifests itself at the limit of being and non-being, as a soft warmth where being dissipates into radiance, like the "pale blush" of the nymphs in the *Afternoon of a Faun,* which "leaps in the air drowsy with thick slumbers," dis-individualizing and relieving itself of its own weight of being, already evanescence and swoon, flight into self in the very midst of its manifestation. And in this flight the other is other, foreign to the world too coarse and too offensive for him.

And yet this extreme fragility lies also at the limit of an existence "without ceremonies," "without circumlocutions," a "non-signifying" and raw density, an exorbitant ultramateriality. These superlatives, better than metaphors, denote a sort of paroxysm of materiality. Ultramateriality does not designate a simple absence of the human in the piles of rocks and sands of a lunar landscape, nor the materiality that outdoes itself, gaping under its rent forms, in ruins and wounds; it designates the exhibitionist nudity of an exorbitant presence coming as though from farther than the frankness of the face, already profaning and wholly profaned, as if it had forced the interdiction of a secret. *The essentially hidden throws itself toward the light, without becoming signification.* Not nothingness—but what is not yet. This unreality at the

---

* ". . . l'Aimé qui est Aimée."

256

threshold of the real does not offer itself as a possible to be grasped; the clandestinity does not describe a gnoseological accident that occurs to a being. "Being not yet" is not a this or a that; clandestinity exhausts the essence of this non-essence. In the effrontery of its production this clandestinity avows a nocturnal life not equivalent to a diurnal life simply deprived of light; it is not equivalent to the simple *inwardness* of a solitary and inward life which would seek expression in order to overcome its repression. It refers to the modesty it has profaned without overcoming. The secret appears without appearing, not because it would appear half-way, or with reservations, or in confusion. The simultaneity of the clandestine and the exposed precisely defines *profanation*. It appears in equivocation. But it is profanation that permits equivocation —essentially erotic—and not the reverse. Modesty, insurmountable in love, constitutes its pathos. Immodesty, always dared in the presentation of wanton nudity, is not something added to an antecedent neutral perception, such as that of the doctor who examines the nudity of the patient. The mode in which erotic nudity is produced (is presented and is) delineates the original phenomena of immodesty and profanation. The moral perspectives they open are situated already in the singular dimension opened by this exorbitant exhibitionism, which is a production of being.

Let us in passing note that this depth in the subterranean dimension of the tender prevents it from being identified with the graceful, which it nevertheless resembles. The simultaneity or the equivocation of this fragility and this weight of non-signifyingness [non-significance], heavier than the weight of the formless real, we shall term *femininity*.

The movement of the lover before this frailty of femininity, neither pure compassion nor impassiveness, indulges in compassion,* is absorbed in the complacence of the caress.

The caress, like contact, is sensibility. But the caress transcends the sensible. It is not that it would feel beyond the felt, further than the senses, that it would seize upon a sublime food while maintaining, within its relation with this ultimate felt, an intention of hunger that goes unto the food promised, and given to, and deepening this hunger, as though the caress would be fed by its own hunger. The caress consists in seizing upon nothing, in soliciting what ceaselessly escapes its form toward a future never future enough, in soliciting what slips away as though it

---

* "... se complaît dans la compassion ..."

were not yet. It *searches,* it forages. It is not an intentionality of disclosure but of search: a movement unto the invisible. In a certain sense it *expresses* love, but suffers from an inability to tell it. It is hungry for this very expression, in an unremitting increase of hunger. It thus goes further than to its term, it aims beyond an existent however future, which, precisely as an *existent,* knocks already at the gates of being. The desire that animates it is reborn in its satisfaction, fed somehow by what *is not yet,* bringing us back to the virginity, forever inviolate, of the feminine. It is not that the caress would seek to dominate a hostile freedom, to make of it its object or extort from it a consent. Beyond the consent or the resistance of a freedom the caress seeks *what is not yet,* a "less than nothing," closed and dormant beyond the *future,* consequently dormant quite otherwise than the *possible,* which would be open to anticipation. The profanation which insinuates itself in caressing responds adequately to the originality of this dimension of absence—an absence other than the void of an abstract nothingness, an absence referring to being, but referring to it in its own way, as though the "absences" of the future were not all future on the same level and uniformedly. Anticipation grasps possibles; what the caress seeks is not situated in a perspective and in the light of the graspable. The carnal, the tender par excellence correlative of the caress, the beloved, is to be identified neither with the body-thing of the physiologist, nor with the lived body [corps propre] of the "I can," nor with the body-expression, attendance at its own manifestation, or face. In the caress, a relation yet, in one aspect, sensible, the body already denudes itself of its very form, offering itself as erotic nudity. In the carnal given to tenderness, the body quits the status of an existent.

The Beloved, at once graspable but intact in her nudity, beyond object and face and thus beyond the existent, abides in virginity. The feminine essentially violable and inviolable, the "Eternal Feminine," is the virgin or an incessant recommencement of virginity, the untouchable in the very contact of voluptuosity, future in the present. Not as a freedom struggling with its conqueror, refusing its reification and its objectification, but a fragility at the limit of non-being wherein is lodged not only what is extinguished and is *no longer,* but what is not yet. The virgin remains ungraspable, dying without murder, swooning, withdrawing into her future, beyond every possible promised to anticipation. Alongside of the night as anonymous rustling of the *there is* extends the night of the erotic, behind the night of insomnia the night of the hidden, the clandestine, the mysterious, land of the virgin, simultaneously uncovered by *Eros* and refusing *Eros*—another way of saying: profanation.

The caress aims at neither a person nor a thing. It loses itself in a being that dissipates as though into an impersonal dream without will and even without resistance, a passivity, an already animal or infantile anonymity, already entirely at death. The will of the tender is produced in its evanescence as though rooted in an animality ignorant of its death, immersed in the false security of the elemental, in the infantile not knowing what is happening to it. But also vertiginous depth of what *is not yet,* which *is not,* but with a nonexistence not even having with being the kinship that an idea or a project maintains, with a nonexistence that does not claim, in any of these ways, to be an avatar of what is. The caress aims at the tender which has no longer the status of an "existent," which having taken leave of "numbers and beings" is not even a quality of an existent. The tender designates a *way,* the way of remaining in the *no man's land* between being and not-yet-being. A way that does not even signal itself as a signification, that in no way shines forth, that is extinguished and swoons, essential frailty of the Beloved produced as vulnerable and as mortal.

But precisely in the evanescence and swoon of the tender the subject does not project itself toward the future of the possible. The not-yet-being is not to be ranked in the same future in which everything I can realize already crowds, scintillating in the light, offering itself to my anticipations and soliciting my powers. The not-yet-being is precisely not a possible that would only be more remote than other possibles. The caress does not *act,* does not grasp possibles. The secret it forces does not inform it as an experience; it overwhelms the relation of the I with itself and with the non-I. An amorphous non-I sweeps away the I into an absolute future where it escapes itself and loses its position as a subject. Its "intention" no longer goes forth unto the *light,* unto the meaningful. Wholly passion, it is compassion for the passivity,* the suffering, the evanescence of the tender. It dies with this death and suffers with this suffering. Being moved [Attendrissement] suffering without suffering, it is consoled already, complacent in its suffering. Being moved is a pity that is complacent, a pleasure, a suffering transformed into happiness— voluptuosity. And in this sense voluptuosity begins already in erotic desire and remains desire at each instant. Voluptuosity does not come

---

* "Toute passion, elle compatit à la passivité . . ."

to gratify desire; it is this desire itself. This is why voluptuosity is not only impatient, but is impatience itself, breathes impatience and chokes with impatience, surprised by its end, for it goes without going to an end.

Voluptuosity, as profanation, discovers the hidden as hidden. An exceptional relation is thus accomplished in a conjuncture which, for formal logic, would arise from contradiction: the discovered* does not lose its mystery in the discovery, the hidden is not disclosed, the night is not dispersed. The profanation-discovery abides in modesty, be it under the guise of immodesty: the clandestine uncovered does not acquire the status of the disclosed. To discover here means to violate, rather than to disclose a secret. A violation that does not recover from its own audacity —the shame of the profanation lowers the eyes that should have scrutinized the uncovered. The erotic nudity says the inexpressible, but the inexpressible is not separable from this saying in the way a mysterious object foreign to expression is separated from a clear speech that seeks to circumscribe it. The mode of "saying" or of "manifesting" itself hides while uncovering, says and silences the inexpressible, harasses and provokes. The "saying," and not only the said, is equivocal. The equivocal does not play between two meanings of speech, but between speech and the renouncement of speech, between the signifyingness [significance] of language and the non-signifyingness of the lustful which silence yet dissimulates. Voluptuosity profanes; it does not see. *An intentionality without vision,* discovery does not shed light: what it discovers does not present itself as *signification* and illuminates no horizon. The feminine presents a face that goes beyond the face. The face of the beloved does not *express* the secret that *Eros* profanes; it ceases to express, or, if one prefers, it expresses only this refusal to express, this end of discourse and of decency, this abrupt interruption of the order of presences. In the feminine face the purity of expression is already troubled by the equivocation of the voluptuous. Expression is inverted into indecency, already close on to the equivocal which says less than nothing, already laughter and raillery.

In this sense voluptuosity is a pure experience, an experience which does not pass into any concept, which remains blindly experience. Profanation, the revelation of the hidden as hidden, constitutes a model of being irreducible to intentionality, which is objectifying even in praxis,

---

* Throughout this section *découvrir* and its cognates suggest that we understand "discovering" as an "uncovering."—Trans.

for not taking leave of "numbers and beings." Love is not reducible to a knowledge mixed with affective elements which would open to it an unforeseen plane of being. It grasps nothing, issues in no concept, does not *issue,* has neither the subject-object structure nor the I-thou structure. Eros is not accomplished as a subject that fixes an object, nor as a pro-jection, toward a possible. Its movement consists in going beyond the possible.

The non-signifyingness of erotic nudity does not precede the signifyingness of the face as the obscurity of formless matter precedes the artist's forms. It already has forms behind it; it comes from the future, from a future situated beyond the future wherein possibles scintillate, for the chaste nudity of the face does not vanish in the exhibitionism of the erotic. The indiscretion in which it remains mysterious and ineffable precisely is attested by the exorbitant inordinateness of this indiscretion. Only the being that has the frankness of the face can be "discovered" in the non-signifyingness of the wanton [lascif].

Let us recall what is involved in signification. The first instance of signification is produced in the face. Not that the face would receive a signification *by relation* to something. The face signifies by itself; its signification precedes *Sinngebung*. A meaningful behavior arises already in its light; it spreads the light in which light is seen. One does not have to explain it, for every explanation begins with it. In other words, society with the Other, which marks the end of the absurd rumbling of the *there is,* is not constituted as the *work* of an I giving meaning. It is necessary to already be for the Other—to exist and not to work only—for the phenomenon of meaning, correlative of the intention of a thought, to arise. Being-for-the-Other must not suggest any finality and not imply the antecedent positing or valorization of any value. To be for the Other is to be good. The concept of the Other has, to be sure, no new content with respect to the concept of the I: but being-for-the Other is not a relation between concepts whose comprehension would coincide, or the conception of a concept by an I, but my goodness. The fact that in existing for another I exist otherwise than in existing for me is morality itself. On all sides it envelops my knowledge of the Other, and is not disengaged from the knowledge of the Other by a valorization of the Other over and above this primary knowledge. Transcendence as such is "conscience." Conscience accomplishes metaphysics, if metaphysics consists in transcending. In all that precedes we have sought to expose the epiphany of the face as the origin of exteriority. The primary phenomenon of signification coincides with exteriority; exteriority is signifyingness itself. And only the face in its morality is exterior. In this epiphany the face is not resplendent as a form clothing a content, as an *image,* but as the nudity of the principle, behind which there is nothing further. The dead face becomes a form, a mortuary mask; it is shown instead of letting see—but precisely thus no longer appears as a face.

We can say it yet otherwise: exteriority defines the existent as existent, and the signification of the face is due to an essential coinciding of the existent and the signifier. Signification is not added to the existent. To signify is not equivalent to presenting oneself as a sign, but to expressing oneself, that is, presenting oneself in person. The symbolism of the sign already presupposes the signification of expression, the face. In the face the existent par excellence presents itself. And the whole body—a hand or a curve of the shoulder—can express as the face. The primordial signifyingness of the existent, its presentation in person or its expression, its way of incessantly upsurging outside of its plastic image, is produced concretely as a temptation to total negation, and as the infinite resistance to murder, in the other qua other, in the hard resistance of these eyes without protection—what is softest and most uncovered. The existent qua existent is produced only in morality. Language, source of all signification, is born in the vertigo of infinity, which takes hold before the straightforwardness of the face, making murder possible and impossible.

The principle "you shall not commit murder," the very signifyingness of the face, seems contrary to the mystery which *Eros* profanes, and which is announced in the femininity of the tender. In the face the Other expresses his eminence, the dimension of height and divinity from which he descends. In his gentleness dawns his strength and his right. The frailty of femininity invites pity for what, in a sense, is not yet, disrespect for what exhibits itself in immodesty and is not discovered despite the exhibition, that is, is profaned.

But disrespect presupposes the face. Elements and things remain outside of respect and disrespect. It is necessary that the face have been apperceived for nudity to be able to acquire the non-signifyingness of the lustful. The feminine face joins this clarity and this shadow. The feminine is the face in which trouble surrounds and already invades clarity. The in appearance asocial relation of eros will have a reference —be it negative—to the social. In this inversion of the face in femininity, in this disfigurement that refers to the face, non-signifyingness abides in the signifyingness of the face. This presence of non-signifyingness in the signifyingness of the face, or this reference of the non-signifyingness to signifyingness—where the chastity and decency of the face abides at the limit of the obscene yet repelled but already close at hand and promising—is the primordial event of feminine beauty, of that eminent sense that beauty assumes in the feminine. The artist will have to convert this beauty into "weightless grace" by carving in the cold matter of color or stone, where beauty will become calm presence, sovereignty in flight, existence unfounded for without foundations.* The beautiful of art *inverts* the beauty of the feminine face. It substitutes an image for the troubling depth of the future, of the "less than nothing" (and not the depth of a world) announced and concealed by the feminine beauty. It presents a beautiful form reduced to itself in flight, deprived of its depth. Every work of art is painting and statuary, immobilized in the instant or in its periodic return. Poetry substitutes a rhythm for the feminine life. Beauty becomes a form covering over indifferent matter, and not harboring mystery.

Thus erotic nudity is as it were an inverted signification, a signification that signifies falsely, a clarity converted into ardor and night, an expression that ceases to express itself, that expresses its renunciation of expression and speech, that sinks into the equivocation of silence, a word that bespeaks not a meaning but exhibition. Here lies the very lasciviousness of erotic nudity—the laughter that deflagrates in Shakespearean witches' sessions full of innuendos, beyond the decency of words, as the absence of all seriousness, of all possibility for speech, the laughter of "ambiguous tales" where the mechanism of laughter is not only ascribable to the formal conditions of the comic such as Bergson, for example, has defined them in his book *Laughter*—there is in addition a content which brings us to an order where seriousness is totally lacking. The beloved is opposed to me not as a will struggling with my own or subject to my own, but on the contrary as an irresponsible animality which does not speak true words. The beloved, returned to the stage of infancy without responsibility—this coquettish head, this youth, this pure life "a bit silly"—has quit her status as a person. The face fades, and in its impersonal and inexpressive neutrality is prolonged, in ambiguity, into animality. The relations with the Other are enacted in play; one plays with the Other as with a young animal.

---

* ". . . existence sans fondements car sans fondations."

The non-signifyingness of the wanton is therefore not equivalent to the stupid indifference of matter. As the reverse of expression of what has lost expression, it thereby refers to the face. The being that presents itself as identical in its face loses its signification by reference to the secret profaned, and plays in equivocation. Equivocation constitutes the epiphany of the feminine—at the same time interlocutor, collaborator and master superiorly intelligent, so often dominating men in the masculine civilization it has entered, and woman having to be treated as a woman, in accordance with rules imprescriptible by civil society. The face, all straightforwardness and frankness, in its feminine epiphany dissimulates allusions, innuendos. It laughs under the cloak of its own expression, without leading to any specific meaning, hinting in the empty air, signaling the less than nothing.

The violence of this revelation marks precisely the *force* of this absence, this *not yet,* this less than nothing, audaciously torn up from its modesty, from its essence of being hidden. A *not yet* more remote than a future, a temporal *not yet,* evincing degrees in nothingness. Hence *Eros* is a ravishing beyond every project, beyond every dynamism, radical indiscretion, profanation and not disclosure of what *already exists* as radiance and signification. *Eros* hence goes beyond the face. Not that the face would cover over something more by its decency, like a mask of another face. The immodest apparition of erotic nudity weighs down the face, weighing a monstrous weight in the shadow of non-sense that is projected upon it, not because another face arises behind it, but because the hidden is torn up from its modesty. The hidden, and not a hidden existent or a possibility for an existent; the hidden, what is not yet and what consequently lacks quiddity totally. Love does not simply lead, by a more detoured or more direct way, toward the Thou. It is bent in another direction than that wherein one encounters the Thou. The hidden—never hidden enough—is beyond the personal and as its reverse, refractory to the light, a category exterior to the play of being and nothingness, beyond the possible, for absolutely ungraspable. Its *way* beyond the possible is manifested in the non-sociality of the society of lovers, their refusal to give themselves over in the midst of their abandon, this refusal to surrender themselves that constitutes voluptuosity, fed by its own hungers, approaching, in vertigo, the hidden or the feminine, a non-personal, but into which the personal will not be engulfed.

The relationship established between lovers in voluptuosity, fundamentally refractory to universalization, is the very contrary of the social relation. It excludes the third party, it remains intimacy, dual solitude, closed society, the supremely non-public. The feminine is the other refractory to society, member of a dual society, an intimate society, a society without language. Its intimacy is to be described. For the unparalleled relation voluptuosity maintains with the non-signifying constitutes a complex that is not reducible to the repetition of this *non,* but to positive traits by which the future and what *is not yet* (and is not simply an existent that remains at the status of the possible) is, so to speak, determined.

The impossibility of reducing voluptuosity to the social, the non-signifyingness upon which it opens, and which is manifested in the indecency of the language that would state voluptuosity, isolates the lovers, as though they were alone in the world. This solitude does not only deny, does not only forget the world; *the common action of the sentient and the sensed* which voluptuosity accomplishes closes, encloses, seals the society of the couple. The non-sociality of voluptuosity is, positively, the community of sentient and sensed: the other is not only a sensed, but in the sensed is affirmed as sentient, as though one same sentiment were substantially common to me and to the other— and not in the way two observers have a common landscape or two thinkers a common idea. An identical objective content does not here mediate the community, nor is the community due to the analogy of feeling; it is due to the identity of the feeling. Reference of love "given" to love "received," love of love, voluptuosity is not a sentiment to the second power like a reflection, but direct like a spontaneous consciousness. It is inward and yet intersubjectively structured, not simplifying itself into consciousness that is one. In voluptuosity the other is me and separated from me. The separation of the Other in the midst of this community of feeling constitutes the acuity of voluptuosity. The voluptuous in voluptuosity is not the freedom of the other tamed, objectified, reified, but his freedom untamed, which I nowise desire objectified. But it is freedom desired and voluptuous not in the clarity of his face, but in the obscurity and as though in the vice of the clandestine, or in the future that remains clandestine within discovery, and which, precisely for this reason, is unfailingly profanation. Nothing is further from *Eros* than possession. In the possession of the Other I possess the Other inasmuch as he possesses me; I am both slave and master. Voluptuosity would be extinguished in possession. But on the other hand, the impersonality of voluptuosity prevents us from taking the relation between lovers to be a complementarity. Voluptuosity hence aims not at the Other but at his voluptuosity; it is voluptuosity of voluptuosity, love of the love of the other. Love accordingly does not represent a particular case of friendship. Love and friendship are not only felt differently; their correlative differs: friendship goes unto the Other; love seeks what does not have the structure of an existent, the infinitely future, what is to be engendered. I love fully only if the Other loves me, not because I need the recognition of the Other, but because my voluptuosity delights in his voluptuosity, and because in this unparalleled conjuncture of identification, in this *trans-substantiation,* the same and the other are not united but precisely—beyond every possible project, beyond every meaningful and intelligent power—engender the child.

If to love is to love the love the Beloved bears me, to love is also to love oneself in love, and thus to return to oneself. Love does not transcend unequivocably—it is complacent, it is pleasure and dual egoism. But in this complacence it equally moves away from itself; it abides in a vertigo above a depth of alterity that no signification clarifies any longer—a depth exhibited and profaned. Already the relation with the child—the coveting of the child, both other and myself—takes form in voluptuosity, to be accomplished in the child himself (as can be accomplished a Desire that is not extinguished in its end nor appeased in its satisfaction). We are here before a new category: before what is behind the gates of being, before the less than nothing that eros tears from its negativity and profanes. It is a question of a nothingness distinct from the nothingness of anxiety: the nothingness of the future buried in the secrecy of the less than nothing.

C. FECUNDITY

The profanation that violates a secret does not "discover," beyond the face, another more profound I which this face would express; it discovers the child. By a total transcendence, the transcendence of trans-substantiation, the I is, in the child, an other. Paternity remains a self-identification, but also a distinction within identification—a structure unforeseeable in formal logic. Hegel in the writings of his youth was able to say that the child *is* the parents, and in *Weltalter* Schelling was able for theological needs to deduce filiality from the identity of Being. Possession of the child by the father does not exhaust the meaning of the relationship that is accomplished in paternity, where the father discovers himself not only in the gestures of his son, but in his substance and his unicity. My child is a stranger (Isaiah 49), but a stranger who is not only mine, for he *is* me. He is me a stranger to myself. He is not only my work, my creature, even if like Pygmalion I should see my work restored to life. The son coveted in voluptuosity is not given to action, remains unequal to powers. No anticipation represents him nor, as is said today, projects him. The project invented or created, unwonted and new, emanates from a solitary head to illuminate and to comprehend. It dissolves into light and converts exteriority into idea. Whence we can define power as presence in a world that by right resolves itself into my ideas. But the encounter with the Other as feminine is required in order that the future of the child come to pass from beyond the possible, beyond projects. This relationship resembles that which was described for the idea of infinity: I cannot account for it by myself, as I do account for the luminous world by myself. This future is neither the Aristotelian germ (less than being, a lesser being) nor the Heideggerian possibility which constitutes being itself, but transforms the relation with the future into a power of the subject. Both my own and non-mine, a possibility of myself but also a possibility of the other, of the Beloved, my future does not enter into the logical essence of the possible. The relation with such a future, irreducible to the power over possibles, we shall call fecundity.

267

Fecundity encloses a duality of the Identical. It does not denote all that I can grasp—my possibilities; it denotes my future, which is not a future of the same—not a new avatar: not a history and events that can occur to a residue of identity, an identity holding on by a thread, an I that would ensure the continuity of the avatars. And yet it is my adventure still, and consequently my future in a very new sense, despite the discontinuity. Voluptuosity does not depersonalize the I ecstatically; it remains ever desire, ever search. It is not extinguished in a term in which it would be absorbed by breaking with its origin in me, even if it does not entirely return to me—to my old age and my death. The I as subject and support of powers does not exhaust the "concept" of the I, does not command all the categories in which subjectivity, origin, and identity are produced. Infinite being, that is, ever recommencing being —which could not bypass subjectivity, for it could not recommence without it—is produced in the guise of fecundity.

The relation with the child—that is, the relation with the other that is not a power, but fecundity—establishes relationship with the absolute future, or infinite time. The other that I will be does not have the indetermination of the possible, which does, however, bear the trace of the fixity of the I that grasps that possible. In power the indetermination of the possible does not exclude the *reiteration* of the I, which in venturing toward this indeterminate future falls back on its feet, and, riveted to itself, acknowledges its transcendence to be merely illusory and its freedom to delineate but a fate. The diverse forms Proteus assumes do not liberate him from his identity. In fecundity the tedium of this repetition ceases; the I is other and young, yet the ipseity that ascribed to it its meaning and its orientation in being is not lost in this renouncement of self. Fecundity continues history without producing old age. Infinite time does not bring an eternal life to an aging subject; it is *better* across the discontinuity of generations, punctuated by the inexhaustible youths of the child.

In fecundity the I transcends the world of light—not to dissolve into the anonymity of the *there is,* but in order to go further than the light, to go *elsewhere.* To stand in the light, to see—to grasp before grasping—is not yet "to be infinitely"; it is to return to oneself older, that is, encumbered with oneself. To be infinitely means to be produced in the mode of an I that is always at the origin, but that meets with no trammels to the renewal of its substance, not even from its very identity. Youth as a philosophical concept is defined thus. The relation with the son in fecundity does not maintain us in this closed expanse of light and dream, cognitions and powers. It articulates the time of the absolutely other, an alteration of the very substance of him who can—his trans-substantiation.

That infinite being not be a possibility enclosed within the separated being, but that it be produced as fecundity, involving, therefore, the alterity of the Beloved, indicates the vanity of pantheism. That in fecundity the personal I has its place indicates the end of the terrors whereby the transcendence of the sacred, inhuman, anonymous, and neuter, menaces persons with nothingness or with ecstasy. Being is produced as multiple and as split into same and other; this is its ultimate structure. It is society, and hence it is time. We thus leave the philosophy of Parmenidean being. Philosophy itself constitutes a moment of this temporal accomplishment, a discourse always addressed to another. What we are now exposing is addressed to those who shall wish to read it.

Transcendence is time and goes unto the Other. But the Other is not a term: he does not stop the movement of Desire. The other that Desire desires is again Desire; transcendence transcends toward him who transcends—this is the true adventure of paternity, of the trans-substantiation which permits going beyond the simple renewal of the possible in the inevitable senescence of the subject. Transcendence, the for the Other, the goodness correlative of the face, founds a more profound relation: the goodness of goodness. Fecundity engendering fecundity accomplishes goodness: above and beyond the sacrifice that imposes a gift, the gift of the power of giving, the conception of the child. Here the Desire which in the first pages of this work we contrasted with need, the Desire that is not a lack, the Desire that is the independence of the separated being and its transcendence, is accomplished—not in being satisfied and in thus acknowledging that it was a need, but in transcending itself, in engendering Desire.

D. THE SUBJECTIVITY IN EROS

Voluptuosity, as the coinciding of the lover and the beloved, is charged by their duality: it is simultaneously fusion and distinction. The maintenance of duality does not mean that in love the egoism of the lover *wills* to obtain the testimony of a recognition in the love received. To love to be loved is not an *intention,* is not the thought of a subject thinking his voluptuosity and thus finding himself exterior to the community of the sensed (despite the cerebral extrapolations of voluptuosity possible, despite the desire for reciprocity guiding lovers to voluptuosity). Voluptuosity transfigures the subject himself, who henceforth owes his identity not to his initiative of power, but to the passivity of the love received. He is passion and trouble, constant *initiation* into a mystery rather than *initiative*. *Eros* can not be interpreted as a superstructure having the individual as basis and subject. The subject in voluptuosity finds himself again as the self (which does not mean the object or the theme) of an other, and not only as the self of himself. The relationship with the carnal and the tender precisely makes this self arise incessantly: the subject's trouble is not assumed by his mastery as a subject, but is his being moved [attendrissement], his effemination, which the heroic and virile I will remember as one of those things that stand apart from "serious things." There is in the erotic relationship a characteristic reversal of the subjectivity issued from position, a reversion of the virile and heroic I which in positing itself put an end to the anonymity of the *there is,* and determined a mode of existence that opens forth the light. In it plays the play of the possibilities of the I, and in this play origin is produced in being in the guise of the I. Being is here produced not as the definitiveness of a totality but as an incessant recommencement, and consequently as infinite. But in the subject the production of origin is the production of old age and death, which mock power. The I returns to itself, finds itself again the same despite all its recommencements, falls back on its feet again solitary, delineates but an irreversible fate. Self-possession becomes encumberment with oneself.

270

The subject is imposed upon itself, drags itself along like a possession. The freedom of the subject that posits itself is not like the freedom of a being free as the wind. It implies responsibility—which should surprise, nothing being more opposed to freedom than the non-freedom of responsibility. The coinciding of freedom with responsibility constitutes the I, doubled with itself, encumbered with itself.

Eros delivers from this encumberment, arrests the return of the I to itself. If the I does not here disappear by uniting with the Other, it does not produce a work either, be it a work perfect as that of Pygmalion but dead, leaving the I alone in the old age it finds at the end of its adventure. *Eros* does not only extend the thoughts of a subject beyond objects and faces; it goes toward a future which *is not yet* and which I will not merely grasp, but I *will be*—it no longer has the structure of the subject which from every adventure returns to its island, like Ulysses. The I springs forth without returning, finds itself the self of an other: its pleasure, its pain is pleasure over the pleasure of the other or over his pain—though not through sympathy or compassion. Its future does not fall back upon the past it ought to renew; it remains an absolute future by virtue of this subjectivity which consists not in bearing representations or powers but in transcending absolutely in fecundity. The "transcendence of fecundity" does not have the structure of intentionality, does not reside in the powers of the I, for the alterity of the feminine is associated with it: the erotic subjectivity is constituted in the common act of the sensing and the sensed as the self of an other, and accordingly is constituted within a relation with the other, within a relation with the face. In this community there plays an equivocation, to be sure: the other presents himself as lived by myself, as object of my enjoyment. This is why, as we have already said, erotic love oscillates between being beyond desire and being beneath need, and why its enjoyment takes its place among all the other pleasures and joys of life. But in addition it takes place beyond all pleasure, all power, beyond all war with the freedom of the other, for the amorous subjectivity is transubstantiation itself. This unparalleled relation between two substances, where a *beyond substances* is exhibited, is resolved in paternity. The "beyond substances" is not open to a power, such as to confirm the I, but neither is it produced in the being of the impersonal, the neuter, the anonymous—infra-personal or supra-personal. This future still refers to the personal from which it is nonetheless liberated: it is the child, mine in a certain sense or, more exactly, me, but not myself; it does not fall back upon my past to fuse with it and delineate a fate. In fecundity subjectivity no longer has the same meaning. Like need, *eros* is bound up with a subject identical with himself, in the logical sense. But the inevitable reference of the erotic to the future in fecundity reveals a radically different structure: the subject is not only all that he will do, he does not maintain with alterity the relationship of thought, possessing the other as a theme, he does not have the structure of speech that calls upon the Other; he will be other than himself while remaining *himself,* but not across a residue common to the former and the new avatar. This alteration and identification in fecundity—beyond the possible and the face—constitutes paternity. In paternity desire maintained as insatiate desire, that is, as goodness, is accomplished. It can not be accomplished by being satisfied. For Desire to be accomplished is equivalent to engendering good being, to being goodness of goodness.

The structure of the subjectivity's identity that is produced in *Eros* takes us outside the categories of classical logic. To be sure, the I, identity par excellence, has often been caught sight of on the margin of identity, an I profiling itself behind the I; thought hearkens to itself. Muse, genius, Socrates' daemon, Faust's Mephistopheles speak in the depths of the I and guide it. Or else the freedom of absolute commencement turns out to be obedience to insidious forms of the impersonal and the neuter: Hegel's universal, Durkheim's social, the statistical laws that govern our freedom, Freud's unconscious, the existential that sustains the existentiel in Heidegger. All these notions represent not an opposition between diverse faculties of the I, but the presence behind the I of a foreign principle which is not necessarily opposed to the I, but which can assume this enemy demeanor. To these influences stands opposed M. Teste, who wishes to be *nothing but myself,* at the absolute origin of all these initiatives, without there being any personality or entity behind him prompting his actions. If our exposition must introduce a notion of subject distinct from this absolute I of M. Teste, it does not lead to the affirmation of an I behind the I, unknown to the conscious I, and fettering it anew. It is precisely as itself that the I is, in the relation with the Other in femininity, liberated of its identity, that it can be other on the basis of self as origin. In the I being can be produced as infinitely recommencing, that is, properly speaking, as infinite.

The notion of fecundity does not refer to the wholly objective idea of the species to which the I comes as an accident. Or else, if one prefers, the unity of the species is deduced from the desire of the I which does not renounce the event of origin in which its being is effected. Fecundity is part of the very drama of the I. The intersubjective reached across the notion of fecundity opens up a plane where the I is divested of its tragic egoity, which turns back to itself, and yet is not purely and simply dissolved into the collective. Fecundity evinces a unity that is not opposed to multiplicity, but, in the precise sense of the term, engenders it.

E. TRANSCENDENCE
AND FECUNDITY

As classically conceived, the idea of transcendence is self-contradictory. The subject that transcends is swept away in its transcendence; it does not transcend itself. If, instead of reducing itself to a change of properties, climate, or level, transcendence would commit the very identity of the subject, we would witness the death of its substance.

It may, certainly, be asked whether death is not transcendence itself; whether among the elements of this world—simple avatars—where change only transforms, that is, safeguards and presupposes a permanent term, death does not represent the exceptional event of a transubstantiation coming to pass, which, without returning to nothingness, ensures its continuity otherwise than by the subsistence of an identical term. But that would be tantamount to defining the "problematic concept" of transcendence. It would shake the foundations of our logic.

For our logic rests on the indissoluble bond between the One and Being, a bond that is incumbent on reflection because we always envisage existing in an existant. Being qua being is for us monadic. Pluralism appears in Western philosophy only as a plurality of subjects that exist. Never has it appeared in the existing of those existants. The plural, exterior to the existence of beings, is given as a number; to a subject that counts it is already subordinated to the synthesis of the "I think." Unity alone is ontologically privileged. Throughout Western metaphysics quantity is scorned as a superficial category. Whence transcendence itself will never be profound; as a "simple relation," it is situated outside of the *event of being*. Consciousness appears as the very type of existing in which the multiple *is* and yet, in synthesis, *is no more,* in which, consequently, transcendence, a simple relation, is less than being. The object is converted into an event of the subject. Light, the element of knowledge, makes all that we encounter be ours. When knowledge takes on an ecstatic signification, when, for Léon Brunschvicg, the spirit-

274

ual I posits itself in refusing itself, affirms generously its personality in negating its egoism, it issues in Spinozist unity, relative to which the I is but a thought. And the alleged movement of transcendence is reduced to a return from an imaginary exile.

In articulating existing as time rather than congealing it in the permanence of the stable the philosophy of becoming seeks to disengage itself from the category of the one, which compromises transcendence. The upsurge or the projection of the future transcends—not by knowledge only, but by the very existing of being. Existing is freed from the unity of the existant. To substitute Becoming for Being is above all to envisage being outside of the *existent*. Interpenetration of instants in duration, openness upon the future, "being for death": these are ways of expressing an existing not in conformity with the logic of unity.

This separation of Being and the One is obtained by the rehabilitation of the possible. No longer backed up behind the unity of the Aristotelian act, possibility harbors the very multiplicity of its dynamism, hitherto indigent alongside of the act accomplished, henceforth richer than it. But the possible is immediately inverted into Power and Domination. In the new that springs from it the subject recognizes himself. He finds himself again in it, masters it. His freedom writes his history which is one; his projects delineate a fate of which he is master and slave. An existant remains the principle of the transcendence of power. A man thirsting for power, aspiring to its divinization, and consequently destined to solitude, appears at the term of this transcendence.

There is in Heidegger's "late philosophy" an impossibility for power to maintain itself as monarchy, to ensure its total mastery. The light of comprehension and truth streams into the darkness of incomprehension and non-truth; power, bound to mystery, avows its impotence. Thereby the unity of the existant seems broken, and fate, as errance, once more mocks the being that in comprehension means to govern it. What is the import of this admission? To say, as M. De Waelhens has tried to affirm in the Introduction to *De l'essence de la vérité,** that errance is not known as such, but experienced, is perhaps to play with words. In Heidegger the human being apprehended as power remains, in reality, truth and light. Heidegger hence disposes of no notion to describe the

---

* Martin Heidegger, *De l'essence de la vérité*, Fr. trans. of *Vom Wesen der Wahrheit* Alphonse De Waehlens (Louvain, 1950).

relation with mystery, already implied in the finitude of *Dasein*. If power is at the same time impotence, it is by reference to power that this impotence is described.

We have sought outside of consciousness and power for a notion of being founding transcendence. The acuity of the problem lies in the necessity of maintaining the I in the transcendence with which it hitherto seemed incompatible. Is the subject only a subject of knowings and powers? Does it not present itself as a subject in another sense? The relation sought, which qua subject it supports, and which at the same time satisfies these contradictory exigencies, seemed to us to be inscribed in the erotic relation.

One might doubt that there is a new ontological principle here. Does not the social relation resolve itself entirely into relations of consciousness and powers? As a collective representation it would in fact differ from a thought only by its content, and not by its formal structure. Participation presupposes the fundamental relations of the logic of objects, and even in Lévy-Bruhl it is treated as a psychological curiosity. It masks the absolute originality of the erotic relation which is, disdainfully, relegated to the biological.

Yet, curiously enough, the philosophy of the biological itself, when it goes beyond mechanism, falls back on finalism and a dialectic of the whole and the part. That the vital impulse propagates itself across the separation of individuals, that its trajectory is discontinuous, that is, that it presupposes the intervals of sexuality and a specific dualism in its articulation, is not seriously taken into consideration. When, with Freud, sexuality is approached on the human plane, it is reduced to the level of the search for pleasure, without the ontological signification of voluptuosity and the irreducible categories it brings into play ever being even suspected. One gives oneself pleasure ready made; one reasons on the basis of it. What remains unrecognized is that the erotic, analysed as fecundity, breaks up reality into relations irreducible to the relations of genus and species, part and whole, action and passion, truth and error; that in sexuality the subject enters into relation with what is absolutely other, with an alterity of a type unforeseeable in formal logic, with what remains other in the relation and is never converted into "mine," and that nonetheless this relation has nothing ecstatic about it, for the pathos of voluptuosity is made of duality.

Neither knowledge nor power. In voluptuosity the Other, the feminine, withdraws into its mystery. The relation with it is a relation with its absence, an absence on the plane of knowledge—the unknown —but a presence in voluptuosity. Nor power: there is no initiative at the birth of love, which arises in the passivity of its pangs. Sexuality is in us neither knowledge nor power, but the very plurality of our existing.

For it is as characteristics of the very ipseity of the I, the very subjectivity of the subject, that the erotic relation is to be analysed. Fecundity is to be set up as an ontological category. In a situation such as paternity the return of the I to the self, which is set forth in the monist concept of the identical subject, is found to be completely modified. The son is not only my work, like a poem or an object, nor is he my property. Neither the categories of power nor those of knowledge describe my relation with the child. The fecundity of the I is neither a cause nor a domination. I do not have my child; I am my child. Paternity is a relation with a stranger who while being Other ("And you shall say to yourself, 'who can have borne me these? I was bereaved and barren . . .'" *Isaiah,* 49) *is* me, a relation of the I with a self which yet is not me. In this "I am" being is no longer Eleatic unity. In existing itself there is a multiplicity and a transcendence. In this transcendence the I is not swept away, since the son is not me; and yet I *am* my son. The fecundity of the I is its very transcendence. The biological origin of this concept nowise neutralizes the paradox of its meaning, and delineates a structure that goes beyond the biologically empirical.

F. FILIALITY AND FRATERNITY

The I breaks free from itself in paternity without thereby ceasing to be an I, for the I *is* its son.

The converse of paternity, filiality, the father-son relationship, designates a relation of rupture and a recourse at the same time.

As rupture, repudiation of the father, commencement, filiality at each moment accomplishes and repeats the paradox of a created freedom. But in this apparent contradiction and in the form of the son being *is* infinitely and discontinuously, historical without fate. The past is recaptured at each moment from a new point, from a novelty that no continuity, such as that which still weighs on the Bergsonian duration, could compromise. For in continuity, where being bears the whole burden of the past (even if in its projection unto the future it should, in defiance of death, recommence), the past limits the infinitude of being, and this limitation is manifested in its senescence.

The recapture of this past can be produced as a recourse. For by existing an existence which still *subsists* in the father the I echos the transcendence of the paternal I who *is* his child: the son *is,* without being "on his own account"; he shifts the charges of his being on the other and thus plays his being. Such a mode of existence is produced as childhood, with its essential reference to the protective existence of the parents. The notion of maternity must be introduced here to account for this recourse. But this recourse to the past, with which the son has nonetheless in his ipseity broken, defines a notion distinct from continuity, a way of resuming the thread of history—concrete in a family and in a nation. The originality of this resumption [renouement], distinct from continuity, is attested in the revolt or the permanent revolution that constitutes ipseity.

But the son's relation with the father across fecundity is not effected only in recourse and the rupture which the I of the son accomplishes as an I already existing. The I owes its unicity as an I to the paternal *Eros*. The father does not simply cause the son. *To be* one's son means

278

to be I in one's son, to be substantially in him, yet without being maintained there in identity. Our whole analysis of fecundity aimed to establish this dialectical conjuncture, which conserves the two contradictory movements. The son resumes the unicity of the father and yet remains exterior to the father: the son is a unique son. Not by number; each son of the father is the unique son, the chosen son. The love of the father for the son accomplishes the sole relation possible with the very unicity of another; and in this sense every love must approach paternal love. But this relation of the father with the son is not *added* to the already constituted I of the son, as a good fortune. The paternal *Eros* first invests the unicity of the son; his I qua filial commences not in enjoyment but in election. He is unique for himself because he is unique for his father. This is precisely why he can, as a child, not exist "on his own." And because the son owes his unicity to the paternal election he can be brought up, be commanded, and can obey, and the strange conjuncture of the family is possible. Creation contradicts the freedom of the creature only when creation is confused with causality. Whereas creation as a relation of transcendence, of union and fecundity, conditions the positing of a unique being, and his ipseity qua elected.

But the I liberated from its very identity in its fecundity cannot maintain its separation with regard to this future if it is bound to its future in its *unique* child. The unique child, as elected one, is accordingly at the same time unique and non-unique. Paternity is produced as an innumerable future; the I engendered exists at the same time as unique in the world and as brother among brothers. I am I and chosen one, but where can I be chosen, if not from among other chosen ones, among equals? The I as I hence remains turned ethically to the face of the other: fraternity is the very relation with the face in which at the same time my election and equality, that is, the mastery exercised over me by the other, are accomplished. The election of the I, its very ipseity, is revealed to be a privilege and a subordination, because it does not place it among the other chosen ones, but rather in face of them, to serve them, and because no one can be substituted for the I to measure the extent of its responsibilities.

If biology furnishes us the prototypes of all these relations, this proves, to be sure, that biology does not represent a purely contingent order of being, unrelated to its essential production. But these relations free themselves from their biological limitation. The human I is posited in fraternity: that all men are brothers is not added to man as a moral conquest, but constitutes his ipseity. Because my position as an I is *effectuated* already in fraternity the face can present itself to me as a face. The relation with the face in fraternity, where in his turn the Other appears in solidarity with all the others, constitutes the social order, the reference of every dialogue to the third party by which the *We* —or the parti—encompasses the face to face opposition, opens the erotic upon a social life, all signifyingness and decency, which encompasses the structure of the family itself. But the erotic and the family which articulates it ensure to this life, in which the I does not disappear but is promised and called to goodness, the infinite time of triumph without which goodness would be subjectivity and folly.

G. THE INFINITY OF TIME

To be infinitely—infinition—means to exist without limits, and thus in the form of an origin, a commencement, that is, again, as an existent. The absolute indetermination of the *there is,* an existing without exist-ants, is an incessant negation, to an infinite degree, consequently an infi-nite limitation. Against the anarchy of the *there is* the existent is pro-duced, a subject of what can happen, an origin and commencement, a power. Unless the origin had its identity of itself infinition would not be possible. But infinition is produced by the existent that is not trammeled in being, that can, while remaining bound to being, take its distances with regard to being: infinition is produced by the existent that exists in truth. Distance with regard to being, by which the existent exists in truth (or ad infinitum), is produced as time and as consciousness, or again, as anticipation of the possible. Across this distance of time the definitive is not definitive; being, while being, is not yet, remains in suspense, and can at each instant commence. The structure of con-sciousness or of temporality—of distance and truth—results from an elementary gesture of the being that refuses totalization. This refusal is produced as a relation with the non-encompassable, as the welcom-ing of alterity—concretely, as presentation of the face. The face arrests totalization. The welcoming of alterity hence conditions con-sciousness and time. Death does not compromise the *power* by which infinition as a negation of being and as nothingness is produced; it menaces power by suppressing distance. Infinition by way of *power* is limited in the return of power to the subject from which it emanates, and which it *ages* by forming the definitive. *The time in which being ad infinitum is produced goes beyond the possible.* In fecundity distance with regard to being is not only provided in the real; it consists in a distance with regard to the present itself, which chooses its possibles, but is realized and has aged somewhat, and consequently, congealed into definitive reality, has already sacrificed possibles. Memories, seeking after lost time, procure dreams, but do not restore the lost occasions.

281

Thus true temporality, that in which the definitive is not definitive, presupposes the possibility not of grasping again all that one might have been, but of no longer regretting the lost occasions before the unlimited infinity of the future. It is not a question of complacency in some romanticism of the possibles, but of escaping the crushing responsibility of existence that veers into fate, of resuming the adventure of existence so as to be to the infinite. The I is at the same time this engagement and this disengagement—and in this sense time, drama in several acts. Without multiplicity and discontinuity—without fecundity—the I would remain a subject in which every adventure would revert into the adventure of a fate. A being capable of another fate than its own is a fecund being. In paternity, where the I, across the definitiveness of an inevitable death, prolongs itself in the other, time triumphs over old age and fate by its discontinuity. Paternity—the way of being other while being oneself—has nothing in common with a transformation in time which could not surmount the identity of what traverses it, nor with some metempsychosis in which the I can know only an avatar, and not be another I. This discontinuity must be emphasized.

The very permanence of the I in the lightest, the least sedentary, the most graceful being, the being most launched toward the future, produces the irreparable, and consequently limits. The irreparable is not due to the fact that we conserve a memory of each instant; on the contrary, memory is founded on this incorruptibility of the past, on the return of the I to itself. But does not the memory arisen in each new instant already give to the past a new meaning? In this sense, better than clinging to the past, does it not already repair it? For in this return of the new instant to the former instant lies the salutary character of succession. But this return weighs upon the present instant, "laden with all the past," even if it is pregnant with the whole future. Its age limits its powers and opens it to the imminence of death.

The discontinuous time of fecundity makes possible an absolute youth and recommencement, while leaving the recommencement a relation with the recommenced past in a free return to that past (free with a freedom other than that of memory), and in free interpretation and free choice, in an existence as entirely pardoned. This recommencement of the instant, this triumph of the time of fecundity over the becoming of the mortal and aging being, is a pardon, the very work of time.

Pardon in its immediate sense is connected with the moral phenomenon of fault. The paradox of pardon lies in its retroaction; from the point of view of common time it represents an inversion of the natural order of things, the reversibility of time. It involves several aspects. Pardon refers to the instant elapsed; it permits the subject who had committed himself in a past instant to be as though that instant had not past on, to be as though he had not committed himself. Active in a stronger sense than forgetting, which does not concern the reality of the event forgotten, pardon acts upon the past, somehow repeats the event, purifying it. But in addition, forgetting nullifies the relations with the past, whereas pardon conserves the past pardoned in the purified present. The pardoned being is not the innocent being. The difference does not justify placing innocence above pardon; it permits the discerning in pardon of a surplus of happiness, the strange happiness of reconciliation, the *felix culpa,* given in an everyday experience which no longer astonishes us.

The paradox of the pardon of fault refers to pardon as constitutive of time itself. The instants do not link up with one another indifferently, but extend from the Other unto me. The future does not come to me from a swarming of indistinguishable possibles which would flow toward my present and which I would grasp; it comes to me across an absolute interval whose other shore the Other absolutely other—though he be my son—is alone capable of marking, and of connecting with the past. But then the Other is alone capable of retaining from this past the former Desire that animated it, which the alterity of each face increases and deepens ever more profoundly. If time does not make moments of mathematical time, indifferent to one another, succeed one another, it does not accomplish Bergson's *continuous duration* either. The Bergsonian conception of time explains why it is necessary to wait "for the sugar to melt": time no longer expresses the unintelligible dispersion of the unity of being, wholly contained in the first cause, in an apparent and phantasmal series of causes and effects; time adds something new to being, something absolutely new. But the newness of springtimes that flower in the instant (which, in good logic, is like the prior one) is already heavy with all the springtimes lived through. The profound work of time delivers from this past, in a subject that breaks with his father. Time is the non-definitiveness of the definitive, an ever recommencing alterity of the accomplished—the "ever" of this recommencement. The work of time goes beyond the suspension of the definitive which the continuity of duration makes possible. There must be a rupture of continuity, and continuation across this rupture. The essential in time consists in being a drama, a multiplicity of acts where the following act resolves the prior one. Being is no longer produced at one blow, irremissibly present. Reality is what it is, but will be once again, another time freely resumed and pardoned. Infinite being is produced as times, that is, in several times across the dead time that separates the father from the son. It is not the finitude of being that constitutes the essence of time, as Heidegger thinks, but its infinity. The death sentence does not approach as an end of being, but as an unknown, which as such suspends power. The constitution of the interval that liberates being from the limitation of fate calls for death. The nothingness of the interval—a dead time—is the production of infinity. Resurrection constitutes the principal event of time. There is therefore no continuity in being. Time is discontinuous; one instant does not come out of another without interruption, by an ecstasy. In continuation the instant meets its death, and resuscitates; death and resurrection constitute time. But such a formal structure presupposes the relation of the I with the Other and, at its basis, fecundity across the discontinuous which constitutes time.

The psychological fact of the *felix culpa*—the surplus reconciliation provides by reason of the rupture it integrates—refers therefore to all the mystery of time. The fact and the justification of time consist in the recommencement it makes possible in the resurrection, across fecundity, of all the compossibles sacrificed in the present.

Why is the beyond separated from the below? Why, to go unto the good, are evil, evolution, drama, separation necessary? Recommencement in discontinuous time brings youth, and thus the infinition of time. Time's infinite existing ensures the situation of judgment, condition of truth, behind the failure of the goodness of today. By fecundity I dispose of an infinite time, necessary for truth to be told, necessary for the particularism of the apology to be converted into efficacious goodness, which maintains the I of the apology in its particularity, without history breaking and crushing this allegedly still subjective concordance.

But infinite time is also the putting back into question of the truth it promises. The dream of a happy eternity, which subsists in man along with his happiness, is not a simple aberration. Truth requires both an infinite time and a time it will be able to seal, a completed time. The completion of time is not death, but messianic time, where the perpetual is converted into eternal. Messianic triumph is the pure triumph; it is secured against the revenge of evil whose return the infinite time does not prohibit. Is this eternity a new structure of time, or an extreme vigilance of the messianic consciousness? The problem exceeds the bounds of this book.

CONCLUSIONS

1. From the Like to the Same

This work has not sought to describe the psychology of the social relation, beneath which the eternal play of the fundamental categories reflected definitively in formal logic would be maintained. On the contrary the social relation, the idea of infinity, the presence in a container of a content exceeding its capacity, was described in this book as the logical plot of being. The specification of a concept the moment it issues in its individuation is not produced by adjunction of an ultimate specific difference, not even if it originates in matter. The individualities thus obtained within the ultimate species would be indiscernible. The Hegelian dialectic is all powerful to reduce this individuality of the τόδε τι to the concept, since the act of pointing to a here and a now implies references to the *situation,* in which the finger's movement is identified from the outside. The identity of the individual does not consist in being like to itself, and in letting itself be identified *from the outside* by the finger that points to it; it consists in being the *same*—in being oneself, in identifying oneself from within. There exists a logical passage from the like to the same; singularity logically arises from the logical sphere *exposed to the gaze* and organized into a totality by the reversion of this sphere into the interiority of the I, the reversion, so to speak, of convexity into concavity. And the entire analysis of interiority pursued in this work describes the conditions of this reversion. Relations such as the idea of infinity, which the formal logic of the gaze cannot let show through without absurdity, and which it prompts us to interpret in theological or psychological terms (as a miracle or as an illusion), have a place in the logic of interiority—in a sort of micro-logic—in which logic is pursued beyond the τόδε τί. Social relations do not simply present us with a superior empirical matter, to be treated in terms of the logic of genus and species. They are the original deployment of the relationship that is no longer open to the gaze that would encompass its terms, but is *accomplished* from me to the other in the face to face.

2. *Being Is Exteriority*

Being is exteriority. This formula does not only mean to denounce the illusions of the subjective, and claim that objective forms alone, in opposition to the sands in which arbitrary thought is mired and lost, merit the name of being. Such a conception would in the end destroy exteriority, since subjectivity itself would be absorbed into exteriority, revealing itself to be a moment of a panoramic play. Exteriority would then no longer mean anything, since it would encompass the very interiority that justified this appellation.

But exteriority is not yet maintained if we affirm a subject insoluble into objectivity, and to which exteriority would be opposed. This time exteriority would acquire a relative meaning, as the great by relation to the small. But in the absolute the subject and the object would still be parts of the same system, would be enacted and revealed panoramically. Exteriority, or, if one prefers, alterity, would be converted into the same. And over and beyond the relation between the interior and the exterior there would be room for the perception of this relation by a lateral view that would take in and perceive (or penetrate) their play, or would provide an ultimate stage on which this relation would be enacted, on which its being would be effected *truly*.

Being is exteriority: the very exercise of its being consists in exteriority, and no thought could better obey being than by allowing itself to be dominated by this exteriority. Exteriority is true not in a lateral view apperceiving it in its opposition to interiority; it is true in a face to face that is no longer entirely vision, but goes further than vision. The face to face is established starting with a point separated from exteriority so radically that it maintains itself of itself, is me; every other relation that would not part from this separated and therefore arbitrary point (but whose arbitrariness and separation are produced in a positive mode as me), would miss the—necessarily subjective—field of truth. The true essence of man is presented in his face, in which he is infinitely other than a violence like unto mine, opposed to mine and hostile, already at grips with mine in a historical world where we participate in the same system. He arrests and paralyzes my violence by his call, which does not do violence, and comes from on high. The truth of being is not the *image* of being, the *idea* of its nature; it is the being situated in a subjective field which *deforms* vision, but precisely thus allows exteriority to state itself, entirely command and authority: entirely superiority. This curvature of the intersubjective space inflects distance into elevation; it does not falsify being, but makes its truth first possible.

One cannot "allow for" this refraction "produced" by the subjective field, so as to thus "correct" it; it constitutes the very mode in which the exteriority of being is effectuated- in its truth. The impossibility of "total reflection" is not due to a flaw in subjectivity. The so-called "objective" nature of the entities that would appear outside of this "curvature of space"—the phenomenon—would, on the contrary, indicate the loss of metaphysical truth, the superior truth—in the literal sense of the term. This "curvature" of the intersubjective space in which exteriority is effectuated (we do not say "in which it appears") as superiority must be distinguished from the arbitrariness of "points of view" taken upon objects that appear. But the latter, source of errors and opinions, issued from the violence opposed to exteriority, is the price of the former.

This "curvature of space" expresses the relation between human beings. That the Other is placed higher than me would be a pure and simple error if the welcome I make him consisted in "perceiving" a nature. Sociology, psychology, physiology are thus deaf to exteriority. Man as Other comes to us from the outside, a separated—or holy—face. His exteriority, that is, his appeal to me, is his truth. My response is not added as an accident to a "nucleus" of his objectivity, but first *produces* his truth (which his "point of view" upon me can not nullify). This surplus of truth over being and over its idea, which we suggest by the metaphor of the "curvature of intersubjective space," signifies the divine intention of all truth. This "curvature of space" is, perhaps, the very presence of God.

The face to face is a final and irreducible relation which no concept could cover without the thinker who thinks that concept finding himself forthwith before a new interlocutor; it makes possible the pluralism of society.

3. *The Finite and the Infinite*

Exteriority, taken as the essence of being, signifies the resistance of the social multiplicity to the logic that totalizes the multiple. For this logic, multiplicity is a fall of the One or the Infinite, a diminution in being which each of the multiple beings would have to surmount so as to return from the multiple to the One, from the finite to the Infinite. Metaphysics, the relation with exteriority, that is, with superiority, indicates, on the contrary, that the relation between the finite and the infinite does not consist in the finite being absorbed in what faces him, but in remaining in his own being, maintaining himself there, acting here below. The austere happiness of goodness would invert its meaning and would be perverted if it confounded us with God. In understanding being as exteriority, in breaking with the panoramic existing of being and the totality in which it is produced, we can understand the meaning of the *finite* without its limitation, occurring within the infinite, requiring an incomprehensible fall of the infinite, without finitude consisting in a nostalgia for infinity, a longing for return. To posit being as exteriority is to apperceive infinity as the Desire for infinity, and thus to understand that the production of infinity calls for separation, the production of the absolute arbitrariness of the I or of the origin.

The traits of limitation and finitude, which separation takes on, do not sanction a simple "less," intelligible on the basis of the "infinitely more" and the unfailing plenitude of infinity; they ensure the very overflowing of infinity, or, to speak concretely, the very overflowing of all the surplus over being—all the Good—that is produced in the social relation. The negativeness of the finite is to be understood on the basis of this Good. The social relation engenders this surplus of the Good over being, multiplicity over the One. It does not consist in reconstituting the wholeness of the perfect being which Aristophanes speaks of in the myth of the *Symposium,* nor in being immersed again in the whole and abdicating into the intemporal, nor in gaining the whole through history. The adventure separation opens is absolutely new with regard to the beatitude of the One and its famous freedom, which consists in negating or in absorbing the other, so as to encounter nothing. The concept of a Good beyond Being and beyond the beatitude of the One announces a rigorous concept of creation, which would be neither a negation nor a limitation nor an emanation of the One. Exteriority is not a negation, but a marvel.

4. Creation

Theology imprudently treats the idea of the relation between God and the creature in terms of ontology. It presupposes the logical privilege of totality, as a concept adequate to being. Thus it runs up against the difficulty of understanding that an infinite being would border on or tolerate something outside of itself, or that a free being would send its roots into the infinity of a God. But transcendence precisely refuses totality, does not lend itself to a view that would encompass it from the outside. Every "comprehension" of transcendence leaves the transcendent outside, and is enacted before its face. If the notions of totality and being are notions that cover one another, the notion of the transcendent places us beyond categories of being. We thus encounter, in our own way, the Platonic idea of the Good beyond Being. The transcendent is what can not be encompassed. This is an essential precision of the notion of transcendence, utilizing no theological notion. What embarrasses the traditional theology, which treats of creation in terms of ontology—God leaving his eternity, in order to create—is incumbent as a first truth in a philosophy that begins with transcendence: nothing could better distinguish totality and separation than the difference between eternity and time. But then the Other, in his signification prior to my initiative, resembles God. This signification precedes my *Sinngebung* initiative.

For the idea of totality, in which ontological philosophy veritably reunites—or comprehends—the multiple, must be substituted the idea of a separation resistant to synthesis. To affirm origin from nothing by creation is to contest the prior community of all thing within eternity, from which philosophical thought, guided by ontology, makes things arise as from a common matrix. The absolute gap of separation which transcendence implies could not be better expressed than by the term creation, in which the kinship of beings among themselves is affirmed, but at the same time their radical heterogeneity also, their reciprocal exteriority coming from nothingness. One may speak of creation to characterize entities situated in the transcendence that does not close over into a totality. In the face to face the I has neither the privileged position of the subject nor the position of the thing defined by its place in the system; it is apology, discourse *pro domo,* but discourse of justification before the Other. The Other is the prime intelligible, since he is capable of justifying my freedom, rather than awaiting a *Sinngebung* or a meaning from it. In the conjuncture of creation the I is for itself, without being *causa sui.* The will of the I affirms itself as infinite (that is, free), and as limited, as subordinated. It does not get its limits from the proximity of the other, who, being transcendent, does not *define* it. The I's form no totality; there exists no privileged plane where these I's could be grasped in their principle. There is an anarchy essential to multiplicity. In the absence of a plane common to the totality (which one persists in seeking, so as to relate the multiplicity to it) one will never know which will, in the free play of the wills, pulls the strings of the game; one will not know who is playing with whom. But a principle breaks through all this trembling and vertigo when the face presents itself, and demands justice.

5. *Exteriority and Language*

We have begun with the resistance of beings to totalization, with an untotaled multiplicity they constitute, the impossibility of their conciliation in the same.

This impossibility of conciliation among beings, this radical heterogeneity, in fact indicates a mode of being produced and an ontology that is not equivalent to panoramic existence and its disclosure. For common sense but also for philosophy, from Plato to Heidegger, panoramic existence and its disclosure are equivalent to the very production of being, since truth or disclosure is at the same time the work or the essential virtue of being, the *Sein* of the *Seiendes* and of every human behavior it would in the last analysis govern. The Heideggerian thesis that every human attitude consists in "bringing to light" (modern technology itself would be but a mode of extracting things or producing them in the sense of "fully bringing to light") rests on this primacy of the panoramic. The break-up of totality, the denunciation of the panoramic structure of being, concerns the very existing of being and not the collocation or configuration of entities refractory to system. Correlatively, the analysis that tends to show intentionality as an aiming at the visible, at the *idea,* expresses this domination of the panoramic as the ultimate virtue of being, the Being of the existent. This trait is maintained in the modern analysis of affectivity, practice, and existence, despite all the suppleness forced upon the notion of contemplation. One of the principal theses of this work is that the noesis-noema structure is not the primordial structure of intentionality (which is not equivalent to interpreting intentionality as a logical relation or as causality).

The exteriority of being does not, in fact, mean that multiplicity is without relation. However, the relation that binds this multiplicity does not fill the abyss of separation; it confirms it. In this relation we have recognized language, produced only in the face to face; and in language we have recognized teaching. Teaching is a way for truth to be produced such that it is not my work, such that I could not derive it from my own interiority. In affirming such a production of truth we modify the original meaning of truth and the noesis-noema structure, taken as the meaning of intentionality.

In effect, the being who speaks to me and to whom I respond or whom I interrogate does not offer himself to me, does not *give* himself so that I could assume this manifestation, measure it to my own interiority, and receive it as come from myself. Vision operates in this manner, totally impossible in discourse. For vision is essentially an adequation of exteriority with interiority: in it exteriority is reabsorbed in the contemplative soul and, as an *adequate idea,* revealed to be a priori, the result of a *Sinngebung.* The exteriority of discourse cannot be converted into interiority. The interlocutor can have no place in an inwardness; he is forever outside. The relationship between separated beings does not totalize them; it is a "unrelating relation," which no one can encompass or thematize. Or more exactly, he who would think it, who would totalize it, would by this "reflection" mark a new scission in being, since he would still tell this total to someone. The relation between the "fragments" of separated being is a face to face, the irreducible and ultimate relation. An interlocutor arises again behind him whom thought has just apprehended—as the certitude of the *cogito* arises behind every negation of certitude. The description of the face to face which we have attempted here is told to the other, to the reader who appears anew behind my discourse and my wisdom. Philosophy is never a wisdom, for the interlocutor whom it has just encompassed has already escaped it. Philosophy, in an essentially liturgical sense, invokes the Other to whom the "whole" is told, the master or student. It is precisely for this that the face to face proper to discourse does not connect a subject with an object, and differs from the essentially adequate thematization. For no concept lays hold of exteriority.

The object thematized remains in itself, but it belongs to its essence to be known by me; and the surplus of the in itself over my knowledge is progressively absorbed by knowledge. The difference between the knowing that bears on the object and the knowing that bears on the in itself or the solidity of the object dwindles in the course of a development of thought which, according to Hegel, would be history itself. Objectivity is absorbed in absolute knowledge, and the being of the thinker, the humanity of man, is therewith conformed to the perpetuity of the solid in itself, within a totality where the humanity of man and the exteriority of the object are at the same time conserved and absorbed. Would the transcendence of exteriority simply indicate an unfulfilled thought, and would it be overcome in the totality? Would exteriority have to be inverted into interiority? Is it evil?

We have broached the exteriority of being not as a form that being would eventually or provisionally take on in dispersion or in its fall, but as its very existing—inexhaustible, infinite exteriority. Such an exteriority opens in the Other; it recedes from thematization. But it refuses thematization positively because it is produced in a being who expresses himself. In contradistinction to plastic manifestation or disclosure, which manifests something *as* something, and in which the disclosed renounces its originality, its hitherto unpublished existence, in expression the manifestation and the manifested coincide; the manifested attends its own manifestation and hence remains exterior to every image one would retain of it, presents itself in the sense that we say of someone that he presents himself by stating his name, which permits evoking him, even though he remains always the source of his own presence. A presentation which consists in saying "It's me"*—and nothing else to which one might be tempted to assimilate me. This presentation of the exterior being nowise referred to in our world is what we have called the face. And we have described the relation with the face that presents itself in speech as desire—goodness and justice.

Speech refuses vision, because the speaker does not deliver images of himself only, but is personally present in his speech, absolutely exterior to every image he would leave. In language exteriority is exercised, deployed, brought about. Whoever speaks attends his manifestation, is non-adequate to the meaning that the hearer would like to retain of it as a result acquired outside of the very relationship of discourse, as though this presence in speech were reducible to the *Sinngebung* of him who listens. Language is the incessant surpassing of the *Sinngebung* by the signification. This presence whose format exceeds the measure of the I is not reabsorbed into my vision. The overflowing of exteriority, non-

---

* "moi, c'est moi."

adequate to the vision which still measures it, precisely constitutes the dimension of height or the divinity of exteriority. Divinity keeps its distances. Discourse is discourse with God and not with equals, according to the distinction established by Plato in the *Phaedrus*. Metaphysics is the essence of this language with God; it leads above being.

6. Expression and Image

The presence of the Other, or expression, source of all signification, is not contemplated as an intelligible essence, but is heard as language, and thereby is effectuated exteriorly. Expression, or the face, overflows images, which are always immanent to my thought, as though they came from me. This overflowing, irreducible to an image of overflowing, is produced commensurate with—or in the inordinateness of—Desire and goodness, as the moral dissymmetry of the I and the other. The distance of this exteriority immediately extends to height. The eye can conceive it only by virtue of position which, as an above-below disposition, constitutes the elementary fact of morality. Because it is the presence of exteriority the face never becomes an image or an intuition. Every intuition depends on a signification irreducible to intuition; it comes from further than intuition, and it alone comes from afar. Signification, irreducible to intuitions, is measured by Desire, morality, and goodness —the infinite exigency with regard to oneself, or Desire of the other, or relation with infinity.

The presence of the face, or expression, is not to be ranked among other meaningful manifestations. The works of man all have meaning, but the human being absents himself from them immediately, and is divined across them; he too is given in the articulation of the "qas." There is a abyss between labor, which results in works having a meaning for other men, and which others can acquire—already merchandise reflected in money—and language, in which I attend my manifestation, irreplaceable and vigilant. But this abyss gapes open because of the en-ergy of the vigilant presence which does not *quit* the expression. It is not to expression what the will is to its work; the will withdraws from its work, delivering it over to its fate, and is found to have willed "a lot of things" it had not willed. For the absurdity of these works is not due to a defect of the thought that formed them; it is due to the anonymity into which this thought immediately falls, to the unrecognition of the worker that results from this essential anonymity.

Jankélévitch is right to say that labor is not an expression.[1] In acquiring
the work I desacralize the neighbor who produced it. Man is really
apart, non-encompassable, only in expression, where he can "bring aid"
to his own manifestation.

In political life, taken unrebuked, humanity is understood from its
works—a humanity of interchangeable men, of reciprocal relations.
The substitution of men for one another, the primal disrespect, makes
possible exploitation itself. In history—the history of States—the
human being appears as the sum of his works; even while he lives he
is his own heritage. Justice consists in again making possible expression,
in which in non-reciprocity the person presents himself as unique.
Justice is a right to speak. It is perhaps here that the perspective of a
religion opens. It diverges from political life, to which philosophy does
not lead necessarily.

7. Against the Philosophy of the Neuter

We have thus the conviction of having broken with the philosophy of
the Neuter: with the Heideggerian Being of the existent whose impersonal neutrality the critical work of Blanchot has so much contributed to
bring out, with Hegel's impersonal reason, which shows to the personal
consciousness only its ruses. The movements of ideas of the philosophy
of the Neuter, so different in their origins and their influences, agree in
announcing the end of philosophy. For they exalt the obedience that no
face commands. Desire in the spell of the Neuter, said to have been
revealed to the Presocratics, or desire interpreted as need, and thus bound
to the essential violence of action, dismisses philosophy and is gratified
only in art or in politics. The exaltation of the Neuter may present itself
as the anteriority of the We with respect to the I, of the situation with
respect to the beings in situation. This book's insistence on the separation of enjoyment was guided by the necessity of liberating the I from the
situation into which little by little philosophers have dissolved it as
totally as reason swallows up the subject in Hegelian idealism.
Materialism does not lie in the discovery of the primordial function of
the sensibility, but in the primacy of the Neuter. To place the Neuter
dimension of Being above the existent which unbeknown to it this Being
would determine in some way, to make the essential events unbeknown to

---

[1] V. Jankélévitch, *L'Austérité et la vie morale* (Paris, 1956), p. 34.

the existents, is to profess materialism. Heidegger's late philosophy becomes this faint materialism. It posits the revelation of Being in human inhabitation between Heavens and Earth, in the expectation of the gods and in the company of men, and sets up the landscape or the "still life" as an origin of the human. The Being of the existent is a *Logos* that is the word of no one. To begin with the face as a source from which all meaning appears, the face in its absolute nudity, in its destitution as a head that does not find a place to lay itself, is to affirm that being is enacted in the relation between men, that Desire rather than need commands acts. Desire, an aspiration that does not proceed from a lack—metaphysics—is the desire of a person.

8. Subjectivity

Being is exteriority, and exteriority is produced in its truth in a subjective field, for the separated being. Separation is accomplished positively as the interiority of a being referring to itself and maintaining itself of itself—all the way to atheism! This self-reference is concretely constituted or accomplished as enjoyment or happiness. It is an essential sufficiency, which in its expansion—in knowledge, whose ultimate essence critique (the recapturing of its own condition) develops—is even in possession of its own origin.

To metaphysical thought, where a finite has the idea of infinity— where radical separation and relationship with the other are produced simultaneously—we have reserved the term intentionality, consciousness of. . . . It is attention to speech or welcome of the face, hospitality and not thematization. Self-consciousness is not a dialectical rejoinder of the metaphysical consciousness that I have of the other. Nor is its relation with itself a *representation* of itself. Prior to every vision of self it is accomplished by holding *oneself* up [*se* tenant] ; it is *implanted in itself* as a body and it keeps itself [se tient] in its interiority, in its home. It thus accomplishes separation positively, without being reducible to a negation of the being from which it separates. But thus precisely it can welcome that being. The subject is a host.

Subjective existence derives its features from separation. Individuation—an inner *identification* of a being whose essence is exhausted in identity, an identification of the same—does not come to strike the terms of some relation called separation. Separation is the very act of individuation, the possibility in general for an entity which is posited in being to be posited not by being defined by its references to a whole, by its place within a system, but starting from itself. The fact of starting from oneself is equivalent to separation. But the act of starting from oneself and separation itself can be produced in being only by opening the dimension of interiority.

9. The Maintenance of Subjectivity
The Reality of the Inner Life
and the Reality of the State
The Meaning of Subjectivity

Metaphysics, or the relation with the other, is accomplished as service and as hospitality. In the measure that the face of the Other relates us with the third party, the metaphysical relation of the I with the Other moves into the form of the We, aspires to a State, institutions, laws, which are the source of universality. But politics left to itself bears a tyranny within itself; it deforms the I and the other who have given rise to it, for it judges them according to universal rules, and thus as in absentia. In welcoming the Other I welcome the On High to which my freedom is subordinated. But this subordination is not an absence: it is brought about in all the personal work of my moral initiative (without which the truth of judgment cannot be produced), in the attention to the Other as unicity and face (which the visibleness of the political leaves invisible), which can be produced only in the unicity of an I. Subjectivity is thus rehabilitated in the work of truth, and not as an egoism refusing the system which offends it. Against this egoist protestation of the subjectivity, against this protestation in the first person, the universalism of Hegelian reality will perhaps prevail. But how could universal, that is, visible principles be opposed with this same pride to the face of the other, without recoiling before the cruelty of this impersonal justice! And then how could the subjectivity of the I not be introduced as the sole possible source of goodness?

Metaphysics therefore leads us to the accomplishment of the I as unicity by relation to which the work of the State must be situated, and which it must take as a model.

The irreplaceable unicity of the I which is maintained against the State is accomplished by fecundity. It is not to purely subjective events, losing themselves in the sands of interiority which the rational reality mocks, that we appeal to in insisting on the irreducibility of the personal to the universality of the State; we appeal to a dimension and a perspective of transcendence as real as the dimension and perspective of the political and more true than it, because in it the apology of the ipseity does not disappear. The interiority opened up by separation is not the ineffable of the clandestine or the subterranean—but the infinite time of fecundity. Fecundity permits the assuming of the actual as the vestibule of a future. It opens the subterranean, where a life called inward or merely subjective seemed to take refuge, upon being.

The subjectivity present to the judgment of truth is therefore not reducible simply to an impotent, clandestine, unforeseeable, and from the outside invisible protestation against totality and objective totalization. And yet its entry into being is not wrought as an integration into a totality the separation had broken up. Fecundity and the perspectives it opens evince the ontological character of separation. But fecundity does not join together the fragments of a broken totality into a subjective history. Fecundity opens up an infinite and discontinuous time. It liberates the subject from his facticity by placing him beyond the possible which presupposes and does not surpass facticity; it lifts from the subject the last trace of fatality, by enabling him to be an other. In eros the fundamental exigencies of the subjectivity are maintained—but in this alterity the ipseity is graceful, lightened of egoist unwieldiness.

10. Beyond Being

Thematization does not exhaust the meaning of the relationship with exteriority. Thematization or objectification is not to be described only as an impassive contemplation, but is to be described as a relation with the solid, with the thing, since Aristotle the term of the analogy of being. The solid is not reducible to the structures imposed by the impassibility of the look that contemplates it; it is to be understood in terms of the structures imposed by its relation with time—which it traverses. The being of the object is perduration, a filling of the time which is empty and inconsolable against death as an end. If exteriority consists not in being presented as a theme but in being open to desire, the existence of the separated being which desires exteriority no longer consists in caring for Being. To exist has a meaning in another dimension than that of the perduration of the totality; it can go beyond being. Contrary to the Spinozist tradition, this going beyond death is produced not in the universality of thought but in the pluralist relation, in the goodness of being for the Other, in justice. The surpassing of being starting from being—the relation with exteriority—is not measured by duration. Duration itself becomes visible in the relation with the Other, where being is surpassed.

11. Freedom Invested

The presence of exteriority in language, which commences with the presence of the face, is not produced as an affirmation whose formal meaning would remain without development. The relation with the face is produced as goodness. The exteriority of being is morality itself. Freedom, the event of separation in arbitrariness which constitutes the I, at the same time maintains the relation with the exteriority that morally resists every appropriation and every totalization in being. If freedom were posited outside of this relation, every relation within multiplicity would enact but the *grasp* of one being by another or their common participation in reason, where no being looks at the face of the other, but all beings negate one another. Knowledge or violence would appear in the midst of the multiplicity as events that realize being. The common knowledge proceeds toward unity, either toward the apparition in the midst of a multiplicity of beings of a rational system in which these beings would be but objects, and in which they would find their being— or toward the brutal conquest of beings outside of every system by violence. Whether in scientific thought or in the object of science, or in history understood as a manifestation of reason, where violence reveals itself to be reason, philosophy presents itself as a realization of being, that is, as its liberation by the suppression of multiplicity. Knowledge would be the suppression of the other by the grasp, by the hold, or by the vision that grasps before the grasp. In this work metaphysics has an entirely different meaning. If its movement leads to the transcendent as such, transcendence means not appropriation of *what is,* but its respect. Truth as a respect for being is the meaning of metaphysical truth.

If, in contradistinction to the tradition of the primacy of freedom, taken as the measure of being, we contest vision its primacy in being, and contest the pretension of human emprise to gain access to the rank of *logos,* we take leave neither of rationalism, nor of the ideal of freedom. One is not an irrationalist nor a mystic nor a pragmatist for questioning the identification of power and *logos.* One is not against freedom if one seeks for it a justification. Reason and freedom seem to us to be founded on prior structures of being whose first articulations are delineated by the metaphysical movement, or respect, or justice—identical to truth. The terms of the conception making truth rest on freedom must be inverted. What justification there is in truth does not rest on freedom posited as independence in regard to all exteriority. It would be so, to be sure, if justified freedom would simply express the necessities rational order imposes on the subject. But true exteriority is metaphysical; it does not weigh on the separated being and commands him as free. The present work has sought to describe metaphysical exteriority. One of the consequences that follows from its very notion is that freedom is posited as requiring justification. The founding of truth on freedom would imply a freedom justified by itself. There would have been for freedom no greater scandal than to discover itself to be finite. To not have chosen one's freedom would be the supreme absurdity and the supreme tragic of existence; this would be the irrational. The Heideggerian *Geworfenheit* marks a finite freedom and thus the irrational. The encounter with the Other in Sartre threatens my freedom, and is equivalent to the fall of my freedom under the gaze of another freedom. Here perhaps is manifested most forcefully being's incompatibility with what remains veritably exterior. But to us here there rather appears the problem of the justification of freedom: does not the presence of the Other put in question the naïve legitimacy of freedom? Does not freedom appear to itself as a shame for itself? And, reduced to itself, as a usurpation? The irrational in freedom is not due to its limits, but to the infinity of its arbitrariness. Freedom must justify itself; reduced to itself it is accomplished not in sovereignty but in arbitrariness. Precisely through freedom—and not because of its limitation—the being freedom is to express in its plentitude appears as not having its reason in itself. Freedom is not justified by freedom. To account for being or to be in truth is not to comprehend nor to take hold of . . . , but rather to encounter the Other without allergy, that is, in justice.

To approach the Other is to put into question my freedom, my spontaneity as a living being, my emprise over the things, this freedom of a "moving force," this impetuosity of the current to which everything is permitted, even murder. The "You shall not commit murder" which delineates the face in which the Other is produced submits my freedom to judgment. Then the free adherence to truth, an activity of knowledge, the free will which, according to Descartes, in certitude adheres to a clear idea, seeks a reason which does not coincide with the radiance of this clear and distinct idea itself. A clear idea which imposes itself by its clarity calls for a strictly personal work of a freedom, a solitary freedom that does not put itself in question, but can at most suffer a failure. In morality alone it is put in question. Morality thus presides over the work of truth.

It will be said that the radical questioning of certitude reduces itself to the search for another certitude: the justification of freedom would refer to freedom. Indeed that is so, in the measure that justification cannot result in non-certitude. But in fact, the moral justification of freedom is neither certitude nor incertitude. It does not have the status of a result, but is accomplished as movement and life; it consists in addressing an infinite exigency to one's freedom, in having a radical non-indulgence for one's freedom. Freedom is not justified in the consciousness of certitude, but in an infinite exigency with regard to oneself, in the overcoming of all good conscience. But this infinite exigency with regard to oneself, precisely because it puts freedom in question, places me and maintains me in a situation in which I am not alone, in which I am judged. This is the primary sociality: the personal relation is in the rigor of justice which judges me and not in love that excuses me. For this judgment does not come to me from a Neuter; before the Neuter I am spontaneously free. In the infinite exigency with regard to oneself is produced the duality of the face to face. One does not prove God thus, since this is a situation that precedes proof, and is metaphysics itself. The ethical, beyond vision and certitude, delineates the structure of exteriority as such. Morality is not a branch of philosophy, but first philosophy.

12. Being as Goodness—the I—Pluralism—Peace

We have posited metaphysics as Desire. We have described Desire as the "measure" of the Infinite which no term, no satisfaction arrests (Desire opposed to Need). The discontinuity of generations, that is, death and fecundity, releases Desire from the prison of its own subjectivity and puts an end to the monotony of its identity. To posit metaphysics as Desire is to interpret the production of being—desire engendering Desire—as goodness and as beyond happiness; it is to interpret the production of being as being for the Other.

But "being for the Other" is not the negation of the I, engulfed in the universal. The universal law itself refers to a face to face position which refuses every exterior "viewing." To say that universality refers to the face to face position is (against a whole tradition of philosophy) to deny that being is produced as a panorama, a coexistence, of which the face to face would be a modality. This whole work opposes this conception. The face to face is not a modality of coexistence nor even of the knowledge (itself panoramic) one term can have of another, but is the primordial production of being on which all the possible collocations of the terms are founded. The revelation of the third party, ineluctable in the face, is produced only through the face. Goodness does not radiate over the anonymity of a collectivity presenting itself panoramically, to be absorbed into it. It concerns a being which is revealed in a face, but thus it does not have eternity without commencement. It has a principle, an origin, issues from an I, is subjective. It is not regulated by the principles inscribed in the nature of a particular being that manifests it (for thus it would still proceed from universality and would not respond to the face), nor in the codes of the State. It consists in going where no clarifying—that is, panoramic—thought precedes, in going without knowing where. An absolute adventure, in a primal imprudence, goodness is transcendence itself. Transcendence is the transcendence of an I. Only an I can respond to the injunction of a face.

The I is conserved then in goodness, without its resistance to system manifesting itself as the egoist cry of the subjectivity, still concerned for happiness or salvation, as in Kierkegaard. To posit being as Desire is to decline at the same time the ontology of isolated subjectivity and the ontology of impersonal reason realizing itself in history.

To posit being as Desire and as goodness is not to first isolate an I which would then tend toward a beyond. It is to affirm that to apprehend oneself from within—to produce oneself as I—is to apprehend oneself with the same gesture that already turns toward the exterior to extra-vert and to manifest—to respond for what it apprehends—to express; it is to affirm that the becoming-conscious is already language, that the essence of language is goodness, or again, that the essence of language is friendship and hospitality. The other is not the negation of the same, as Hegel would like to say. The fundamental fact of the ontological scission into same and other is a non-allergic relation of the same with the other.

Transcendence or goodness is produced as pluralism. The pluralism of being is not produced as a multiplicity of a constellation spread out before a possible gaze, for thus it would be already totalized, joined into an entity. Pluralism is accomplished in goodness proceeding from me to the other, in which first the other, as absolutely other, can be produced, without an alleged lateral view upon this movement having any right to grasp of it a truth superior to that which is produced in goodness itself. One does not enter into this pluralist society without always remaining outside by speech (in which goodness is produced)— but one does not leave it in order to simply *see oneself* inside. The unity of plurality is peace, and not the coherence of the elements that constitute plurality. Peace therefore cannot be identified with the end of combats that cease for want of combatants, by the defeat of some and the victory of the others, that is, with cemetaries or future universal empires. Peace must be my peace, in a relation that starts from an I and goes to the other, in desire and goodness, where the I both maintains itself and exists without egoism. It is conceived starting from an I assured of the convergence of morality and reality, that is, of an infinite time which through fecundity is its time. It will remain a personal I before the judgment in which truth is stated, and this judgment will come from outside of it without coming from an impersonal reason, which uses ruse with persons and is pronounced in their absence.

The situation in which the I thus posits itself before truth in placing its subjective morality in the infinite time of its fecundity—a situation in which the instant of eroticism and the infinity of paternity are conjoined —is concretized in the marvel of the family. The family does not only result from a rational arrangement of animality; it does not simply mark a step toward the anonymous universality of the State. It identifies itself outside of the State, even if the State reserves a framework for it. As source of human time it permits the subjectivity to place itself under a judgment while retaining speech. This is a metaphysically ineluctable structure which the State would not dismiss, as in Plato, nor make exist in view of its own disappearance, as Hegel would have it. The biological structure of fecundity is not limited to the biological fact. In the biological fact of fecundity are outlined the lineaments of fecundity in general as a relation between man and man and between the I and itself not resembling the structures constitutive of the State, lineaments of a reality that is not subordinated to the State as a means and does not represent a reduced model of the State.

Situated at the antipodes of the subject living in the infinite time of fecundity is the isolated and heroic being that the State produces by its virile virtues. Such a being confronts death out of pure courage and whatever be the cause for which he dies. He assumes finite time, the death-end or the death-transition, which do not arrest the continuation of a being without discontinuity. The heroic existence, the isolated soul, can gain its salvation in seeking an eternal life for itself, as though its subjectivity, returning to itself in a continuous time, could not be turned against it—as though in this continuous time identity itself would not be affirmed obsessively, as though in the identity that remains in the midst of the most extravagant avatars "tedium, fruit of the mournful incuriosity that takes on the proportions of immortality" did not triumph.

INDEX